Praise for *The Execution Challenge*

"All businesses must maintain their relevance in ever-changing market conditions and do so with greater confidence that their chosen strategy can be realized. Too often, companies have a disconnect between their strategy and their change investments, compromising their operating plan and financial performance. Cameron and Kuehn promote a well-researched, comprehensive, educational insight into the essential discipline of strategic business architecture that provides the red thread between strategy and execution, ultimately helping organizations succeed in their chosen journey."

—**Peter Elsdon**, *Head of Strategic Transformation Planning, Strategy Office, A.P. Moller-Maersk*

"In today's complex, fast-changing environments, effective strategy execution is not just about the 'what,' but also the 'how.' Cameron and Kuehn provide a practical, insightful, and invaluable guide, offering proven techniques to translate ambitious strategies into coordinated action and momentum. For an emerging leader, they provide the tools that allow you to create a path forward, helping you navigate the execution challenges with agility, structure, and organization. For seasoned leaders, they provide a compass prompting a reevaluation of established practices, fostering adaptability and better decision-making, and encouraging a culture of continuous improvement. A must-read for executives, strategists, and business leaders who seek to bridge the gap between strategy and successful execution."

—**Jessica Saba,** *Pharm. D., MMGT, BCGP, Director, Business and Operation Strategy Realization, Highmark Health*

"Based on a career that included business leadership in three Fortune 500 companies, leadership of a multibillion-dollar private family-owned company, and growing up in a smaller family business, I developed a passion for business leadership and strategy. I saw good strategy development with less-than-stellar execution. As a business leader, I believe you actually start by developing good business execution processes in the organization before you start strategic planning. Once you have them in place you can step back and develop clear strategies. After that, you link them together. Once you have this in place it can be very powerful.

Many well-formulated strategies fall apart without strong organizational buy-in and the transformation of ideas into action. This book provides a fresh approach into the 'how' of strategy with a focus on execution. This comes down to the strategy process, and the book presents great tools and techniques to develop and execute great strategies. Move this one to the top of your reading list!"

—**Rick Merluzzi,** *Executive Vice Chairman, Metal Exchange Corporation*

"Strategy without execution is meaningless. Yet, many companies are so focused on strategy that they forget the most important part of strategy is execution. The business environment has never been more volatile and unpredictable, making execution more critical than ever. While the business challenges of successful strategy execution are well known, I believe the playbook for how to do it is not well developed in most organizations. In *The Execution Challenge,* Cameron and Kuehn provide an indispensable guide for *how* to link strategy with the organization's capabilities and deliver it through the entire value chain. The Execution Challenge is a practical, real-world framework to understand and manage complexity. This book is a must-read for business leaders, strategic planners, and managers at all levels who must lead their teams and organization through change."

—**Brad Smith,** *Vice President, Portfolio Management, Innovation and Insights, CJ Schwan's*

"As part of our mission to drive innovation in graduate business programs, the Graduate Business Curriculum Roundtable was pleased to sponsor a recent study by Brian Cameron and Whynde Kuehn to investigate how, if at all, strategy execution is taught in these programs. The study found that most strategy execution/implementation courses focus heavily on the human and organizational elements of strategy but do not discuss in any real detail *how* to translate or execute strategy or manage ongoing changes to it. This book squarely addresses that gap with a comprehensive approach to strategy execution that links the project execution layer with business strategy and keeps them aligned as organizations evolve in today's dynamic landscape. *The Execution Challenge* should be considered part of every graduate business curriculum and is a must-read for business leaders of today and tomorrow."

—**Jeff Bieganek,** *Executive Director,*
Graduate Business Curriculum Roundtable

"The translation of a winning strategy into a superior performance is perhaps one of the greatest challenges of organizational leaders in today's ever-changing corporate arena. How do we help our people maintain razor-sharp focus on strategy execution amid so much organizational complexity? Cameron and Kuehn help us bridge the gap between strategy formulation and execution—how refreshing it is to have such an in-depth exploration of the 'how' of implementing strategy successfully!"

—**David L. Dinwoodie,** *Center for Creative Leadership;*
Coauthor of Becoming a Strategic Leader: Your Role in Your Organization's Enduring Success

"Despite years of research and strategy methodologies, many organizations continue to be challenged in strategy execution to achieve their strategic outcomes. *The Execution Challenge: Delivering Great Strategy at Scale* aims to bridge this gap and comes at a time when effective strategy execution will not be just for business performance, but for future survival. Cameron and Kuehn provide invaluable insights and a pragmatic approach, drawing from extensive experience and organizations successfully embracing their teachings to fill the gap between strategy and execution. For strategy executives navigating today's complexities, this book is indispensable."

—**Kartik Ravel,** *Head of Value Realization, N.A., Fujitsu America, Inc.*

"In *The Execution Challenge: Delivering Great Strategy at Scale,* Cameron and Kuehn provide an expert playbook for effective strategy execution, with a focus on proven, real-world implementation. In the intricate dance between vision and reality, strategy execution wields the conductor's baton. This book not only reveals the notes but also teaches us how to orchestrate them into a symphony of success, something that has been missing in other books about strategy. In the current volatile, uncertain, complex, and ambiguous (VUCA) landscape, Cameron and Kuehn introduce strategic business architecture, the missing link in ensuring the successful realization of organizational strategies."

—**Jenn Hood,** *HR Transformation PMO Director, UGI Corporation*

"*The Execution Challenge* provides keys to businesses and leaders who want to move from a 'ready, fire, aim' approach to 'ready, aim, fire.'"

—**Miranda Meyer,** *Director of Strategy Management and Chief of Staff, Health Insurance Company*

"This book is a must-read for leaders who are looking for a proven, pragmatic approach to executing business strategy. The often missing 'line of sight' linkage between strategy and tactical execution becomes visible when you leverage the practical frameworks and techniques outlined in this book."

—**Tanisha Fitts,** *General Manager, T. Rowe Price*

"Cameron and Kuehn offer the tools to make a strategic plan that is actionable—not merely theoretical. This book provides a way to navigate the tension that is inherent in developing a concept and its execution at once. Most strategic plans morph along the way to implementation—if they even make it that far—so much so that the end result may have little in common with the vision. Using their strategic business architecture, organizations can create an integrated, comprehensive way forward that leverages the best of their teams, talents, and opportunities."

—C.J. Wise, *Senior Vice President, Finance & Strategy, New York Center for Child Development*

"When I started reading this book, I could not stop. It effectively addresses the strategy to execution gaps using strategic business architecture. With my experience in strategy, business architecture, and agile project management, I am excited to see the practical, straightforward, and easy-to-consume methods presented in this book. In my opinion, if you follow these methods, you will be able to execute your strategy successfully."

—Mulanga Machaba, *Strategist, Leading Financial Institution in South Africa*

"As a leader, I am always striving to add more tools to my skill set to drive better strategic planning and execution. *The Execution Challenge* is a must-read for all leaders looking to close the gap between strategy ideation and execution excellence. Cameron and Kuehn provide clear visibility to the challenges of strategy execution and how to keep leaders focused on coordinated efforts to deliver strategy execution at scale."

—Shawn T. Condon, *Chief Operating Officer, Schuman Cheese*

"*The Execution Challenge* represents a superb resource for business executives. It distills in simple but powerful, deep-rooted strategic principles the drivers that allow organizations to deliver on their value propositions, hence paving the road to wealth creation and long-term economic growth. A must-read for any current or aspiring business leader."

—Jose Eduardo Salgado Ballesteros,
CEO, Curfimex S.A. de C.V.

"Brian Cameron and Whynde Kuehn break through the philosophic and high-level strategic concepts of transformation and provide practical insights on how to operationalize these initiatives by leaning on business architecture as the consistent thread. A one-of-a-kind primer, here is a book that serves to make us wiser digital transformation leaders."

—Jessica Carroll, *Chief Experience Officer,*
Acuative & Institute for Digital Transformation Fellow

"One of the keys to effective strategic delivery is the ability to 'see' the big picture and translate aspiration into meaningful action. Well-executed business architecture paints that picture. Joining the dots across complex organizations and systems enables everyone within them to see and do things differently, harnessing the real power of shared vision-aligned collective effort. This book provides a practical 'how-to' guide to creating strategic business architecture, which effectively links delivery to purpose at scale."

—Jacqueline Ambrose, *Head of Change,*
The University of Sheffield

"If you're in search of a guide to achieve successful strategy execution, then *The Execution Challenge* is the book you need. This insightful read has it all, bridging the gap between developing a solid strategy and effectively executing it. It provides a clear road map, highlighting the benefits of establishing a strategic business architecture function and integrating it with strategic planning. Along the way, it demystifies the application of the most effective strategy frameworks and tools. Additionally, it offers an organizational assessment tool that allows readers to evaluate the maturity of their existing strategy execution processes. Whether you're an executive, strategist, or simply curious about strategy execution, *The Execution Challenge* is a must-read for you!"

—**Deborah Billingham,** *Organisational Change Professional, Western Power Corporation*

"This is the book I would have loved to have on my desk as a strategic and transformational leader. Executing on the strategy is one of the biggest challenges business leaders have, and this book gives a great perspective on how to include strategic business architecture to maximize execution capabilities. Great book."

—**Lene Østerberg,** *CEO and Founder, Linconomy*

"The authors have identified the natural dichotomy that occurs between organizational strategy and execution. While many others have written about the development of business strategy, Cameron and Kuehn have focused on techniques to ensure successful implementation of those strategies. Followers of this work will be seen as key delivery enablers."

—**Gary Buck,** *Global CIO, Retired*

"Everyone in leadership understands the importance of developing strategic goals within their organization. Unfortunately, the majority of leaders never successfully execute such strategies. This book will stand apart from all the other leadership books that you own, as it illustrates challenges from traditional thinking and explores new approaches that can get you closer to effective strategy development and execution. In leadership, there are no excuses, just results!"

—**Aaron Parker,** *Manager, Labor Relations, Amtrak*

"In leading a scientific/technically focused function within a large biotech and medical device corporation, a major challenge has been evolving the organization to address expanding internal product portfolio needs and external environmental drivers (customer and regulatory requirements). Urgency often demands a targeted response to the immediate need, with limited consideration given to optimization of resultant department architecture, transactional processes, or true cohesive strategy to drive effective service delivery and execution. This book offers a very thorough foundation in the relevant theory, development of actual applications, and ultimately distillation into practical actionable frameworks to address performance. The authors' depth and breadth of expertise on how to build a cohesive strategy and translate it into coordinated execution is clear and obvious, as is their true commitment to sharing this knowledge for the benefit of clients and readers. I'm sure you will find the same as you delve into this book."

—David W. Eaker, *Ph.D., DABT, Vice President, Corporate Preclinical Development and Toxicology, Becton Dickinson (BD)*

"Successfully transforming an organization is about having the ability to adapt, pivot, and transform organizational DNA and culture. We need a mechanism to pool our cross-functional experience and skills to collaborate on dealing with whatever crisis arises, be it financial, technological, environmental, regulatory, or health related. *The Execution Challenge* gives us that mechanism by articulating the comprehensive journey from strategy formulation through its seamless execution."

—Peter Cully, President, *Association of Change Management Professionals ANZ, Inc.*

"*The Execution Challenge: Delivering Great Strategy at Scale* transcends the conventional boundaries of strategic literature, emerging as a seminal guide that masterfully navigates the translation of intricate strategy into tangible outcomes. Where existing discourse on strategy execution often finds itself ensnared in the dichotomy of theory versus practice, this work stands out for its thoughtful exploration of the alchemy required to transform meticulously crafted strategy into harmonious, impactful execution. The authors imbue this book with an abundance of wisdom and practical advice, offering a treasure trove of insights for both seasoned strategy execution practitioners and those aspiring to mastery in this domain. It serves as an indispensable toolkit, designed to streamline efforts, mitigate conflict, and foster a productive dynamic that guides every step from strategic ideation to its pragmatic realization. This book promises not just to educate its readers but to equip them with the means to effect meaningful business impact through strategic excellence."

—Suleiman Barada, *President,*
Lebanon Chapter at the Global Innovation Institute

"*The Execution Challenge* is a must-read for current and future leaders. It serves as the how-to we need on implementing the business architecture framework, the true secret to strategic success. This thought-provoking body of work will be helmed as the guide for leadership teams who strive to take their corporations to the next level. It bridges the gap between premier strategy and profitable execution. Cameron and Kuehn's research creates a powerful body of work and shows just why they are the ones to watch and learn from in the field!"

—Rosa Barringer, *United States Air Force, Retired*

"Every business should be in the business of growth—and growth requires not only clear strategic vision but a framework to align every individual in the organization toward the goal. *The Execution Challenge* delivers a brilliant and comprehensive road map for businesses of all sizes to deliver on even the most ambitious, far-reaching strategies."

—Eileen Love O'Donnell, *Founder and Co-CEO,*
Odonnell Company

"Many companies strategize but struggle to translate their plans into transformative outcomes. *The Execution Challenge* breaks this pattern, delving deeper to address the vital connection between the execution layer and business strategy, while adeptly managing ongoing changes. It not only showcases expertise but also demonstrates a dedication to offering a thorough understanding of strategy execution, thus ensuring projects stay aligned with overarching business objectives in dynamic environments."

—**Jackie Parkinson,** *Senior Global Enablement Manager, Technical Pre-Sales, Adobe*

"In a world where strategic execution can mean the difference between success and stagnation, *The Execution Challenge: Delivering Great Strategy at Scale* emerges as a vital compass for leaders navigating the complexities of corporate and IT strategy. Having served as both a Chief Strategy Officer (CSO) and Chief Enterprise Architect, I've witnessed firsthand the challenges and imperatives of aligning strategy with execution across vast and varied teams. Coauthors Brian Cameron and Whynde Kuehn have masterfully distilled decades of experience into an insightful guide that demystifies the oft-overlooked art of strategy execution. Their pragmatic approach, blending strategic business architecture with actionable frameworks, is a beacon for those aiming to translate visionary strategy into tangible outcomes. This book not only equips leaders with the tools to bridge the perennial gap between strategy development and its execution but also fosters a culture of alignment, agility, and innovation."

—**Raymond Bordogna,** *Chief Enterprise Architect, WPP*

"Effective strategy execution is crucial for every organization's success and its ability to adapt and thrive in today's dynamic and disruptive business environment. However, many organizations struggle to bridge the gap between strategy and execution, facing challenges such as time-consuming planning processes and disconnected teams and tools. *The Execution Challenge* helps us reimagine a better way. With its comprehensive approach to strategy execution, it demonstrates how to establish continuous alignment from strategy to execution in a transparent, cohesive, connected, and efficient way—enabled by a holistic view of an organization. *The Execution Challenge* is an instant classic on strategy execution—and essential reading for anyone serious about delivering strategy and transformation at scale."

—**Geeta Pyne,** *SMD, Chief Architect, TIAA*

"*The Execution Challenge* represents a much-needed paradigm shift from business to IT alignment into an evolution and mindset of execution and realization. Business leaders and technologists globally will find a gripping real-world approach, decomposing business architecture as a business to execution practice through the enterprise strategic lens. Readers will find pragmatic composition of internal and external factors and considerations to scale 'go dos' for target state capabilities and continuous achievement of the business results."

—**Pamela Wise-Martinez,** *MEM, Author; Inventor; Executive Director, Global Head of the Enterprise Architecture, Whirlpool Corporation*

"Brian Cameron and Whynde Kuehn present an effective solution to the challenge faced by executives in all industries to bridge strategy and execution and activate change needed continually in twenty-first-century organizations. This captivating book is a gift for leaders at all levels to not only deliver a great strategy but also scale it to grow and transform their organizations. This is not just a book but a manual containing step-by-step practical tools. A reader will be able to implement the tools right away by utilizing the tips and tricks from the lifetime work of the authors with deep expertise in the exciting and ever-growing field of strategic business architecture. Highly recommended!"

—**Guru Chadha,** *SVP Business Architecture, Citi*

"*The Execution Challenge* provides a pragmatic view into concrete ways for how to achieve enterprise strategy plans. Where strategy formulation and change journey management set the stage, the drama of enterprise transformation plays out in the programs and projects where strategic execution occurs—or fails. My 30 years of transformations taught that lesson through hard learnings in the field. As disruptive technology change now compels leaders to set new strategies and execution challenges to meet, this practical guide is vital for new and experienced change agents alike."

—Patrick Engelking, *Vice President of Business Architecture & Transformation, Advantage Solutions*

"How well companies, both large and small, can execute great plans will increasingly become a survival factor. This requires translating big ideas into blueprints for successful change implementation. Brian Cameron and Whynde Kuehn offer actionable ways of cracking the code to the *how* of strategy execution."

—Juliane Berger, *Head of Business Architecture, Allianz Commercial*

"As a proponent and practitioner of business architecture for more than two decades, I am thrilled to read Brian Cameron and Whynde Kuehn articulate such a pragmatic and applicable approach to strategy execution. Their delineation of business architecture across strategic and execution tiers provides valuable insight for organizations struggling with the optimal placement of their business architecture practice. Moreover, the tools and logical steps outlined in this book will empower business architects to derive value across various strategic, value stream, or capability levels. *The Execution Challenge* also tackles head-on, the organizational hurdles associated with harmonizing business transformation, technology, and architecture functions when executing strategy."

—Harminder Blackburn, *Head of Enterprise Business Architecture, Liberty Specialty Markets*

"Execution is the most difficult, yet least understood and documented phase of any major transformation program. This comprehensive work, based on direct experience, is the skeleton key to making the complex simple and delivering the right outcomes in a controlled manner via strategic business architecture. It shows not only how but why certain approaches are necessary and aptly places often confused transformation concepts that can otherwise create early communication challenges."

—**Steve Carter,** *Head of Business Architecture, Insurance Company in AUSPAC*

"Business architecture plays a critical role for organizations that want to differentiate themselves amidst competitors, enhance their operational performance, and innovate on a large scale. However, many organizations fail to leverage the full potential of business architecture by limiting its role to an execution level within their enterprise architecture practice. To unlock exponential value, organizations need to embrace strategic business architecture as well. This book provides a comprehensive guide to establishing both strategic and execution-level business architecture, along with practical steps to bridge the gap between the two. Aspiring and experienced business architecture professionals alike will find immense value in this insightful read."

—**Kavitha Narayanan, VP,** *Head of Business Architecture, Large Financial and Insurance Company*

"During the two decades I have worked in strategy, business architecture, and portfolio management, the debate has unfortunately been more about who does what and when, and who decides and who is right, rather than collaborative value creation. In *The Execution Challenge,* Brian Cameron and Whynde Kuehn shed light on *how* to execute strategy, while prioritizing shared objectives and coherence across functions. Then 'who does it' is no longer at the center of the debate because strategic business architecture provides a mindset and a way of connecting the dots across the strategy execution continuum that transcends individual roles. Their pragmatic and agile approach, complemented by a brilliantly presented step-by-step maturity assessment tool, allows you to target exactly where to start within your organization. This guide, devoid of technical jargon and dogmatic concepts, is pertinent to all leaders and practitioners across the strategy execution continuum, and I am confident that it will positively influence the success of our organizations."

—Amélie Régimbal, *Senior Advisor in Organizational Transformation and Strategic Business Architecture Leader, Desjardins Group*

"One of the questions I've been asked frequently as an educator, coach, and consultant in business architecture and leading strategy formation is, 'How do we actually do this work, practically speaking?' We've been able to convey the 'why' and the 'what' of business architecture and strategy planning in our teaching over the last decade—making the case, laying out the conceptual, and then hoping to use our skills with the models to navigate through blockers and achieve real benefit.

Now, with *The Execution Challenge,* we've been given the unequivocal 'how.' My esteemed colleagues, Brian Cameron and Whynde Kuehn, have created the literal recipe book to instruct practitioners in the daily work of executing to deliver the strategic intentions of the organization using business architecture and other tools. With the why and what as the backdrop, they have brought us the step-by-step guidebook for how, which I think, if followed in earnest, will lead to new opportunities for predictable success for both the practitioner and the organization."

—Linda Finley, *Founder and President, The Twin Cities Business Architecture Forum*

"The making of strategies and their actual execution are interdependent processes. *The Execution Challenge* acknowledges this interdependence—highlighting the importance of aligning business architectures with the competitive and/or cooperative nature of the underlying strategy. The authors demonstrate the importance of design to sustain strategy, including cooperative ventures where interactions and capabilities associated with value cocreation are promoted. Execution is an essential part in understanding how single organizations are or can become part of evolving networks and emerging ecosystems."

—Lars Huemer, *Professor of Strategy,*
BI Norwegian Business School

"Ineffective business books merely present content. Good business books introduce new subjects. Great business books explain the reasons behind things. Exceptional business books inspire us. . . . This book is one of these! This is a must-read for all executives, entrepreneurs, business leaders, and academics looking for answers and aiming to understand the intersection between technology, strategy, business models, and exponential growth."

—Javier Tovar Márquez, *Professor INALDE Business School,*
Speaker, and Business Consultant

"The authors of *The Execution Challenge* offer a simplistic case for change by hitting on the shortcomings of traditional methods, then progress into how to determine the comprehensive change required to make strategies successful—from people, process, information, and technology lenses. Their insights on achieving horizontal enterprise alignment and informing strategic planning are truly groundbreaking, offering a path forward where before it seemed like an abstract ideal. I firmly believe that this book has the potential to create a paradigm shift in how organizations approach strategy translation and redefine the field for architecture innovation."

—Amy Browning, *Strategic Business Architect, CBA®*

"In the journey of achieving meaningful purpose, the path from strategic vision to tangible results is an exhilarating adventure. It begins with a steadfast commitment to execution. *The Execution Challenge: Delivering Great Strategy at Scale* equips you with a powerful toolkit, forged from real-world experience, to bridge the gap between strategy and execution. These audience-friendly strategic business architecture tools can be seamlessly customized to fit your industry and organizational culture.

As you embark on this transformative voyage, remember your *why*—the driving force behind your aspirations. With this book as your compass, chart a course toward *how*—the practical steps that turn vision into reality. Are you ready to conquer the execution challenge? Dive in, embrace the journey, and make your strategy soar!"

—**Lindsey Funair,** *MMGT, Global Business Architect, Orbia Connectivity Solutions (Dura-Line)*

"Executive-level strategy oftentimes gets lost in translation as it is disseminated across the enterprise, and attempts to align ongoing work with this strategy are hopeful at best. *The Execution Challenge: Delivering Great Strategy at Scale* addresses this existing gap in an easy-to-understand way. In my many years of experience, I have never seen a set of stepping stones to define the path from strategy declaration to appropriate project prioritization, initialization, or shutdown. In the past, we have learned about strategy development, portfolio management, solution delivery, etc., which all seem to come up short, but utilizing business architecture as described in *The Executive Challenge* seems to fill that void. This is a must-read for all levels of management."

—**Kurt Nelson,** *Enterprise Architect, The Boeing Company*

"An overwhelming majority of businesses fail at strategy execution. Why? Because they lack the ability to turn their strategy into a coherent, actionable, and manageable plan for change, where everyone is on the same page. That's where strategic business architecture can provide the golden thread, linking the vision for what an organization wants to be with a clearly defined path to get there. Going beyond your standard business strategy book, *The Execution Challenge* also tackles the important topic of business education, taking the conversation to a new level. For companies to develop the muscle they need to survive in today's uncertain and complex business ecosystems, leaders need the know-how to reliably turn vision into reality. This highly pragmatic approach to solving strategy execution challenges provides current and aspiring leaders with that knowledge."

—Darryl Carr, Editor,
Enterprise Architecture Professional Journal

The Execution Challenge

The Execution Challenge

Delivering Great Strategy at Scale

Brian H. Cameron
Whynde Kuehn

WILEY

Published by John Wiley & Sons, Inc., Hoboken, New Jersey.
Published simultaneously in Canada.

For general information on our other products and services or for technical support, please contact our Customer Care Department within the United States at (800) 762-2974, outside the United States at (317) 572-3993 or fax (317) 572-4002.

Wiley also publishes its books in a variety of electronic formats. Some content that appears in print may not be available in electronic formats. For more information about Wiley products, visit our web site at www.wiley.com.

Library of Congress Cataloging-in-Publication Data is Available:

ISBN 9781394210435 (Cloth)
ISBN 9781394210442 (ePub)
ISBN 9781394210459 (ePDF)

Cover Design: Wiley
Cover Image: © Gerasimov174/Getty Images
Author Photos: Courtesy of the Author

SKY10075837_052824

To the bold leaders and visionaries who dare to think differently and have the courage to drive change and shape a new tomorrow. We hope that this book provides you with the tools and perspective to make lasting change.

Brian Cameron and Whynde Kuehn

Contents

Foreword

The late Stephen Covey once said, "Most leaders would agree that they'd be better off having an average strategy with superb execution than a superb strategy with poor execution." Similarly, noted authority Michael Porter observed that more than 80 percent of organizations do not successfully execute their business strategies and that in 70 percent of these cases, the reason was not the strategy itself but bad execution.

In my four-plus decades of work as a professor of strategic leadership and an active consultant to organizations around the world, I can attest to both sets of observations. I have experienced first-hand that it is far easier for organizations to create a strategy than it is for them to implement it.

Even in business schools, we teach courses on strategy formulation and courses on strategy implementation/execution, but typically they are separate courses, with the latter being more focused on leadership and change as opposed to devising an architecture to make a strategy real, implementable, and measurable. That architecture for implementation has long been a missing link in the field of strategy.

I first met Brian Cameron more than 30 years ago when I was Associate Dean for Executive Education at the Smeal College of Business at Penn State. Brian became a valued member of our staff and helped us to incorporate newly developing technologies into our management processes. We stayed in touch as his career unfolded, and I followed his work as it evolved into a focus on business architecture in which technology played a role, but strategy execution was the goal. Brian introduced me to Whynde Kuehn, and the two of them impressed and engaged me with their approach to strategic business architecture and to creating "lines of sight" that directly link strategy development to strategy execution.

In *The Execution Challenge,* Brian and Whynde present a handbook for strategy implementation with strategic business architecture as the enabling platform. Throughout the book, they share their tested approach to strategy execution, beginning with an explanation of strategic business architecture as a discipline, then unveiling an array of approaches, frameworks, tools, and assessments that enable readers to understand and apply the discipline to strategy execution in their own organizations.

The authors share their experiences, both as contributors to the establishment of strategic business architecture as a proven discipline and also as consultants who have helped organizations globally to create the crucial "line of sight" processes linking strategy with execution. These processes have enabled those organizations to evolve their strategies from ideation, through well-designed and coordinated projects, into well-defined results.

Creating the capacity to execute has long been the missing link in the strategy process. This book bridges that gap, showing us how to create the connection between strategy development and strategy execution. The authors provide us with a road map for how to turn the promise of strategy into the reality of results.

Dr. Albert A. Vicere
Smeal College of Business
The Pennsylvania State University

Preface

My over 20-year journey with strategy execution evolved as I moved into strategy-oriented IT leadership roles and, more recently, through my ongoing research and work with enterprise and business architecture groups and strategic planning groups in a variety of organizations and industries. I started this journey with the indoctrination that direct alignment between business and IT strategy was the "holy grail," but I also saw that this alignment was not happening in most organizations and I began to explore why this was the case. At the same time, I ran across a quote from Michael Porter stating that 80 percent of organizations fail to execute their business strategy, which was consistent with my experience. I also saw that in many of these organizations, the failure of IT to align with business strategy was often blamed as a primary cause of this failure to execute strategy. I asked myself if this was the real root cause of the strategy execution problems or something more. My conclusions offer a pragmatic and proven approach to strategy execution and alignment that challenges some of the traditional literature and thinking.

In short, direct alignment between IT and business strategies is not possible for reasons we will discuss in detail in this book. An interim "Rosetta stone" alignment mechanism is needed for effective and sustainable alignment over time—this interim mechanism is the core business capabilities of the organization. We will discuss in detail how business capabilities form the foundation of the "strategic business architecture" of the organization and provide the foundation for effective strategy execution and ongoing strategy alignment.

During this journey, I uncovered the emerging discipline of strategic business architecture and the many modeling approaches and tools that fall under this broad umbrella that enable the in-depth organizational understanding needed to develop the enterprise-wide perspectives that are critical for creating (and maintaining) line-of-sight linkages between business strategies and tactical execution (typically in the form of project portfolios). The development and usage of these perspectives made so much sense that I assumed that the strategic planning profession has a similar approach and set of tools for facilitating effective strategy execution but perhaps called it something other than strategic business architecture. After talking to many people in the strategic planning profession and exploring what the strategic planning professional organizations had to offer, I learned that no such comprehensive approach to strategy execution exists, though pieces are referenced from time to time when discussing strategy execution. It was clear to me that a marriage between strategic business architecture and strategy execution would be the "holy grail" that many in the strategy execution arena were searching for—but I wanted to test out my findings a bit more before doing something like writing a book.

Next, I did a few things in parallel to get additional input and validation. First, I developed and launched an online graduate course in strategic business architecture that focuses on utilizing the practice of strategic business architecture as a driver of effective strategy execution. I started this course at Penn State in 2018 as a required course in our online enterprise architecture and business transformation master's program and as an elective course in our online MBA program and online master's in strategic management and executive leadership master's program (this master's program is populated with many strategic planning–related executives). The course started with 25 students from the enterprise architecture master's program and has grown to two offerings per year with more than 125 students per year, over two-thirds of whom come from the online MBA program and online master's in strategic management. The strategic planning people who take the course tell me that it is what they have been searching for—a pragmatic approach to the *how* of strategy execution. As a result of this course, several students have received job offers from their strategic planning organizations to bring a strategic business architecture perspective to their strategy execution efforts.

Many students have asked if we could provide a series of short courses that they could have others in their organizations take to get everyone thinking along the same lines and "singing from the same sheet of music," as not everyone can take a 15-week graduate course. In response to these requests, we developed an executive education short-course series that will launch in fall 2024.

As I saw the popularity of the graduate course grow, I became an advisor to the Business Architecture Guild® and emphasized the importance of framing the discipline of business architecture primarily around strategy execution. I also attempted to bring the main professional organization for strategic planning people together with the main business architecture professional organization. As I learned, professional organizations have established revenue models and are often reluctant to collaborate as it may mean a change in or potential disruption to their revenue models. I quickly realized that this route was unlikely to go very far.

It was around this time that I came to know Whynde Kuehn. We realized that we were two kindred spirits and saw the untapped potential for the application of strategic business architecture practices to enable effective strategy execution. Our discussions led to several collaborations, including this book.

I also suspected that part of the problem with the issues plaguing strategy execution was the manner in which the topic was covered in most graduate business programs. I decided to explore how strategy execution was taught/approached in higher education at the graduate level. My hypothesis was based on my experiences and was: "If strategy execution was covered in a curriculum, it was done at a high-level that focuses primarily on the *what* and *why* of strategy execution with very little detail on the *how*." The *how* is hard and often messy. I organized a research study sponsored by the Business Architecture Guild and the Graduate Business Curriculum Roundtable to explore this question. Whynde and I collaborated on this study. We discuss the results in detail in this book, but the bottom line was that my hypothesis was correct: We found mostly lip service on strategy execution with no detail on *how* to effectively align project-level execution with business strategy (and keep them aligned over time).

The findings of this study reminded me of a story told to me during an international consulting engagement: Two bunny rabbits were not happy and wanted to change their lives. They were always running from predators that wanted to eat them, and life was not good. They went to the Oracle at Delphi and said: "Oh, mighty Oracle, our lives are horrible. Everyone wants to eat us, and we can't go on this way. Can you help us?" The Oracle thought about it for a few minutes and responded, "Become hedgehogs—they have hard exteriors and nobody wants to eat them." The rabbits were very happy and started to leave the temple when one rabbit said to the other, "Exactly how to we become hedgehogs?" The other rabbit said, "I don't know. Let's go back and ask the Oracle." The rabbits went back to the Oracle and said, "Oh, mighty Oracle, exactly how to we become hedgehogs? The Oracle responded, "That's execution, I only do strategy."

The client was sending me a message—they expected more than a high-level strategy with no pragmatic means to execute/implement. Unfortunately, this story resonates with far too many people. The *how* is hard, and often it's just given lip service.

This book is the next step in the journey. It provides pragmatic and needed perspectives on the issues that have plagued strategy execution for decades and provides a proven, pragmatic approach to creating (and maintaining) a line of sight between high-level business strategy and project-level execution. Without this line of sight, effective strategy execution will remain incomplete and elusive.

—Brian H. Cameron

I have had the honor of working with organizations all around the world, from the largest global organizations and governments to start-ups and nonprofits. Regardless of size, industry, sector, or location, they were challenged by the same thing: the inability to execute strategy well. I witnessed a big gap between the high-level direction of strategy and the coordinated execution at scale required to turn that direction into action. I realized that no matter how brilliant a strategy or business model may be, it doesn't matter if an organization can't make it real.

I fell in love with this gap and helping organizations to bridge it by building a new capacity for change—for turning strategy into reality. In our connected, digital world of constant change, I can't think of anything more important for our organizations, institutions, and societies to survive and thrive.

As a systemic thinker grounded with a background in science, I have always been drawn to holistic approaches. It led me to the discipline of strategic business architecture for which I have become a recognized global thought leader and advocate, and a cofounder of the Business Architecture Guild. I have also been one of the pioneers who has leveraged this discipline for enterprise-wide strategy execution and transformation at a massive scale.

Through my experiences, I also realized the power of thinking holistically and intentionally about strategy to execution as a process. I saw how a process and purpose could bring teams together to build a brand-new muscle: the capacity to execute strategy and create organizational agility from top to bottom. I have been truly inspired by what is possible, and how bold leadership and a new mindset can entirely change the way an organization works.

But throughout this journey, I have relentlessly asked: *Why?* What are the root causes of the strategy execution challenge and why does it exist so ubiquitously for organizations? There are countless strategic management frameworks, disciplines, and techniques that are intended to address these issues—and the investment globally in adopting agile methods for delivery is staggering. So, why is there still a gap between strategy and execution?

Meeting Brian Cameron was like finding a kindred spirit. We saw the advantage of effective strategy execution for organizations along with the untapped potential of strategic business architecture as a critical enabler. We both saw similar contributors to poor strategy execution outcomes, such as the fragmentation of organizational structures, processes, and accountabilities. We were also both passionate and curious to research and uncover the true root causes of the strategy execution challenge. The gaps around strategy execution identified in our study of graduate business curriculums (referenced earlier) was a big aha moment for me.

Our collaborations became a turning point as I continued to realize that *what got us here won't get us there*. To really succeed at strategy execution—and with the discipline of strategic business architecture—we need to think and act differently. We have approached the design and change of our organizations in a siloed and reactive way for far too long. It's time to take a view of the whole and to connect the dots across the functions and disciplines involved in strategy execution. Strategy execution is a comprehensive, multidisciplinary function as important as any other, and it requires focused business leadership and commitment.

In this book, we cast a vision for a strategy execution function and approach that is based on holistic thinking, underpinned by the golden thread of strategic business architecture to translate and align strategy and execution. Importantly, we also give practical, tried-and-true methods and a toolkit to help you move into action on this vision.

We hope that this book will reshape the way that we all think about strategy execution. We envision a future where the business students and leaders of tomorrow have a strong command of *how* to deliver great strategy at scale, guided by a well-informed, holistic view—and that strategy execution as an enterprise-wide function with accountability for outcomes becomes the standard. We invite your bold leadership and action to contribute to the realization of this future.

—Whynde Kuehn

About the cover: This graphic represents the many parts of the organization that need to be understood and effectively work together to execute strategy. It also represents the different strategic business architecture layers and perspectives that need to work together to produce this organizational understanding. It suggests the light that is produced if you get it right.

Introduction

Why write another book on strategy execution? Strategy execution/implementation books and courses have been around for quite a while, and any web search will produce an abundance of options. However, effective strategy execution remains a major concern within many organizations today with the statistics to prove it. In Chapter 1, we discuss a study conducted by the Graduate Business Curriculum Roundtable and the Business Architecture Guild® that suggests that a big part of the reason for the poor track record with strategy execution may rest with how strategy execution is taught in graduate business programs (and with the materials used in these courses).

The strategy execution/implementation courses in this study focused heavily on the human and organizational elements of strategy implementation—managing people, resistance to change, building effective teams, navigating/understanding politics, types of power, change management strategies, importance of communication, organizational structure, information and decision processes, rewards, people, and leading change without formal authority.

These topics are covered most often in strategy execution–related books and are often taught in strategy execution/implementation–related courses.

While these topics are important for successful strategy execution, they are far from the comprehensive set of skills, knowledge, and processes needed for successful strategy execution. None of the courses in the study (and the books used in these courses) discussed *how* to link the execution layer (projects) with business strategy and manage ongoing changes to business strategy. Without this linkage, the execution (project) layer falls out of alignment with strategy.

For these reasons, we have focused this book on the *how* of strategy execution. This book focuses on how to translate strategy into coordinated action across an entire organization and effectively create the line of sight between enterprise project portfolios and business strategy to ensure that the organization is doing the "right" projects that are aligned with current business strategy. The book also focuses on *how* to keep the enterprise project portfolios aligned with ongoing changes to strategy. Additionally, the book lays out a comprehensive, end-to-end approach from strategy to execution entailing many functions and disciplines working in partnership to help realize strategy.

Fragmented organizational structures, processes, and accountabilities are among the leading causes of ineffective strategy execution, so strategy execution must be underpinned by a cohesive approach to succeed. None of this is easy, and the difficulty associated with the *how* of strategy execution is likely the reason it is often glossed over or omitted from most strategy execution books and courses. The complexities of *how* to execute strategy require a dedicated book to fully explore and understand this critical and multifaceted business function.

Our intent with this book is not to rehash the common human and organizational elements of strategy implementation that have been discussed for decades. Focusing solely or primarily on these and related topics has not moved the needle on strategy execution success. While we touch on many of these topics in the book, we do so in the context of the *how* of strategy execution.

This book is the result of years of research, consulting, and teaching strategic planning and strategy execution professionals across a wide range of organizations and industries around the world. These people consistently tell us that what follows in this book is what has been missing in their strategy execution journeys and uniquely addresses the missing *how* of strategy execution. We look forward to sharing a pragmatic, comprehensive approach to business strategy execution. As part of this process, we will explore how the discipline of strategic business architecture creates the enterprise perspectives, understanding, and connections needed for effective strategy development and execution.

About This Book

The Execution Challenge is a real-world guide to strategy execution for executives, strategists, transformation and innovation leaders, strategic planners, managers, directors, entrepreneurs, and other business leaders. It provides a practical and contemporary new take on how to approach strategy execution comprehensively and effectively in today's complex, fast-changing environments. The book provides an excellent foundation for leaders and their teams to build a common foundation of knowledge around cross-organizational strategy execution. It also provides tools to assess how effectively strategy execution is working within an organization and provides concrete steps to move into action on opportunities and gaps.

In Chapter 1, we look at traditional approaches to strategy development, alignment, and execution and issues with these traditional approaches. In Chapter 2, we begin to explore how strategic business architecture creates the enterprise perspective and understanding needed for effective strategy development and execution. In Chapter 3, we look at how the strategic business architecture of an organization is typically represented to create the enterprise-wide understanding needed to create the line of sight between businesses strategy and project-level execution. In Chapter 4, we walk through how to translate business strategy through the strategic business architecture to define an organized set of actions for execution across people, processes, information, and technology; this illustrates how the various frameworks and views interrelate and work together from end to end across strategy, architecture, and execution. In Chapter 5, we discuss the role of enterprise portfolio management in detail as a critical component of effective strategy execution. In Chapter 6, we discuss how strategic business architecture links and aligns with other business functions and disciplines within a strategy execution context. In Chapter 7, we discuss integrating the strategic business architecture perspective with strategic planning, skills and competencies needed, success factors, and how to measure and communicate value back to key parts of the organization. Chapter 8 provides guidance on how to create a strategic plan for scaling and maturing a strategic business architecture function that can successfully support strategy execution across an organization. Finally, in Chapter 9, we share a glimpse of some possible future directions for strategic business architecture and strategy execution.

Moving into Action

Please visit www.theexecutionchallenge.com to take the online Strategy Execution Organizational Assessment to assess your organization's readiness for and effectiveness with strategy execution. You will also find resources to help you interpret your results and move into action on the concepts described in this book.

Chapter 1

Strategy Development, Alignment, and Execution

Most organizations have a business strategy—some good, some that could be improved. In their book *The Balanced Scorecard: Translating Strategy into Action,*[1] authors Robert Kaplan and David Norton note that 90 percent of organizations fail to execute their strategies successfully. They go on to state that the reason for this failure is often not the strategy itself, but bad execution. According to Kaplan and Norton, this failure to execute strategy is one of the most significant management challenges facing public and private organizations in the twenty-first century.

In their 2000 book, *The Strategy-Focused Organization: How Balanced Scorecard Companies Thrive in the New Business Environment,*[2] Robert Kaplan and David Norton report that a mere 7 percent of employees fully understand their company's business strategies and what's expected of them in order to help achieve company goals. While this data has been around for a while, our experience suggests that it still rings true today. Furthermore, in most industries, strategy is not static and is tweaked as conditions on the ground change—no plan survives contact with the enemy. This is particularly true today, as the rate of change has accelerated in most organizations and industries.

How can we hope to successfully execute something that is changing and that a very low percentage of people fully understand? This question is at the heart of the problem—organizations today, for the most part, are no better at executing their business strategies than they were 20 years ago. This lack of clear strategic understanding throughout the organization leads to statistics such as "66% of HR and IT organizations develop strategic plans that are not linked to the enterprise strategy" cited by Robert Kaplan and David Norton (*Harvard Business Review*).[3] Here are a few challenges commonly experienced by organizations:

- Various strategies within an organization (for example, corporate/organizational, business unit, operational) are conflicting or misaligned.
- Articulation of strategy is unclear and becomes diffused as it filters down throughout an organization.
- Prioritization can be difficult, so everything becomes a priority and resources are stretched.
- Heuristics for prioritization and other decision-making lack accountability and are skewed toward certain outcomes (for example, investments in core areas versus innovation or large business units versus small).
- Redundant, conflicting, inconsistent, or nonintegrated solutions are implemented.
- The totality of execution does not achieve business strategies and objectives and may lead to suboptimizing parts of the organization versus doing what is best for the entire enterprise.
- Disciplines and teams are disconnected and lack the motivation and mechanisms for enterprise collaboration.
- *Tribal knowledge* (any unwritten knowledge within an organization that is not widely known) is relied upon, and full data is lacking for decision-making.

- Initiative results are difficult to measure against original business objectives, so they are measured primarily based on meeting timelines and budget.

One of the key root causes underlying these challenges is that the translation of strategies into business and technology solutions and plans is performed in siloes. Ultimately, these challenges can lead to inconsistent, fragmented, or unsatisfactory customer experiences, as well as organizational redundancy and complexity, which increases cost and decreases future agility.

We've seen decades of research and teaching in the area of strategy execution yet little improvement in our ability to execute business strategy. The strategy execution issue is a complex problem—if it were simple to resolve, there would be no need for this book.

Before we discuss the *how* of strategy execution in later chapters, this chapter discusses the typical strategy development process and the issues with traditional approaches to strategy alignment and execution.

What Is Strategy?

Generally speaking, *strategy* is defined as the direction, market position, and scope of the organization to promote survival and competitive advantage. The *direction* of an organization involves deciding what future state the organization is trying to achieve and where it wants to be in the long term. The *market position* includes the markets the organization wants to compete in. The *scope* consists of the activities the organization performs.

Strategies may exist at several levels of an enterprise, including corporate (or organizational), business unit, and operational. *Corporate/organizational strategy* defines the overall mission, vision, direction, and scope of the enterprise to address environmental issues and prosper both now and in the future. This level of strategy guides corporate strategic decision-making. *Business unit strategy* is concerned with how a specific aspect of the enterprise competes successfully in a particular market. Business strategies dictate the choice of products and how the customer wants and needs will be met. *Operational strategy* focuses on how each part of the organization is structured and organized to support the business strategy. Operational strategy is concerned with issues surrounding people, processes, and resources, and how these may be leveraged to support higher-level organizational objectives. These levels of strategy apply to all types of organizations and the names may change depending on the type of organization.

Why Is Strategy Needed?

Organizations are faced with an increasing number of options and challenges to deal with in a continuously changing environment, or what is sometimes referred to as the *business context*. Today's enterprise is confronted with globalization, the need to integrate all aspects of the business, aggressive competitors, new and emerging technologies, and an ever-changing regulatory environment. As a result, most enterprises need to innovate and adapt quickly to environmental opportunities and threats. Strategy and strategic planning are designed to account for the business context; point the organization in the right direction; coordinate all activities, processes, and functions; and position the enterprise in the market and among competitors in such a way that the organization survives and thrives.

Strategy and Strategic Planning

A *business strategy* specifies what an organization wants to achieve, where it will compete, and how it will win, whereas a *strategic plan* specifies the detailed activities that an organization will undertake to deliver its strategy.

Strategic management is the set of activities that include creating, implementing, and evaluating cross-organizational decisions to enable an enterprise to achieve success in its long-term goals.

Strategic planning involves specifying the enterprise's vision, mission, goals, and objectives, and then devising the plans, policies, programs, projects, and architectures needed to achieve them. Strategy guides the allocation of resources needed to implement all aspects of the overarching plan and its associated projects, programs, policies, and architectures.

Many organizations use multiple terms interchangeably to describe how work is defined and managed. For clarity and context, the following are definitions of key terms used in this book:

- **Project:** A *project* is a temporary endeavor undertaken to achieve a specific goal or objective. A project is managed with a clear end date in mind, adhering to a set scope and budget.
- **Program:** A *program* is a collection of two or more projects sharing a common goal.
- **Project portfolio:** A *project portfolio* is a group of related initiatives, projects, and/or programs that attain wide-reaching benefits and impacts.
- **Initiative:** An *initiative* is a broader, strategic effort that provides a framework for managing and coordinating various endeavors to achieve overarching objectives. For example, an initiative might include an organization's digital transformation initiative, corporate sustainability initiative, or organizational culture change program.

While both projects and initiatives involve organized efforts to achieve goals, projects are typically more focused, temporary endeavors with clear deliverables, while initiatives are a larger strategic umbrella that encompasses multiple programs and projects.

In this book, when we discuss projects, we encompass various styles of project management. To be clear, we are not implying a waterfall approach with the term *project*. While the waterfall model has been used widely in the past, this linear and sequential approach to project management has given way to a continuous and iterative approach called *agile*. Most organizations have evolved to this modern style of project management, where work is delivered in small, consumable increments to adapt to changing circumstances and deliver value continuously.

The Business Strategy Development Process

The *strategy development process* starts with an exploration of where the organization wants to be in the future and an analysis of where the organization is currently. From this picture, a strategic plan is developed to transition the organization from its current state to its desired future state.

Most organizations go through some type of formal strategy development process. This section explores the common phases of business strategy development and the information and typical areas of consideration that comprise each phase.

Phase I: Assess (Where Are We Now?)

Typical areas of analysis during the Assess phase include:

1. External environment
   - What is impacting the market?
   - What technology trends are occurring?
   - What is affecting our customers?
   - What are our competitors doing?
   - What is the strength of our advantage(s) versus our competitors?
   - What is the height of the barrier to new entrants in our market(s)?
   - How intense is the market competition?

External Environment Areas of Analysis	
Political	• New ecological and environmental issues • Regulatory bodies and procedures • Foreign distribution policies

External Environment Areas of Analysis	
Economic	• Domestic and international economic trends • General taxation issues • Consumer seasonality • Market and trade cycles
Social	• Life-cycle trend • Product demographics • Brand and company image • Consumer buying patterns
Technological	• Competing technology • Research and development activity • Intellectual property rights issues • Patents and licenses

2. Internal environment

- What are our weaknesses?
- Do we have operation issues?
- How are we performing?

Internal Environment Areas of Analysis	
Process Performance	• Level of agility • Performance against key performance indicators • Governance
Information and data performance	• Accessibility of information • Availability of information
Technology standards and maturity	• State of business application • State of infrastructure • Technology and infrastructure road maps
People performance	• Headcount • Skills and competencies • Longevity and advocacy
Strategic performance	• Performance against goals and objectives • Business unit performance
Compliance	• Regulatory • Risk assessment • Security assessment

3. Organization capacity
    - What is our capacity for change?
    - What have we already committed to?
    - What operational change has been requested?

Organization Capacity Areas of Analysis	
Demand Management	• Strategic initiatives • Innovation initiatives • Operational demand
Resource Utilization	• Resources being used • Resources available • Resource supply
Backlog of Commitments	• Strategic projects approved • Operational projects approved
Planned Delivery	• Benefit realization • Delivery dates

Phase II: Define Target (Where Do We Want to Be?)

Typical areas of analysis during the Define Target phase include:

1. Mission
    - What is the overriding purpose of the organization as a whole?
    - What is its "reason for being"?
2. Vision
    - What does the organization want to achieve in the next ten years (vision)?
    - What specific goals does the organization want to achieve in the next three to five years (financial, customers, employees, community goals)?
3. Values
    - What should every employee of the organization value and represent?
    - What distinguishes the organization from others?

What Is It?		Time Frame	Example
Mission	The overarching purpose of an organization Will never be outgrown	Indefinite	3M: "To solve unsolved problems innovatively." Walt Disney: "To make people happy."
Vision	The future the organization aims to deliver Achievable in a CEO's time horizon	Ten years (goals are typically three to five years)	Walmart (1990): "Become a $125 billion company by the year 2000." Honda: "We will crush, squash, and slaughter Yamaha."
Values	The principles that guide day-to-day behavior	Day-to-day	Walt Disney: • No cynicism • Nurturing and promulgation of "wholesome American values" • Creativity, dreams, and imagination • Fanatical attention to consistency and detail • Preservation and control of the Disney "magic"

4. Stakeholder

- What are the main groups of stakeholders (for example, customers, employees, suppliers)?
- What is the most practical and effective method of communicating to each stakeholder group?

5. Target scope

The *target scope* defines where we want to be in the future and how we are going to measure success and achievement of this goal. Example: "Become the leading U.S. provider of XYZ services."

- Financial—deliver financial growth to 2020:
  - Economic value added: 25 percent
  - Revenue: Approximately 25 percent, greater relative contribution from Division A and Division B
  - Net operating profit after tax: 37 percent
  - Measure performance across the entire value chain via Balanced Scorecard
- Clients—Target individuals and corporates to position Client ABC as a lifetime provider of XYZ services.
- Employees—Minimize duplication across business units and increase value added by building functional support to delivery units. Staff will be respected professionals in their area of expertise.
- Community—Support community initiatives that align with Client ABC's activities.

6. Target communication plan

A well-developed communication plan is needed to effectively communicate the desired target state for the organization to all levels of the organization, as well as to external stakeholders.

Target for Communicators	Level	Sponsor	Stakeholder	Media	Frequency
Internal	Group-wide	Corporate Level	Person A	Corporate email	Quarterly
	Division	Division Leads	Person B Person C Person D	Division email Presentation	Monthly
	Business unit (BU)	BU Leads	Person E Person F Person G	BU presentation newsletter	BU specific weekly
External	Customers	Corporate Level	Person A	Flyer Website	As required
	Customers	Corporate Level	Person A	Flyer Website	As required

Phase III: Assess Choices (What Choices Do We Have?)

In this phase of the strategy development process, strategic choices are assessed. Typical areas of analysis include:

1. Identify options.
    - What options exist for competition in chosen segments (for example, strengthen competitive position, skew mix to certain segments, and so on)?
    - What are competitors doing?
    - What is the best practice (domestic, international, other comparable segments)?
2. Assess options.
    - Which options have the highest return and lowest risk (weighted according to starting competitive position)?
    - Which options are the most economically sustainable?
    - What is the likely competitor response to each option?
    - What are the likely outcomes from each option (for example, five to seven big things)?
3. Assess feasibility.
    - How do competitive options add to the organization's value proposition (by market and by segment)?
    - How do competitive options improve the organization's strengths (for example, cost/scale, differentiation, customer intimacy, and so on)?

Strategic levers are also assessed. Typical areas of analysis include:

1. Competitive options
    - Generate strategic options for competition in chosen segments, for example:
        - Strengthen our competitive position.
        - Shift our mix to more attractive segments.
        - Improve attractiveness of key segments.
        - Incorporate international trends and best practices.

2. Strategy choice
   - Evaluate and make choices on "how to compete" on the basis of risks and returns.
   - Determine strategies required to deliver (the five to seven big things).
   - Develop clearly linked economics to overall targets.
   - Determine internal organizational changes required.
   - Determine position sustainability.
3. Definition of strategy
   - Document overall strategic goal and high-level targets.
   - Clarify the offering in each segment/value proposition.
   - Clarify the basis of advantage.

Possible future business strategies for the organization are discussed and assessed. Examples of generic strategies include:

<table>
<tr><th>Strategies</th><th>Categories</th><th>Specific Options</th></tr>
<tr><td>Strengthening our competitive position in attractive segments</td><td>• Widen or overcome cost or differentiation advantages.
• Create new sources of advantage.</td><td rowspan="3">• Scan trends internationally.
• Use benchmarks to target improvements.
• Foster creativity and innovation.
  • Share information and diagnosis (especially customer research)
  • Brainstorming</td></tr>
<tr><td>Shifting our mix toward more attractive segments</td><td>• Gain share of attractive segments.
• Withdraw from unattractive ones.</td></tr>
<tr><td>Increasing segment attractiveness</td><td>• Raise entry barriers.
• Reduce rivalry.
• Reduce pressure from substitutes, buyers, and suppliers.</td></tr>
</table>

Strategic options are evaluated for the best fit for the organization's future competitive position. This process typically involves the following components:

1. Evaluate.
   - "Do nothing" versus other options: magnitude and timing of returns

- Scenario modeling (what-if modeling of risks)
- Competitor response (competitor role-playing): Given possible competitor responses, what is the likely magnitude and timing of returns from alternative strategies?

2. Strategize
- Five to seven big things required to deliver
- May be in the form of "strategic themes/initiatives" (for example, focus on branding)

3. Set targets
- Clearly link economics to overall targets.

4. Org structure
- Determine internal organizational changes required: structure, staffing levels, skills, monitoring and reward systems
- Review operating policies: sales and marketing, production, purchasing, research and development (R&D), assets, information technology (IT)
- Feasibility
- Determine position sustainability

This phase concludes with the production of a recommendations report that defines the recommended strategic direction. This report typically contains the following components:

Section	**Detail**
Executive Summary	Summarize the major challenges, initiatives, and outcomes.
Assessment	• Draws out fact-based insights on our profit by segment, attractiveness, and competitive position. • Clarify our offerings in each segment/value proposition. • Clarify our basis of advantage—cost/scale, differentiation, innovation, customer intimacy.
Vision and Goals	• Mission: a statement of purpose. • Overall strategic goal (for example, attain X position in Y segments by time T).

Section	Detail
Rationale	• Outline preferred strategy and rationale for discarding alternatives. • Describe timing and contingency plans.
Operational Impact	Identify the supporting actions/timing required to implement the operational changes identified—Human Resources (HR), Sales, Assets, and so on.
Financials	Document the five-year financial and other key performance outcomes expected from the plan.

Phase IV: Define Road Map (How Are We Going to Get There?)

Typical areas of discussion and analysis during the Define Road Map phase include:

1. Get buy-in.
   - Stakeholders are clearly identified—internal and external.
   - Communication method/collateral appropriate to each group is available.
   - A communications plan is developed and executed.
   - Awareness and support are achieved from stakeholder groups.
2. Define projects.
   - Individual projects to support each strategy are developed.
   - A project template is completed for each project.
   - The economic model is linked to align bottom-up project economics with strategies and overall goals.
3. Monitor progress.
   - Targets for each project are established in terms of timing, progress to drivers, and progress to economic goals.
   - Clear single-point accountability is established for each project.
   - A tracking system is established and regularly monitored showing progress of each project and gap to overall goals.

The road map will typically consist of a portfolio of projects designed to achieve the desired target state for the organization. Sample goals for the project portfolio may include:

- Financial
  - Economic value added: 25 percent
  - Revenue: About 25 percent, greater relative contribution from Division A and Division B
  - Net operating profit after tax: 37 percent
- Clients
  - Target individuals and corporates to position Client ABC as a lifetime provider of XYZ services
- Employees
  - Minimize duplication across business units and increase value added by building functional support to delivery units
- Community
  - Support community initiatives that align with Client ABC's activities

Defining Project Focus Areas

Project focus areas where projects will be undertaken in order to achieve the desired future state are typically defined. These focus areas are defined to organize and manage projects that are designed to benefit a particular part of the business strategy. These areas will be the primary areas for business analysis and progress tracking within the overall road map project portfolio.

Sample Focus Areas

Brand

- Project 1
- Project 2
- Project 3

Customer

- Project 1
- Project 2
- Project 3

Quality

- Project 1
- Project 2
- Project 3

Distribution

- Project 1
- Project 2
- Project 3

Prioritize Projects

While there are many ways to prioritize projects, a common way is to prioritize by the ease of implementation and impact on profits or revenue, as shown in Figure 1.1.

Build and Monitor the Project Road Map

A project portfolio road map is developed, managed, and tracked. Projects are monitored and evaluated over time regarding alignment with current business strategy. As business strategy evolves, priorities within the project portfolio may change.

The benefits of a well-developed project monitoring and evaluation process include the following:

- It tracks benefits and drives accountability in business units to deliver.
- It creates a clear and separated view of focus areas and projects to improve decision-making capability.
- It ties benefits tracking directly back to key strategy/business drivers.
- It ensures regular monitoring of progress for each project and gap to overall goals.

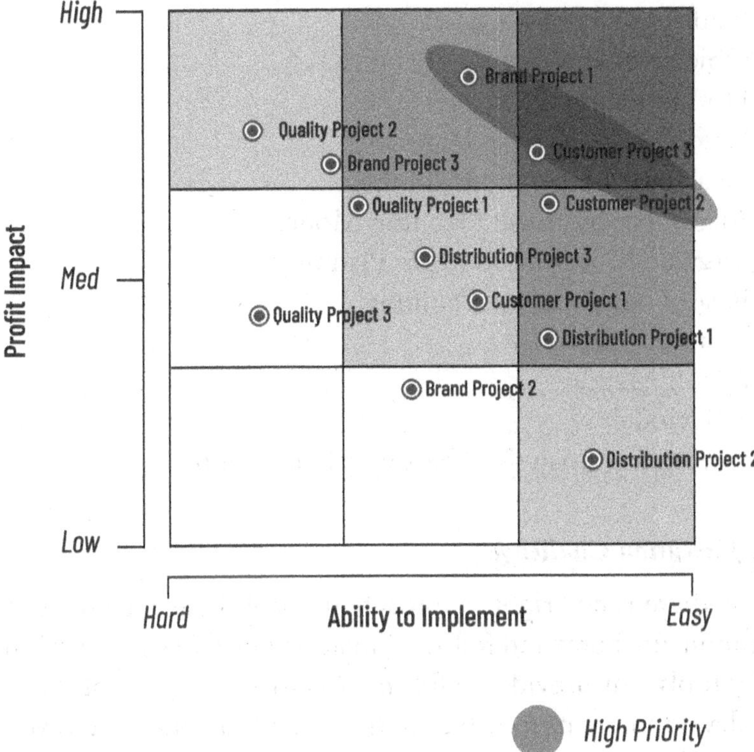

Figure 1.1 Project prioritization.

What Is the Best Approach to Strategy Development?

There are many strategy development approaches, frameworks, and methodologies in use today. Examples of some of the more popular approaches include:

- Balanced Scorecard
- Strategy Map
- Strengths, Weaknesses, Opportunities, Threats (SWOT) Analysis
- Political, Economic, Social, Technological (PEST) Model
- Gap Planning
- Blue Ocean Strategy
- Porter's Five Forces
- Value, Rarity, Imitability, Organization (VRIO) Framework

- Baldridge Framework
- Objectives and Key Results (OKRs)
- Hoshin Planning
- Issue-Based Strategic Planning
- Goal-Based Strategic Planning
- Alignment Strategic Planning Model
- Organic Model of Strategic Planning
- Real-Time Strategic Planning
- Scenario Planning
- Ansoff Matrix
- 7-S Model
- Constraints Analysis (Theory of Constraints)

The Execution Challenge

While there is no "right" approach, most of these approaches have common attributes and follow similar patterns. Several of them are really tools that provide useful insights that feed parts of the strategy development process but do not provide a comprehensive process for formulating strategy. None of these approaches provides a comprehensive process for strategy development and execution.

To illustrate this point, let's examine a few of the more popular approaches and discuss what high-level information and perspectives they provide and some areas where they fall short in terms of strategy execution. ***Note:*** There are many sources of information on pros and cons of these approaches and tools, but for the purposes of this book, we will focus on the execution-related components.

Balanced Scorecard

According to the Balanced Scorecard Institute (https://balancedscorecard.org), "The balanced scorecard (BSC) is a strategic planning and management system that organizations use to:

- Communicate what they are trying to accomplish
- Align the day-to-day work that everyone is doing with strategy

- Prioritize projects, products, and services
- Measure and monitor progress towards strategic targets"[4]

This all sounds very good, and use of this approach has been attempted to varying degrees by countless organizations (though reports of successful implementations are infrequent). However, when we look at the details of the *how* to align day-to-day work with strategy, *how* to prioritize projects, and so on, we are left wanting. There's very little real detail on *how* to effectively implement this high-level approach and no real focus on external factors and competitors.

Hoshin Planning

Hoshin Kanri is a seven-step strategic planning process that aims to ensure that the strategy of a company gets executed across the hierarchy. The process claims to be able to effectively connect strategic planning to project execution. The seven steps to the Hoshin Planning process are:

1. Establish the vision and assess the current state.
2. Develop breakthrough objectives.
3. Define annual objectives.
4. Cascade goals throughout the organization.
5. Execute annual objectives.
6. Conduct monthly reviews.
7. Conduct annual reviews.

These steps are similar to many of the other popular strategic planning approaches. Hoshin Planning has been widely rejected by the agile community because it is very linear and does not easily allow for rapid changes to strategy and adjustments to today's dynamic world.

Step 5 deals with execution via a method known as *Catchball.* The next step is to deploy your annual objectives using a technique called *Hoshin Kanri Catchball,* which is designed to create consensus about how objectives will be met through a top-down system of two-way feedback loops between managers and their direct reports.

Again, this all sounds very good, and this approach provides more guidance than most, but when we look at the details of *how* to align day-to-day work with strategy, we find little real detail on how to effectively create and maintain line of sight between the projects in which the organization is investing its resources and the business strategy of the organization. This line of sight enables the organization to adjust its project portfolio in a timely manner to reflect changes in strategy, so we have true alignment (and effective strategy execution). This type of agile strategy execution process is lacking from most of the popular strategy development approaches.

Blue Ocean Strategy

The goal of a Blue Ocean Strategy is for organizations to find and develop *blue oceans* (uncontested, growing markets) and avoid *red oceans* (overdeveloped, saturated markets). A company will have more success, fewer risks, and increased profits in a blue ocean market.

Great, but *how* do you execute this blue ocean strategy once you've identified it? Again, there's no guidance on the *how* of execution.

Porter's Five Forces

Porter's Five Forces is not a strategy development framework but a model (or tool) that identifies and analyzes five competitive forces that shape every industry and helps determine an industry's weaknesses and strengths. Five Forces analysis is frequently used to identify an industry's structure to inform strategy development.

Porter's Five Forces are as follows:

1. Competition in the industry
2. Potential of new entrants into the industry

3. Power of suppliers
4. Power of customers
5. Threat of substitute products

Again, this is a tool to help inform strategy development and no relation to the *how* of strategy execution.

We could do this type of discussion with each of the popular strategy development approaches but you get the idea—none is effective with strategy execution. With all of these "expert" strategy development approaches available, each claiming to be superior to the others, it's very difficult for organizations to make sense of the pros and cons of each and determine the right course of action for the organization.

Conceptually, all of the strategy development approaches make sense at a high level, but just as the advice to the rabbits in the Introduction to this book made sense, the devil is in the *how* of the implementation details. Some of these approaches mention elements of the strategy execution equation such as capabilities, managing projects, business models, or strategy maps, but none goes into much detail and none presents a holistic approach to linking business strategy with execution. In fact, by not taking a comprehensive approach to strategy execution, the popular strategy development approaches can cause concepts such as strategies, business models, and tactics to be used synonymously, which can lead to poor decision-making (more on this in later chapters).

Many organizations will develop their own hybrid approach that may combine aspects of several of the popular approaches. Most of the popular process-based approaches adhere to some basic phases:

1. Analysis of the current internal and external environments
2. Development of high-level strategy and basic organizational level strategic plan
3. Translation of the high-level strategic plan into more operational planning and action/execution items (more in the following section)

4. Ongoing evaluation, refinement, and management of various facets of strategic management such as performance, communications, culture, and so on

How Do the Popular Strategy Development Approaches Handle Strategy Execution?

Interestingly, most of the popular strategy development approaches only discuss strategy execution at a high, cursory level—*if they discuss it at all.* Execution is hard and messy—this is why most consultants will tell you they try to get out before execution. This is also why most strategy development approaches veer away from any substantiative discussion of strategy execution.

None of the popular strategy development approaches get into the details on *how* to successfully execute strategy, and almost treat strategy execution as a lesser consideration and focus primarily on the strategy development process. No matter how good the strategy is, it's worthless if it can't be successfully executed.

Let's look at two strategy development approaches that specifically mention strategy execution.

Example 1 The following are the steps involved in the strategic planning process according to one strategy development approach:

1. Determine your strategic position.
2. Prioritize your objectives.
3. Develop a strategic plan.
4. Execute and manage the plan.

This sounds very similar to the general strategic planning phases outlined previously, and execution is specifically mentioned in Step 4. However, when you explore Step 4 further, you see that it provides no real guidance on the *how* of strategy execution.

Example 2 The following are the steps involved in the strategic planning process according to another strategy development approach:

1. Outline expectations. Define the enterprise and business context for all stakeholders.
2. Verify the business context. Set enterprise mission and vision.
3. Set goals and objectives.
4. Develop an action plan.
5. Assess your capabilities.
6. Set measures and metrics.
7. Put your strategy on one page.
8. Drive the plan home. Evangelize the objectives and strategy across your function and company.
9. Prepare to respond to change. Measure progress against the objectives, revisit and monitor the plan to ensure it remains valid, and adapt the strategy as business conditions change.

This one has more steps and Steps 8 and 9 are where high-level aspects of execution are mentioned. But again, it has only high-level references to some of the aspects of strategy execution and no details on *how* to effectively execute strategy.

Many of the popular strategy development approaches advocate that all members of an organization need to have a good understanding of the objectives and strategic goals of the organization and have their roles tightly aligned with these goals and objectives. Again, this all sounds great, and most people would say it makes sense—the problem is that there is little to no information on *how* to make all of this happen.

Strategy Alignment: Issues with Traditional Approaches and a Pragmatic Approach

Now that we've introduce the general strategy development process and associated issues with strategy execution, let's explore the notion of strategy alignment and issues that impact effective strategy execution.

What Is Alignment? We've been talking about strategy alignment for decades but what does it really mean to be aligned? Is true alignment even possible? What does alignment look like? Are there different types of alignment? How do you measure it? Can you be 50 percent aligned? Eighty percent? Twenty percent? The questions could go on.

Over the last few decades, we've been conditioned to believe that direct alignment with business strategy is not only possible but something that we all should be continually striving to achieve. However, how can we directly "align" (whatever that means) with something that is changing and evolving (maybe rapidly in some industries) and that only a very small percentage of people in a given organization understand at any point in time? The answer is that you can't—at least not directly. We need a more pragmatic approach to "aligning" business strategy (and changes to strategy) with tactical-level (project-level) execution.

First, we need a general definition of what we mean by strategic alignment. According to Trevor and Varcoe,[5] strategic alignment "means that all elements of a business—including the market strategy and the way the company itself is organized—are arranged in such a way as to best support the fulfillment of its long-term purpose."

We'd like to offer that there are two main aspects to alignment:

- Is the organization structured and designed with intent to deliver on its strategy?
- Is there a continuous line of sight between strategy and the organization's project portfolio?

Our perspective on strategic alignment is that most of us are employed by our organizations to assist in executing the strategy of the organization. This execution typically manifests in the form of projects and project portfolios. If there is line of sight between the projects in which the organization is investing its resources and the business strategy of the organization, and this line of sight enables the organization to adjust its project portfolio in a timely manner to reflect changes in strategy, we have true alignment (and effective strategy execution). This adjustment to the project portfolio may entail adding new projects, changing existing projects, or discontinuing projects that are no longer needed.

Now the question is: How do we do this? Many organizations are doing the wrong projects today. We'll answer this question in detail in the coming chapters. But before we delve into this question, we need to discuss the traditional thinking around strategic alignment a bit more to fully understand the issues with the traditional alignment approaches. We will use the traditional IT and business alignment discussion to illustrate the problems with traditional alignment thinking. Even though IT is used as an example, the concepts and issues discussed apply to any part of the organization that is attempting to "align" with business strategy.

IT/Business Alignment

People with an IT background have been conditioned to believe that the direct alignment of IT strategy with business strategy is not only a goal but an achievable goal. When this goal fails to materialize, the blame is often focused on the IT organization.

Many analyst firms cite the high percentage of IT projects that fail to one degree or another. Today, most (if not all) projects have a healthy technological component. Given these statistics, it is understandable that IT may often be cited as a contributing factor in poor strategy execution, and if the IT organization would just align better with the rest of the business, our strategy execution success would greatly improve.

Is this an accurate and fair conclusion? Is the direct alignment of IT strategy with business strategy really the holy grail? Let's look at the traditional IT/business alignment argument and the problems with this argument.

The Traditional Alignment Rationale

Much of the traditional IT/business alignment thinking can be traced back to the Strategic Alignment Model (SAM) developed by Henderson and Venkatraman (1993).[6] This model, shown in Figure 1.2, suggests that the inability to realize value from IT investments is due to the lack of alignment between business and IT strategies of organizations. The model suggests that direct alignment between IT strategy and business strategy is possible and desirable. According to SAM, business and IT may be functionally

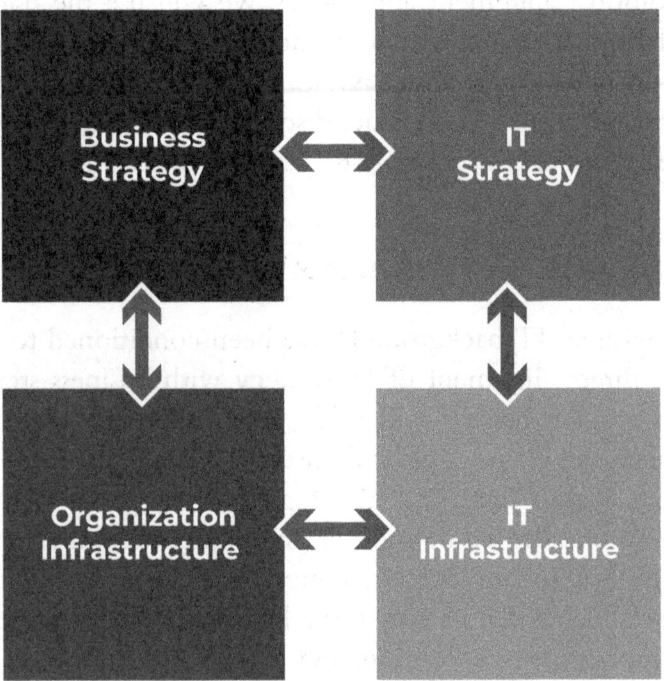

Figure 1.2 Functional integration and alignment.

Source: Adapted from Henderson and Venkatraman, 1993

integrated, but if the external and internal components of IT strategy are out of sync, investments in IT don't bring about the intended results.

On the surface, this all seems to make sense. The IT strategy has to align with the business strategy, right? Why have an IT strategy otherwise? Experience has shown many flaws with this argument and thinking.

As we discussed previously, according to Kaplan and Norton, 90 percent of organizations fail to execute their strategies successfully. They go on to state that the reason for this failure is often not the strategy itself, but bad execution. Kaplan and Norton also reported that a mere 7 percent of employees today fully understand their company's business strategies at any point in time. Again, we ask: How can we hope to successfully execute something that is changing and that a very low percentage of people fully understand?

In addition, an IT strategy is a seriously weighty thing to put together. It's hard to write a strategy that dictates the direction of things that are expensive and hard to change (like tools, platforms, applications, and architecture) based on the business telling IT that "next year we're going to leverage key learnings in our core competencies and maximize customer value by augmenting synergy in the value chain."

So, what's the frame of reference for the IT strategy, if it's not the business strategy? What is the interim mechanism for linking (a better word than aligning) the IT strategy with the business strategy (and changes to the business strategy)?

The job of the IT strategy isn't to *align* to the business strategy. It's to give the businesspeople who create it as many options to change tack as possible. It's a provider of *capability*—capability to react to market changes a bit easier and faster—that can have a big impact on the competitive position of the organization. Now IT is a platform for opportunity and the discussions are now around business opportunities and not about how hard it is to do what the business needs.

This is very difficult to do where IT is attempting to align strategy directly with business strategy. In the world of alignment, IT is always struggling to understand and react to the current state of the business strategy and is never able to "align." This mindset doesn't allow the chief information officer (CIO) and IT to influence business strategy and help determine which projects have the most business value and be a partner in the setting of business strategy and creation of business value. Focusing on IT strategy alignment distracts the IT organization from the real work of understanding and promoting the goals and objectives that matter to the rest of the organization. In addition, using language that focuses on IT alignment with the business is damaging because such language implies that IT stands apart from "the business" instead of being an integral part of it.

This change in thinking around alignment creates a need to rethink how we measure and communicate value. In the traditional alignment mindset, IT would communicate its value around how money is being spent and cost containment and would communicate things like network use, applications supported, projects completed on time, head count, and so on. The more pragmatic approach where IT is thought about as another part of the business changes the focus to metrics that define how IT is contributing to the growth of the business such as contribution to sales and how IT has contributed to drive revenue. Focusing on metrics that define value creates a very different conversation and relationship from those typically created when the conversation is focused on doing things cheaper and faster. We will discuss value measurement and value communication in detail in coming chapters.

So, what is a more effective alternative to align IT, or any other part of the organization, with the business strategy? An interim linking mechanism is needed. The business capabilities of the organization provide the pragmatic, sustainable link to ensure that the IT strategy and IT as a provider of agile services and capabilities is aligned with the current needs of the business strategy. We will explore business and IT alignment in more depth in Chapter 5.

Linking IT and Business Strategies

Using our IT strategy example, we've established that any "alignment" directly with business strategy is very difficult, if not impossible, to establish and maintain over time. We've also established that the alignment mindset can actually be damaging to the organization. An interim linking/alignment mechanism is needed to link the IT strategy as a provider of agile services and capabilities to the current needs of the business strategy. The core business capabilities of the organization provide this pragmatic, sustainable link.

A *business capability* defines the organization's capacity to successfully perform a unique business activity. Business capabilities:

- Are the building blocks of the business
- Represent stable abilities of the business
- Are unique and independent from each other
- Are abstracted from the organizational model
- Capture the business's interests

Business capabilities are typically represented in a conceptual model of all the organization's capabilities called a *capability map* and can be related to the people, processes, and technology that enable them.

Let's look at a simple example to help solidify the concept of a business capability—we will discuss this concept in more detail in later chapters as well.

Figure 1.3 illustrates a Develop Product value stream for a global apparel company that we explore further in Chapter 3. The value stream delivers a manufacturing-ready product design for a piece of apparel. Business capabilities enable each stage of the value stream. For example, the capabilities of Product Information Management, Product Material Management, and Product Design are key to enabling the Design Product stage. We will explore business capabilities and many other topics in more detail later in this book. For now, let's focus on how the core business capabilities of the organization are used to link to business strategy.

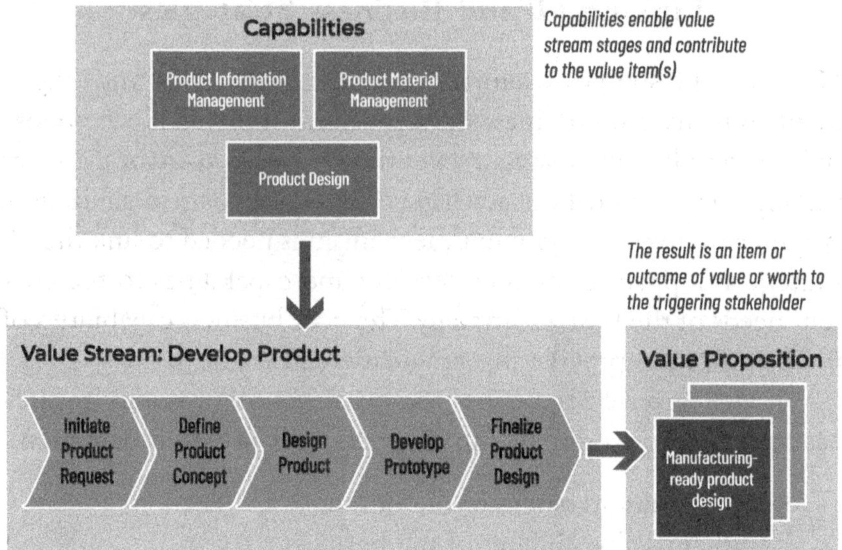

Figure 1.3 Business capabilities are the core components to all products and services.

The owners of the core business capabilities are typically in business strategy–related discussions and understand the current state of the business strategy and what corresponding changes are needed in the business capabilities of the organization. These changes could entail developing new business capabilities, modifying how existing business capabilities are implemented, or discontinuing business capabilities that are no longer needed. These changes to the organizational business capability portfolio often require a series of projects to implement the modifications. These projects (and project portfolios) are the execution layer for the business strategy. In this world, that IT organization is a provider of services (capabilities) to the business capability owners (who are in turn "aligned" with the current state of the business strategy). The business capabilities provide the interim linking/alignment mechanism to create the line of sight between the project execution level and the business strategy (and changes to the business strategy). As business strategy changes, these changes are reflected in corresponding changes to the business capability portfolio that are then reflected in corresponding changes to the project portfolio. The IT organization, in turn, provides the agile services needed to make these changes and react to market changes in a timely manner. We will discuss *how* to create this line of sight and create and sustain these linkages later in this book.

> At this point, we should clarify the two ways that the word *capability* is used in this example (a potential source of confusion to those that are new to business capabilities). When we say that the IT organization is a provider of capability, we mean that the IT organization is providing the ability to do something to the organization (sometimes known as *small c capabilities*). This is different from how the word *capability* is used when we're talking about the core business capabilities of the organization from a strategic perspective. Here we're talking about major areas of the organization, typically those that are central to what our organization does (sometimes known as *big C capabilities*)—see the definition of business capabilities at the start of this section.

Many other aspects/components of the organization must be modeled and understood, in addition to the core business capabilities, in order to create the linkages and line of sight between project-level execution and the business strategy. Figure 1.4 (in the following section) illustrates the major components and how they interrelate. The process of developing and maintaining this organizational perspective and understanding is generally known as *business architecture*. We will discuss the *how* of developing this enterprise-wide perspective in later chapters.

A More Pragmatic Approach to Strategy Execution

We have highlighted some key challenges with strategy execution thus far. First, while many valuable tools and approaches exist, none provides a comprehensive or cohesive process for strategy development *and* execution. Second, there is often a missing link needed to effectively align different parts of the organization back to the business strategy. However, that same missing link exists at strategy level, leading to a significant gap between strategy and execution. After defining a strategy, most organizations interpret, plan, and execute their response to that strategy in organizational silos with loose coordination. This gap is encoded into many of the existing approaches that tie the strategic focal points to projects with nothing in between.

Effective strategy execution requires clear intent to be translated into organized effort across people, processes, and technology. Fragmented strategy translation is the source of countless issues that manifest downstream in execution, including misaligned investments, suboptimal experiences for people, and the creation of duplicate solutions, complexity, and technical debt.

Figure 1.4 lays out a perspective to help bridge this gap and address the challenges that often exist. Here we introduce a five-stage strategy execution perspective to help frame the discussion. Each stage represents activities that need to happen, though this is an intentionally simplified approach that does not represent nuances of timing, waterfall versus agile delivery, feedback loops, or other details. Any type of business direction can flow through the approach, such as strategies, business transformations, innovation ideas, merger-and-acquisition integration activities, regulatory

Figure 1.4 Strategy execution stages.

changes, or other major operational changes, and at any level of detail, from enterprise level to business unit level. One can think of multiple "instances" of this strategy execution path occurring at one time.

In an ideal situation, business direction and objectives are rationalized in the Develop Strategy stage. Even when business direction is formulated in business units or other silos, there is intentional collaboration, especially in cases where multiple areas are interpreting enterprise-level direction.

In the Architect Changes stage, the *collective* impact of the objectives on the organization is cataloged using value streams, capabilities, and other business perspectives (for example, business units, stakeholders, products, policies), along with IT architecture and operating model perspectives (system applications, software services, processes, and so on). Where applicable, this stage allows the architecting or rearchitecting of aspects of the organizational environment to be done together across business units or other silos, such as in the case of an enterprise-wide business transformation or shared capabilities related to customers. This stage may produce a target business and IT architecture(s) that can be communicated widely to align people to a common picture of the future.

Here we recognize that *business capabilities* comprise the bridge that serves to link and align the components of the strategy execution process. This "bridge" is often missing or incomplete in many organizations. Business capabilities are a central component of a holistic view of an organization called a *business architecture,* which we will discuss in detail in the upcoming chapters.

In the Plan/Adjust Portfolios/Projects stage, business and technology changes are organized into the most effective set of projects and project portfolios with mutually exclusive scopes and are logically sequenced to reflect dependencies and integration points. Each project, whether large or small, is framed by the capabilities (in a value stream context) that are being uplifted from a people, process, and/or technology perspective. This means that the value streams and capabilities become *the* connection point across projects, which can be beneficial for many reasons. For example, teams can be readily informed of other teams or projects that are working on the same capability so that they can coordinate as needed to ensure a consistent customer experience, build reusable solutions, share knowledge and resources, and manage the amount of change impacting stakeholders.

During the Plan/Adjust Portfolios/Projects stage, proposed projects can be aligned to business objectives, as well as value streams and capabilities (to be discussed in depth in Chapter 3), producing heat maps that reflect strategic alignment and potentially reveal redundant or misaligned projects. This stage helps portfolio managers rationalize and prioritize all potential investments for decision-making both within and across portfolios.

In the Execute Solutions stage, teams are accelerated by receiving the big-picture context, a clear scope, fully agreed-upon business vocabulary, and an approach for identifying requirements.

Finally, in the Measure Success stage, project results can be compared back to the original business objectives, by referring to the end-to-end traceability available in the business architecture knowledge base. This traceability also facilitates dynamic replanning as well. For example, if the market shifts and a strategy is no longer a priority, the projects tied to it can be readily identified and paused.

The adoption of some sort of strategy execution approach (such as the one shown in Figure 1.4) not only helps an organization to communicate and coalesce around a vision but also provides the context for different teams to interact. This information provides a starting point for discussions about where various teams focus, the value they deliver, their inputs and outputs, and how they interact with other teams.

Figure 1.5 recognizes that this perspective is not a one-and-done process and that strategy is constantly adjusted as environmental conditions change. This fact requires a process that not only initially aligns execution (projects) with strategy but also is

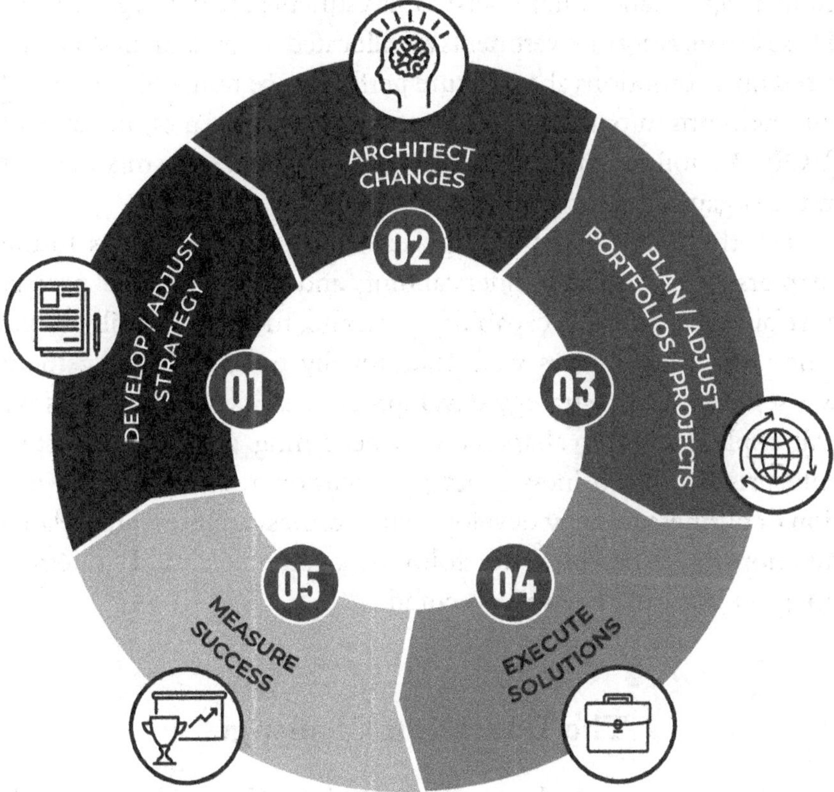

Figure 1.5 Strategy execution stages as a continuous process.

designed to keep the project portfolio aligned with changes in the strategy—something that is not easy to accomplish and something that is typically glossed over (or not addressed at all) by most of the popular strategy development approaches.

The Role of Portfolio Management in Strategy Execution

The concept of portfolio management is derived from financial portfolio management where we manage the assets of the organization (projects, business capabilities, processes, technology assets, human capital, and other assets) as investments for the organization. These organizational investments are allocated to investment strategies based on assumptions about future performance to maximize value/risk trade-offs in optimizing the organization's return on investment (ROI). Portfolio management attempts to optimize the mix of assets in the organization's portfolios.

For the purposes of strategy execution, we will focus future chapters primarily on understanding and managing the project portfolio and business capability portfolio, though we will discuss other asset portfolios as well. Traditionally, portfolio management was separated from strategy development and execution, but as we will explain in later chapters, it is becoming clear that effective enterprise-wide business strategy execution requires an integration of business strategy development, business architecture–related functions, and enterprise portfolio management. A solid strategy is no good if it can't be well executed.

The Education Challenge

A study conducted by the Graduate Business Curriculum Roundtable and the Business Architecture Guild®[7] suggests that part of the reason for the poor track record with strategy execution may rest with how strategy execution is taught in graduate business programs. The study consisted of a short survey designed to better understand to what depth strategy execution is covered in graduate business programs. This survey was sent to administrative leads of graduate programs from a broad cross-section of colleges and universities, and 78 responses were received.

The main focus of the survey was to learn (a) whether strategy execution was taught as a required component of business graduate programs and, if so, (b) how strategy execution was taught in these programs and the associated topics covered. The main part of the survey asked, "Do any of your professional master's programs and/or MBA programs offer a course on strategy execution?" For those that answered yes, the survey then asked, "Is the course required or an elective in your professional master's and MBA programs?" The survey then asked the respondent to upload an outline of the topics covered and/or a copy of the course syllabus; a total of 38 syllabi were submitted. This paper focuses on the findings from the submitted syllabi.

The 38 syllabi came from a variety of colleges and universities. Thirty-six of the schools in this group were U.S.-based institutions; the remaining 2 were from Canada. There was a fairly even mix of public and private schools (22 public, 16 private). There was also a fairly even mix of large universities and small and midsize schools (17 large universities, 21 small/midsize schools). Even though all submitted syllabi claimed to be strategy execution courses, only four had strategy execution/implementation in the title of the course.

Most of the courses in this analysis covered strategic management and leadership topics and only focused one or two weeks on strategy execution/implementation. These courses focused primarily on topics such as organizational culture and structure, change management, team dynamics, rewards and incentives, power and influence, and effective communications. These topics were often discussed in the context of case studies.

The courses with strategy execution/implementation in their titles focused heavily on the human and organizational elements of strategy implementation—managing people, resistance to change, building effective teams, navigating/understanding politics, types of power, change management strategies, importance of communication, organizational structure, information and decision processes, rewards, people, and leading change without formal authority. These topics were taught by the use of case studies that focus on one or more of these areas.

While these topics are important for successful strategy execution, they are far from the comprehensive set of skills, knowledge, and processes needed for successful strategy execution. None of these courses discusses *how* to link the execution layer (projects) with business strategy and manage ongoing changes to business strategy. Without this linkage, the execution (project) layer falls out of alignment with strategy.

This analysis suggests that an incomplete strategy execution picture is presented in many business curricula today. This incomplete picture could be a contributing factor to the persistent problem of strategy execution seen in many organizations today.

Where Do We Go from Here?

Now that we've presented the challenges with the traditional thinking regarding strategy development, alignment, and execution, it is time to begin the discussion on a more pragmatic, comprehensive approach to business strategy execution.

In Chapter 2, we will begin to explore how strategic business architecture creates the enterprise perspective and understanding needed for effective strategy development and execution. In Chapter 3, we will look at how the strategic business architecture of an organization is typically represented to create the enterprise-wide understanding needed to create the line of sight between businesses strategy and project-level execution. In Chapter 4, we will walk through how to translate business strategy through the strategic business architecture to define an organized set of actions for execution across people, processes, information, and technology. This will also illustrate how the various approaches and views interrelate and work together from end to end across strategy, architecture, and execution. In Chapter 5, we will discuss the role of enterprise portfolio management in detail as a critical component of effective strategy execution.

Strategy Execution Organizational Assessment

About the Assessment

The purpose of this assessment is to provide you with an initial understanding of your organization's current level of effectiveness with strategy execution. This assessment aims to highlight where your organization excels, faces challenges, and has opportunities to improve strategy execution capabilities and effectiveness.

The complete assessment is spread across all chapters of this book, and we recommend that you complete each set of chapter-related questions after you finish reading each chapter.

While initially you may complete this assessment individually, we recommend at some point conducting this assessment together with a team that reflects diverse perspectives and roles across strategy execution roles and functions within your organization. This collaborative approach will not only maximize the results but also create shared understanding and commitment to the next steps for improved strategy execution.

For a deeper level of assessment, please visit www.theexecutionchallenge.com. *We offer a tailored assessment for in-house teams, leveraging a more detailed instrument. We also unpack the findings with your team and provide recommendations and a road map to move into action.*

Scoring

For each question, score your answers using a scale of 0 to 5.

A score of 0 generally indicates a *no* response. For example, if your organization does *not* have a strategy development/

(continued)

formulation group or function at all anywhere in the organization, you would score a 0 for the following question:

Our organization has a strategy development/formulation group or function, and it is effective.

Otherwise, score from 1 (least true/poor) to 5 (most true/excellent). These questions require some discussion and decisions. Consider the aggregate set of conditions stated in the question, and score based on how well your organization meets all of them.

For example, given the following question, if none of the conditions are true, score 0. If your organization has a defined, end-to-end approach that is leveraged at an enterprise-level, consider scoring a 3. If it also works effectively, consider scoring a 4. If it is also iterative and adaptive, consider scoring a 5.

Our organization has defined a comprehensive end-to-end approach from strategy development through strategy execution, and it is effective and iterative.

There may also be situations in which the conditions within a question apply to some parts of the organization, but not the entire enterprise. Give credit for the presence of the condition, but score higher when it is present enterprise-wide. For example, if the concepts of capabilities and value streams have been started in one business unit but not adopted enterprise-wide and for strategy execution, consider scoring a 2 for the following question.

Our organization has a documented, business-owned strategic business architecture baseline (comprised of an enterprise-wide capability map based on defined information concepts, a minimum set of enterprise-wide value streams, and a cross-mapping between the two).

> Consider capturing notes for each question during your team assessment discussion. In many cases, the conversation and takeaways can be as important as the scores themselves.

In Chapter 6, we discuss how strategic business architecture links and aligns with other business functions and disciplines within a strategy execution context. In Chapter 7, we move to a discussion on integrating the strategic business architecture perspective with strategic planning, skills and competencies needs, success factors, and how to measure and communicate value back to key parts of the organization. We round out the book in Chapter 8 with guidance on how to create your own strategic plan for scaling and maturing a strategic business architecture function that can successfully support strategy execution across an organization. We provide a strategic business architecture maturity model to help you assess your organization's maturity on critical components for success. We will also look at the necessary ongoing change management and governance practices, as well as essential leadership skills for strategy execution. This comprehensive approach will leave you with the foundation needed to not only effect successful strategy execution but also become a valued resource for informing strategy development. Finally, in Chapter 9 we will share a glimpse of some possible future directions for strategic business architecture and strategy execution.

STRATEGY EXECUTION ORGANIZATIONAL ASSESSMENT

Reflect on the following questions to assess how well strategy execution is working in your organization based on the concepts from Chapter 1.

1. Our organization has a strategic planning group or function (which includes strategy development/formulation), and it is effective.
2. Our organization has a strategy execution group or function, and it is effective.
3. The levels of strategy are aligned across our organization (for example, corporate/organizational, business unit, operational).
4. Our strategy development process is defined and effective.
5. Our strategy development process is dynamic, adaptive, and ongoing.
6. Our strategy development approach is defined and effective.
7. Strategy is effectively communicated and understood throughout all areas and layers of the organization.
8. Our organization has the ability to execute strategy consistently, cohesively, effectively, and at the pace needed for our business.
9. The levels of strategic plans (that is, the detailed activities undertaken to deliver strategy and transition the organization from its current state to the desired future state) are aligned across our organization (for example, corporate/organizational, business unit, operational).
10. Our organization has defined a comprehensive end-to-end approach from strategy development through strategy execution and it is effective and iterative.

Chapter 2

The Role of Strategic Business Architecture in Strategy Development and Execution

As discussed in Chapter 1, we've seen decades of research and education in the area of strategy execution, yet little improvement in our ability to execute business strategy. The chapter also introduced a study that suggests that part of the reason for the poor track record with strategy execution may rest with the set of topics typically covered when addressing strategy execution and the lack of any real guidance on the *how* of strategy execution—specifically, how to link the execution layer (projects) with business strategy and manage ongoing changes to business strategy. Without this linkage, the execution layer quickly falls out of alignment with current strategy.

Much of the traditional thinking regarding strategy development, alignment, and execution is incomplete and lacks specifics on the crucial *how* of strategy execution. In this chapter, we begin the discussion on a more pragmatic, comprehensive approach to business strategy execution and explore how the discipline of strategic business architecture creates the enterprise perspectives, understanding, and connections needed for effective strategy development and execution.

What Is Strategic Business Architecture?

A strategic business architecture is a holistic view of an organization that creates common understanding and aligns strategy and execution.[1] It helps us understand how an organization is structured to deliver value to its customers and support its operations.

Business architecture is the one go-to place where we can see what an entire organization and its business ecosystem does at a macro level—and it provides a shared language for everyone to understand and describe the enterprise. In our world of complexity and detail, the business architecture perspective is often an entirely unique one: It represents an organization *as a whole*. This perspective is invaluable for designing, planning, and activating strategic change across an organization. Business architecture aims to *consolidate and maintain* a conceptual, multidimensional view of an organization in order to better define the target state of the firm and facilitate strategy execution.

The Contemporary Practice of Business Architecture

Business architecture traces its roots back to a variety of frameworks and practices, so different perspectives and definitions of business architecture still exist today. Some people see business architecture as a part of the enterprise architecture discipline (execution-level business architecture), while others see business architecture as a strategic discipline as part of strategic planning (strategic business architecture). The latter perspective is gaining momentum today in many organizations.

Business architecture was traditionally represented as one of the main elements within enterprise architecture, along with data architecture, application architecture, and technical architecture. This legacy view of business architecture is being challenged today as business architecture has evolved beyond its technical roots in enterprise architecture to become a strategic business discipline and an enterprise-wide resource. Strategic business architecture is commonly leveraged to enable strategy execution, design organizations for effectiveness and agility at a macro level, and inform holistic decision-making in a variety of business scenarios. As a result, strategic business architecture increasingly reports to a business function such as strategy, strategic planning, strategy execution, or transformation.

From our own experiences and interactions with organizations and associations such as the Business Architecture Guild®, we know that ten years ago approximately 60 percent of business architecture practices reported to traditional enterprise architecture groups with approximately 40 percent reporting to a business function. Today, those percentages have flipped—approximately 60 percent of business architecture practices report to a business function, and we see this percentage increasing over time. This evolution of the discipline of business architecture is critical to realize strategic business architecture's full potential as an effective facilitator of enterprise-wide strategy execution.

All of this means that the contemporary practice of business architecture crosses, and bridges, two worlds: on one side, strategy development and execution, and on the other side, the enterprise architecture discipline. Business architecture plays a role in the middle as a part of both. This evolution of business architecture helps to explain why people sometimes understand and define business architecture in different ways. We simply look at the world through slightly different lenses depending on our experiences and education.

The role of strategic business architecture in strategy development and execution is to provide the missing framework and role needed to translate strategy cohesively and align it with execution.

It provides an integrative framework and role to transcend silos and offers additional insights for holistic decision-making. On the other hand, informed by strategic business architecture, the role of execution-level business architecture within the enterprise architecture discipline is to provide the business direction, priority, language, and context for technology decision-making.

Strategic business architecture still needs to work closely with enterprise information technology (IT) as most projects today have hefty technological components. As you will see throughout this book, strategic business architecture lays the solid foundation for effective use of IT and effective digital transformation.

Here are a few examples:

- Identifying business capabilities that can be enabled by disruptive technologies and business designs
- Identifying the key disruptive digital technologies and services that could enhance key business capabilities
- Assessing the digital enterprise opportunity and the key business benefits looking at growth, services, costs, and agility
- Prioritizing business capabilities and associated disruptive digital technologies based on analysis of business value and impact

Figure 2.1 introduces the major components of the strategic business architecture ecosystem. These are the major components that help us understand the environment in which our organization operates and are the major components that provide the information needed to align strategy with project-level execution and keep them aligned over time. We will cover each of these components in detail in Chapter 3.

Traditional Execution-Level Business Architecture versus Strategic Business Architecture

At this point, we feel that it is important to distinguish between traditional execution-level business architecture and strategic business architecture. As mentioned previously, the discipline of business

Components that primarily communicate strategic direction and inform strategy development
Components that primarily represent the business and inform strategy execution
Components that primarily implement strategy execution
VALUE NETWORKS
VALUE CHAINS
BUSINESS MOTIVATION MODEL
STRATEGY MAPS
BUSINESS MODEL CANVAS
OPERATING MODEL CANVAS
VALUE PROPOSITION CANVAS
CAPABILITIES
STRATEGIC PORTFOLIO MANAGEMENT
PROJECTS
BUSINESS PROCESSES
VALUE STREAMS
provide context for
inform(s)
enable
manages/governs
manage/govern
implement
deliver changes to

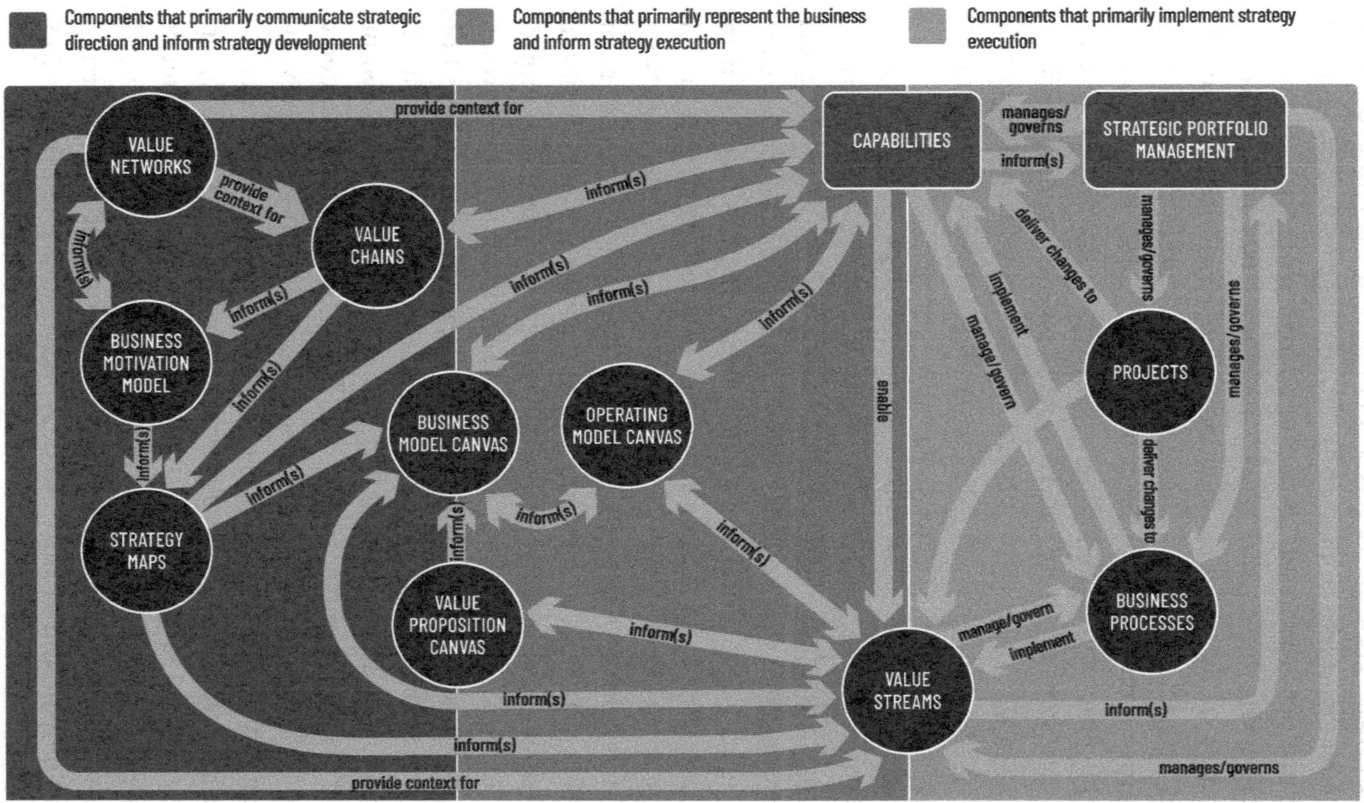

Figure 2.1 The strategic business architecture ecosystem.

architecture "grew up" as part of an IT strategic planning discipline known as *enterprise architecture*. Traditional legacy business architecture practices that reside as part of a larger enterprise architecture practice will be known as execution-level business architecture practices or functions in this book. These traditional execution-level practices are typically technically oriented and often focus on process and/or capability modeling for the IT organization for the purpose of understanding a part of the organization in order to implement or change an IT system, project, or initiative. These practices are not enterprise-wide in their scope (reporting to the IT organization) and are not closely affiliated with strategic planning or enterprise strategy execution.

Strategic business architecture practices have an organization-wide perspective, are business oriented, and are typically part of the strategic planning function. For many, these strategically oriented practices represent the critical component needed for effective strategy execution and a component that is missing in many organizations today. Strategic business architecture creates the line of sight between enterprise project portfolios and business strategy and helps to ensure that the organization is doing the "right" projects that are aligned with current business strategy. Traditional execution-level business architecture helps to ensure that projects are implemented correctly and achieve their desired objectives.

It is possible (and likely) that an organization may have both an execution-level business architecture practice within the IT organization and a strategic business architecture practice within the strategic planning organization. The scope and skills needed to be effective at execution-level business architecture are very different from those associated with strategic business architecture. The execution-level business architecture practice will likely utilize a narrow range of business architecture tools and techniques while the strategic business architecture practice will likely rely on a much wider range of tools and techniques to inform strategy development and facilitate strategy execution. The primary tools

Table 2.1 The Major Differences between Execution-Level and Strategic Business Architecture

	Scope	**Reporting**	**Primary Orientation**	**Primary Stakeholders**
Execution-level business architecture	Project/ program/ level	IT organization/ enterprise architecture	Technical systems	IT organization and IT architects
Strategic business architecture	Enterprise-level strategy execution/ enterprise portfolio level	Strategic planning	Strategy execution	Strategic planning, strategy execution stakeholders

that comprise the strategic business architecture ecosystem are discussed in detail in Chapter 3.

The five-stage strategy process in Figure 1.4 from Chapter 1 could be used by both types of practices, but their scopes and perspectives will be very different. In addition, the skills and backgrounds of the members of the two practices will be very different, as will the structures of the practices. We will discuss the needed skills and suggested organizational structure for an effective strategic business architecture practice in Chapters 7 and 8.

Table 2.1 illustrates some of the major differences between an execution-level business architecture practice and a strategic business architecture practice.

Strategy and Enterprise Architecture

Strategy and enterprise architecture are closely intertwined. Strategy should guide the design of architectural elements to ensure that the business is fulfilling its strategic objectives. Strategy dictates the present and future actions of the firm. In reality, strategies impact and leverage architectural elements of the organization and must be understood, referenced, and made readily accessible. Once the changes to the business and IT architecture layers have been identified to support the strategy, they are then translated into a set of coordinated, business-driven projects.

Figure 2.2 illustrates the traditional main domains of enterprise architecture, including execution-level business architecture, data/information architecture, application architecture, and technical/infrastructure. This model is sometimes known as the Business Architecture, Information Architecture, Application Architecture, Technology Architecture (BIAT) Model and implies that each of these areas is of equal weight and importance. In addition, many

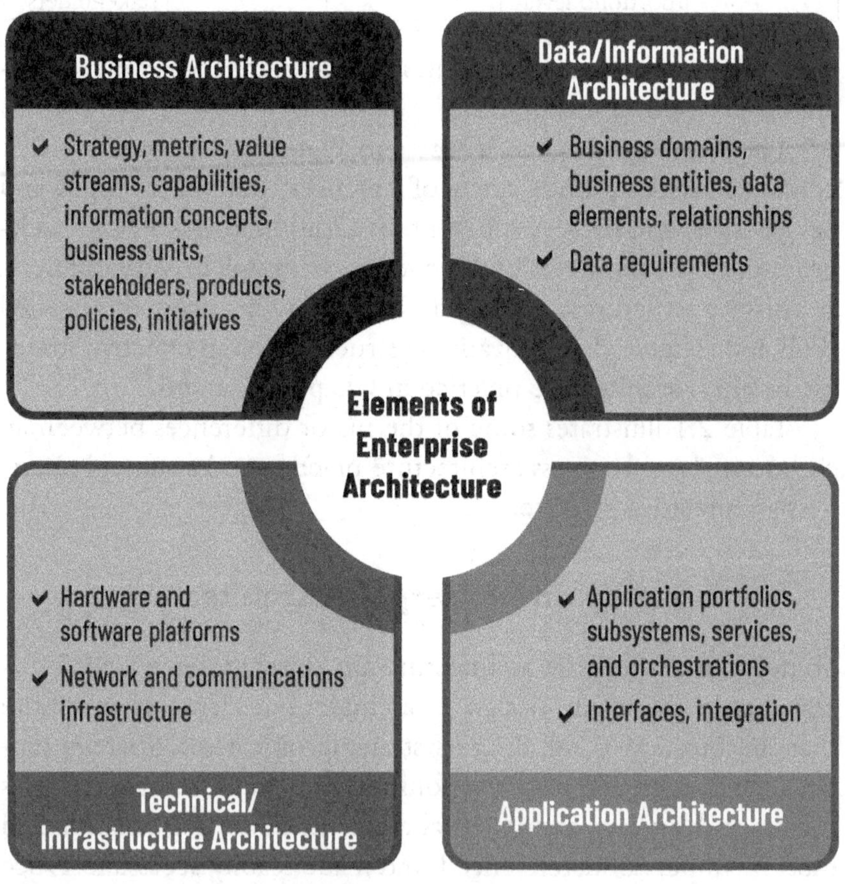

Figure 2.2 The traditional domains of enterprise architecture.

traditional views of execution-level business architecture are primarily focused on process modeling and often view process modeling as the main component of business architecture.

Execution-level business architecture is the foundation for the more technical layers of enterprise architecture. If business architecture is missing or done poorly, the information and technology layers will be poorly developed and ineffective. Many argue that this traditional view of enterprise architecture is no longer valid and that business architecture should be the core focus of enterprise architecture efforts.

As Figure 2.3 demonstrates, the execution-level business architecture drives the formulation of the information architecture of an organization, which in turn drives the applications and infrastructure architectures needed to support the information architecture.

A robust strategic business architecture can be the linchpin to bridge strategy to execution. As Figure 2.4 suggests, effective strategic business architecture is the key to enabling the enterprise to address orders-of-magnitude increases in complexity and in the rate of change.

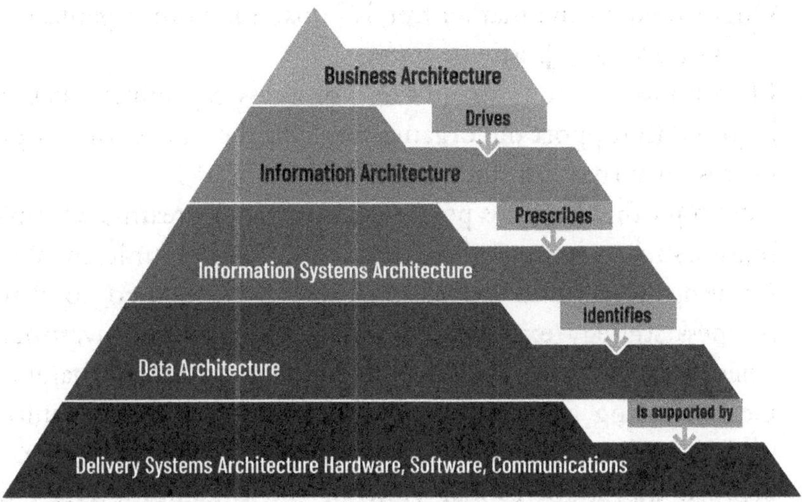

Figure 2.3 Business architecture drives the technical layers of enterprise architecture.

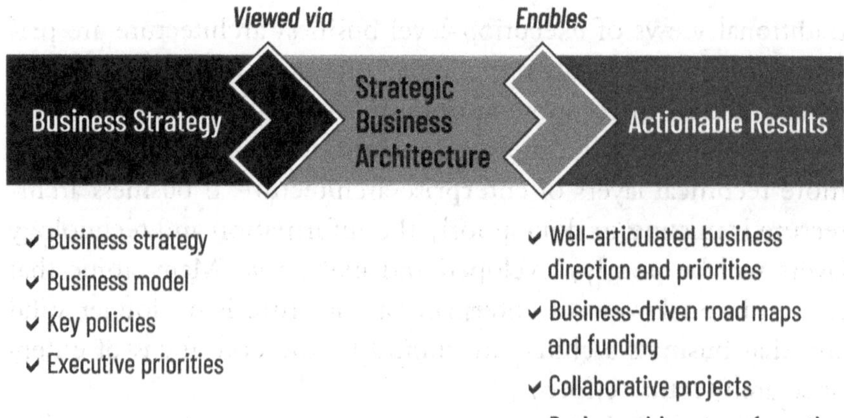

Figure 2.4 Business architecture translates strategy into actionable results.

At a high level, leveraging *strategic* business architecture includes:

- Understanding your organization's business ecosystem, business model, and operating model
- Understanding your organization's business strategy and desired outcomes
- Understanding the market trends impacting your organization and its associated business strategy
- Identifying the value streams and business capabilities that are required to support the organization and the impact on people, process, information, and technology
- Aligning other business perspectives to value streams and capabilities, such as strategies, initiatives, and business units involved
- Creating views and deliverables that can be used to drive business strategy execution, business case analysis, investment analysis, and a wide range of other strategic decision-making
- Consolidating and maintaining business architecture information within a reusable repository that ensures that the conceptual, multidimensional view of the organization can be leveraged to facilitate strategy execution on an ongoing basis

These are the general, high-level benefits that a strategic business architecture function can bring to an organization. There are many other dimensions to strategic business architecture that we will delve into in coming chapters. Figure 2.5 shows the "bridge" role that links strategy and execution that a well-developed strategic business architecture practice provides to the organization.

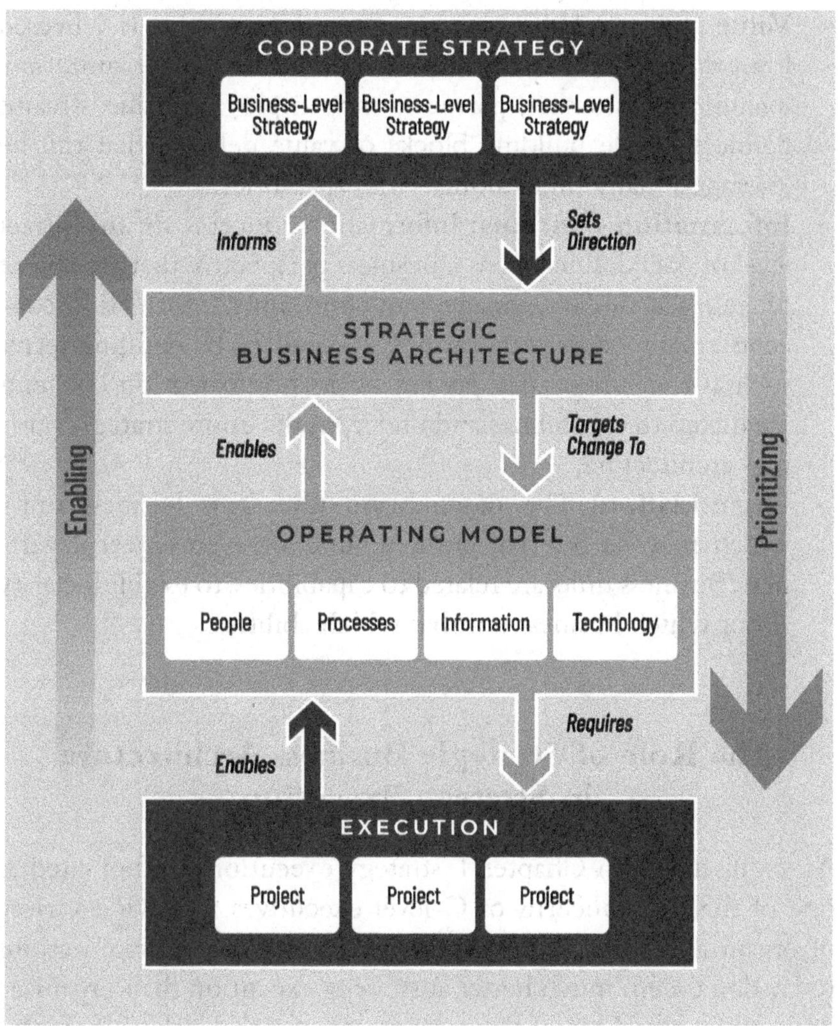

Figure 2.5 Strategic business architecture bridges strategy and execution.

There are four core dimensions of a business architecture, which we will explore further in Chapter 3:

- **Capabilities:** Capabilities are the unique abilities that an organization performs to deliver value and support its operations. They can be thought of as the reusable building blocks of the business, and they produce concrete outcomes. Capabilities define what an organization does, not how.
- **Value streams:** Value streams represent how value is delivered from end to end to the key stakeholders of an organization, including customers, partners, and employees. Value streams define reusable building blocks of value delivery that can be leveraged many times along with capabilities.
- **Information concepts:** Information concepts are an abstract level of data defined from a business perspective that are absent of technical or data management constraints. Information concepts create a common business vocabulary by defining terms such as *customer, product, partner,* or *asset*. Information concepts are linked to capabilities and underpin the entire strategic business architecture.
- **Organization:** The organization represents business units, which may be internal business units or even external partners. Business units are related to capabilities, to establish clarity about which business unit has which abilities.

The Role of Strategic Business Architecture in Strategy Execution

As we discussed in Chapter 1, strategy execution is often cited as one of the top concerns of C-level executives in a wide variety of organizations today. This is not a new problem—organizations today don't seem much better at strategy execution than organizations of the past. One of the main reasons for this lack of improvement in the ability to execute business strategy is a missing or poorly functioning "bridge" between high-level business strategy and the execution layer of the organization. Strategic business architecture (if properly positioned in the organization and properly staffed) could and should be this missing bridge between high-level business strategy and tactical execution. According to Michael Porter, more than 80 percent of organizations do not successfully execute their business strategies. He estimates that in 70 percent of these cases, the reason was not the strategy itself, but bad execution.[2]

There are many reasons for strategy execution failure. Some common reasons cited are:

- Not everyone thinks strategically; thus, they act reactively to events.
- The wrong people are making strategic decisions.
- Leaders are not being held accountable for execution.
- Decisions are being made based on insufficient information.
- Incorrect or little risk assessment is being done.
- There is a lack of collaboration during strategy development.

In our opinion, the main reasons why the strategy execution gap exists include:

- **We were not necessarily taught how to do strategy execution.** As the survey of graduate business curriculums referenced in Chapter 1 illuminated, strategy execution is often taught in a cursory manner, not covering the topic comprehensively or deeply enough to prepare leaders. Business education often includes topics such as strategy formulation and change management but does not provide an in-depth *how-to* of strategy execution.
- **The approach to strategy execution is often unformalized and fragmented.** Strategy execution goes far beyond a department, a framework, or a time-boxed process. It requires integrating many different teams and creating end-to-end transparency and accountability for the results, yet most organizations approach it in a fragmented and informal way.

- **Strategy execution–related decisions are typically approached in silos.** Decisions about investments, priorities, initiatives, projects, and solutions are often made in silos, which is particularly detrimental in today's environment, where organizations are trying to build for simplicity, agility, and cohesive experiences.
- **Our business knowledge base has not been comprehensive enough.** An organization's strategic business architecture can be used to connect and manage all components from strategy to architecture to projects and solutions for strategy translation and alignment. However, organizations have historically not invested in creating a strategic business architecture. This means that the set of information needed to underpin strategy execution from end to end typically exists in disparate places. Furthermore, organizations often focus on delivering laundry lists of potentially disjointed projects versus strategically building enterprise capabilities to deliver on their strategies.
- **We lack an effective means to link projects to changes in strategy.** This is the heart of our perspective on strategy execution. If we can't keep the execution layer (projects) aligned with changes in strategy, we will never be able to execute strategy effectively.

Challenges with Strategic Planning

Strategic planning includes all the activities for developing strategic goals and defining the business process, technology, and organizational changes required to achieve them. Ideally, an entire organization participates in this process, with top-to-bottom assessment and target state definition and across-the-board execution.

In real life, however, organizations are large, multiple roles contribute according to different operational cycle times, and, of course, this idealized process must be scaled accordingly. According to Porter, less than 10 percent of the people in any given organization understand the current business strategy.

This fact leads to many problems. The basic strategic planning and execution process looks something like Figure 2.6.

Figure 2.6 Basic strategic planning and execution process.

This process often ends up looking something like Figure 2.7, where strategic business architects working with project execution

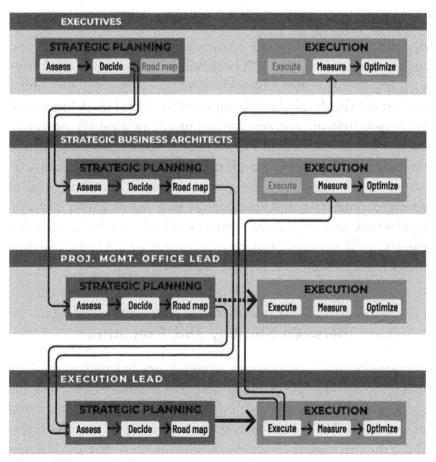

Figure 2.7 Translating strategy to execution.

leads translate strategy into execution and report measurable results to upper levels in the organization.

Why Does This Happen?

1. Executives revise and "hand down" strategic objectives, at least on an annual basis, often more frequently.
2. Strategic business architecture and project management office teams independently use these revised objectives to shape their own strategies, perhaps quarterly.
3. Execution groups (project level) do their best to harmonize conflicting inputs on some other schedule.

Many organizations lack a clear and actionable business strategy and confuse or conflate business vision, goals, objectives, and strategy. Business strategy fails because strategic planners don't have a clearly defined and actionable strategy or because they don't understand the detailed implications of their strategy. A big part of leveraging strategic business architecture is helping the organization realize its strategy. This often requires guiding and facilitating business and IT leaders through the process of recognizing, articulating, and documenting their strategic plans, including what is intended, deliberate, and emergent. It also includes tying strategic focal points such as goals, objectives, and strategies to the impacted aspects of the strategic business architecture, which helps to define the changes needed to carry out the strategy.

Strategic Business Architecture as a Bridge between Strategy and Execution

Strategic business architecture brings a needed perspective and skill set to the strategic planning table. The evolution toward digital business; the lack of clear, actionable strategy; and the integration of business and IT are all forces that are opening the door for leveraging the discipline of business architecture and strategic business architecture practitioners to define, clarify, translate, and execute an actionable business strategy. Strategic planning can be a complex exercise, politically and culturally, as well as a management discipline because there often are many "unknown unknowns."

Typically, more uncertainty and greater assumptions are required with longer strategy time frames. Today, with exponential rates of change and a subsequent need to rapidly adapt business models, strategic planning is typically broken into different planning horizons:

- The long-term planning horizon often focuses on three or more years and often focuses on how future business success will be achieved, often through the use of information and technology.
- The midterm planning horizon often focuses on 12 to 18 months in the future and focuses on key assets and capabilities and the associated investment portfolio plans and high-level development road maps.
- The short-term planning horizon often focuses on 6- to 12-month time frames and associated operational plans.

The relationship of strategic business architecture to corporate strategy is an ongoing conundrum in many organizations today. There are many views on how the interrelationship between strategy and strategic business architecture should work. There are few companies today where strategic business architecture is leveraged as a discipline, and business architects have a seat at the corporate strategy table to play a respected role in the shaping and translation of corporate strategy.

Gartner and other analysts suggest that a gap exists between the high-level, directional nature of strategy and the detailed, implementation focus of execution[3] (see Figure 2.8). Strategic business architecture helps close this gap by providing simple, stable views of the organization and business model while creating a common language among decision-makers.

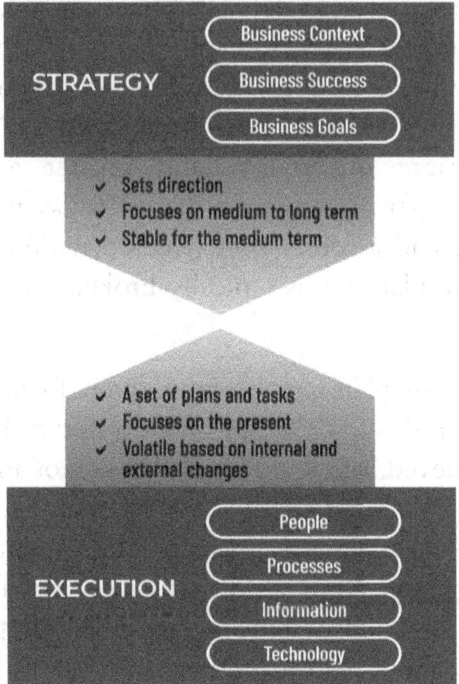

Figure 2.8 Many organizations face an execution gap due to no shared understanding of the organization and lack of a common language across the organization.

The lack of shared understanding creates a gap between strategy and execution. There is a natural dichotomy between strategy and execution in most organizations:

- Strategy sets direction; execution is a set of plans and tasks.
- Strategy is focused on the medium to long term; execution is now.
- Strategy should be largely stable for the medium term; execution is volatile, based on internal and external changes.

This dichotomy leads to difficulties in translating strategy into execution, and a gap often forms between long-term enterprise goals and short-term plans and priorities.

As Figure 2.9 suggests, if the strategic business architecture practice is positioned correctly in the organization and staffed

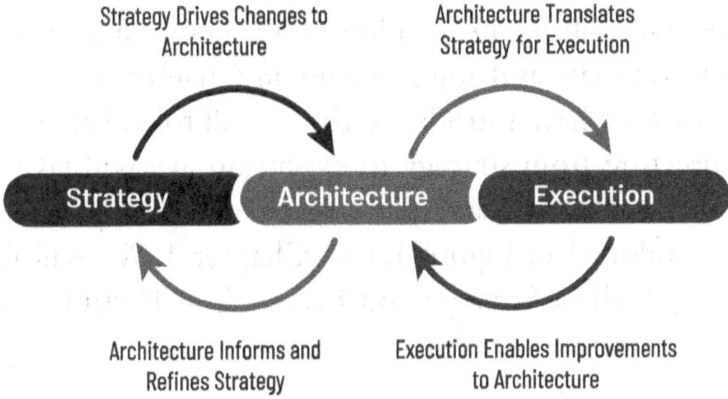

Figure 2.9 Architecture translates strategy to execution.

appropriately, it becomes a critical input into the formulation of an effective corporate strategy that is actionable and executable. It also underscores the iterative nature of these three phases. Strategy drives changes to the architecture, and the architecture and strategic business architects can be consulted to inform strategy on a continual basis. Architecture translates strategy into a set of defined business and technology changes for execution, and execution enables improvements to the implementation of the architecture.

Figure 2.1 (presented earlier) represents some common components and views within the strategic business architecture ecosystem that are used to represent different aspects of the enterprise. The diagram shows how these various components interrelate and exchange information. Each component is categorized within the main phases of strategy development, architecture, or execution. However, it is important to note that many of the strategic business architecture ecosystem components are utilized to varying degrees in multiple phases of the strategy development and execution process. The diagram also emphasizes the central roles of project portfolio management and capability portfolio management in the strategy execution process.

Together, these components combine to create the line of sight between business strategy and project-level execution. This line of sight is updated to reflect changes in business strategy and helps to ensure that the organization is doing the right projects at the right time. We will further explore how these components work together to translate and align strategy in Chapter 4.

Now that we have introduced the overall role of strategic business architecture from strategy to execution, we will take a closer look at its involvement and value within a few key stages of the process introduced in Figure 1.4 in Chapter 1. We will focus on the Develop/Adjust Strategy and Plan/Adjust Portfolios/Projects stages.

The Role of Strategic Business Architecture in the Develop/Adjust Strategy Stage

Recall the following phases of business strategy formulation. The level of confidence increases as you move through these phases, as people in different parts of the organization become comfortable with this process, and as people become more confident in the strategic business architecture team's ability to guide them effectively through the process.

- Assess: Where are we now?
  - What is happening in our business environment?
  - How are we performing?
  - What is our capacity to change?
- Define target: Where do we want to be?
  - What performance do we want?
  - Where do we want to be?
  - How will we know we are there?
- Assess choices: What choices do we have?
  - What are our options?
  - What capabilities and competencies are needed?
  - Can we deliver?
- Define road map: How can we get there?
  - What are our priorities?
  - What investments are needed?
  - When do we need to deliver?

While leaders and strategists are responsible for strategy formulation, strategic business architects can be invaluable partners to help inform strategy with insights about the external and internal environment, as well as the holistic impacts of strategic options and choices. Strategic business architects can also facilitate the process to clarify and translate business strategy. They provide the processes, tools, information, and facilitation skills needed to move the organization through the strategy formulation process, as well as the strategy execution process.

To help gain consensus on the future state of the organization, as well as increase the business focus and scope for strategic business architecture, strategic business architecture practitioners should take the key first step of defining a business outcome statement and review with leaders, strategists, and other stakeholders as applicable. This step must be completed to drive the efforts of any project leveraging strategic business architecture. A business outcome statement should be a short three- to five-page document or a 10- to 15-slide presentation. It should include the following:

- A statement of business direction (business strategy and operations)
- A statement of disruptive trends
- Business and IT executive concerns
- Target business outcomes
- A high-level (contextual) view of the future business state
- A call to action

When defining the business outcome statement, the business outcomes should be focused on what is relevant to the organization, and steer away from standard advice, such as "reduce costs" or "increase efficiencies." Although these two are business outcomes, this is the opportunity to bring clarity as to where in the organization the project team will focus their efforts (for example, "reduce manufacturing costs in bottling or increase sales efficiencies to speed conversion times for client acquisition").

Business Outcome Statement

Strategic business architecture practitioners have found that developing a business strategy on one page can help people across the organization quickly and clearly take in the high-level view of the organization's strategy, business outcomes, business capability enhancements, and projects. It reduces the complexity of the organization to a single picture that shows the key elements, priorities, and interrelationships. This one-page business strategy also helps enterprise architecture and technology innovation leaders who are communicating and building relationships with business executives. A one-page business strategy often forms the focal point for executive discussion and decision-making.

A one-page business strategy aims to highlight the key elements of an organization's strategy from a strategic business architecture perspective, which include:

- **Business strategy:** Short statements of the organization's strategy.
- **Business outcomes:** What key outcomes the strategy is trying to drive.
- **Business capabilities:** What capabilities the organization will need to underpin its strategy.
- **Success measures:** What a successful strategy looks like and how it will be measured.
- **Projects:** What projects are needed to move the organization from the current state to the future state.
- **Management questions:** What questions key stakeholders are asking, or should be asking, regarding the business strategy. The management questions are critical for strategy execution, as these questions and concerns can be used to directly guide the creation of both diagnostic and actionable deliverables.

Strategic business architects might leverage scenario planning to help access opportunities to compete more effectively in the future, as shown in Figure 2.10. This example leverages some of the techniques used in *The Art of the Long View* by Peter Schwartz.

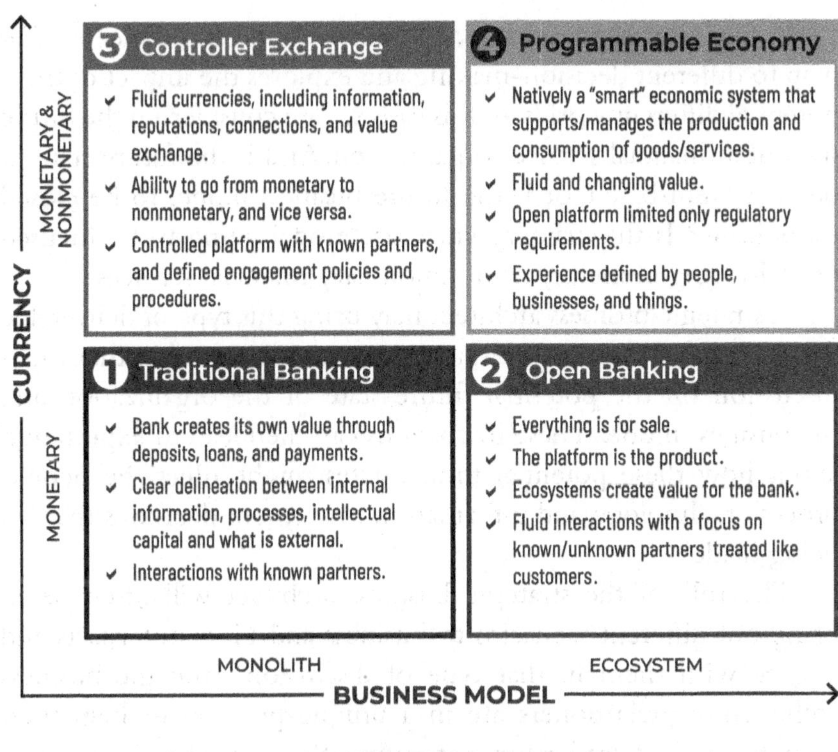

Figure 2.10 Scenario planning example.

Scenario planning considers different opposing concepts that map to different decision-making and explores the impact of these potential different worlds. In this case, we are considering the future state of a financial services organization. And is the future state to be ecosystem based, or is the future business model to be closed monolithic? Is the primary currency model going to be focused on delivering monetary or nonmonetary financial services?

A strategic business architect may bring this type of deliverable forward to business counterparts as a way of engaging them in a discussion on the potential future state of the organization and the business model. These discussions can then lead to exploration about how these potential future states might affect the people, process, technology, and information investment decisions that are being made.

The role of the strategic business architect will often be to bring out different scenarios to business and IT counterparts and engage with them in that type of discussion. Strategic business architecture practitioners are in a unique position to help their own teams and leadership determine the critical business outcomes that are aligned with the business strategy.

Business strategy is executed through a series of business projects that are focused on delivering specific business outcomes. Business outcomes should be expressed as specific and measurable results that include: (1) a measurable business benefit, (2) achievement within a time frame, and (3) support of the business strategy and objectives. For example, a business outcome statement may look something like this: "Streamlining sales processes (business outcome) to shorten the sales cycle by 30 percent (business metric) in 12 months (time frame), which decreases the cost of sales by 10 percent (financial value)."

Strategic business architecture practitioners help clarify and define targeted business outcomes that are used to focus the strategic business architecture and overall project efforts, ensure the organization is executing on the defined and emerging strategic vision, and demonstrate the value of investments.

The Role of Business Architecture in the Plan/Adjust Portfolios/Projects Stage

Now we will take a look at the involvement and value of strategic business architecture within the Plan/Adjust Portfolios/Projects stage, as it pertains to capability portfolio management and project portfolio management.

Capability Portfolio Management

Business capabilities are the new nexus for business performance management. Capabilities bridge the gap between strategy and outcomes via traceability and management of value.

As shown in Figure 2.11, business capabilities facilitate strategy execution by:

- Translating high-level goals describing how the business will win, into detailed opportunities and constraints involved in how the business needs to execute

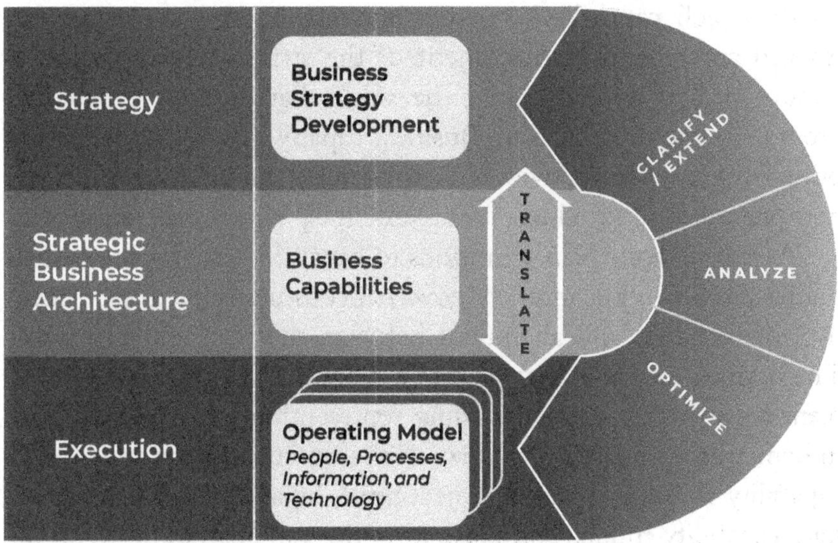

Figure 2.11 Business capabilities translate, clarify, extend, analyze, and optimize strategy execution.

- Clarifying and extending the strategy when planning the business and the contribution of different parts of the organization
- Analyzing priorities and their impact when executing the business plan/strategy
- Optimizing the use of resources when reviewing the plan

With a common view of what the business does and needs to do—a view that is organizationally and functionally independent—senior decision-makers can focus on the value the business delivers to customers. To bridge the gap between high-level business strategy and tactical execution (typically in the form of projects), an understanding is needed of what the business does today, what it must do in the future, and what the implications will be—in terms everyone can understand.

Business capabilities are at the core of defining what must be done to achieve the enterprise strategy. Their simplicity and stability make them especially effective at communicating actions in the value chain that are essential to achieving competitive advantage or business success. It is important not just to identify business capabilities, but to understand how they deliver value, because this clarifies each capability's relative importance and context. Value streams are a central component of the strategic business architecture and in understanding the value that business capabilities provide to the organization. Business capabilities can be related to other business perspectives, such as business information and business processes, to provide a complementary view of the enterprise.

As the strategic plan transitions to execution, the business capabilities provide input into key governance issues (such as prioritization of demand) and alignment between the plan and execution. The business capability perspective can be used to support execution planning in many ways, including representing changes to process information or technology perspectives on current and future state capability views, mapping a project portfolio assessment to a future-state capability model, and illustrating the gap analysis between the implementation of current- and future-state capabilities.

By classifying people, processes, information, and technology based on the business capabilities they support, *leaders can clarify how to prioritize the strategy execution project portfolio.*

When reviewing the strategy and execution stages of the plan, business capabilities can be combined with other information sources—such as the project portfolio, value streams, and processes—to identify potential inefficiencies and redundancies in operations that may prevent the successful execution of the strategy.

As strategic business architects and strategic planning leaders review the progress of the execution plan, they should continually look for ways to optimize performance and reduce inefficiency. *The business capability perspective provides a simple way of identifying and communicating where inefficiency may exist in processes, competencies or other organizational aspects, and applications.*

Before business capabilities can be used as a decision support tool, they must establish a common language for business leaders to discuss planning and execution. Business capabilities create a common language for understanding the organization by:

- Providing a "hierarchy of abstraction."
- Creating a high-level strategic view, which is useful for discussions with senior leaders.
- Creating models that show the big picture of what an enterprise does and how it differentiates itself. These models become important communication devices for understanding, comparing, and evaluating all parts of the organization.

When applied proactively during strategic planning, business capabilities can do more than simply guide execution; they can enrich the business strategy in the following ways:

- **Check how we win.** Validating whether the strategic posture of the business model (that is, how it sets out to win) is realistic or needs modification, given current business capabilities and the ability to build new ones.

- **Change where we play.** Assessing where business capabilities can drive new business opportunities or capability-based extensions such as product line and brand extensions. Similarly, capability-based thinking may cause the organization to withdraw from certain lines of business.

Project Portfolio Management

The strategic business architecture ecosystem diagram in Figure 2.1 depicts how the business capabilities (and changes to those capabilities) inform project portfolio management. This is the heart of the strategy execution equation.

As business strategy changes and evolves, the implementation of business capabilities may be expanded, changed, or discontinued to support the current business strategy. Capabilities may even be added in cases where the organization has introduced significant changes, such as a shift in business model. The changes in the business capability portfolio then drive corresponding changes in the project portfolio. At a high level, this is the line of sight between business strategy (and changes in strategy) and project-level execution. A well-integrated project portfolio management practice is crucial for effective strategy execution; this concept will be discussed in more detail in coming chapters.

The Journey to Leverage Strategic Business Architecture for Value

The journey to leveraging strategic business architecture and business architects as a critical strategic resource and "bridge" in the strategy execution process does not happen overnight—this is a marathon, not a sprint. It takes a series of actions that demonstrate the ability of strategic business architecture to add value to the strategy execution process.

A few of these actions might entail:

- Developing a suite of tools that will assist and influence decision-makers
- Developing and maintaining a live repository of knowledge of the organization and its business environment (the business architecture knowledge base)
- Identifying opportunities to apply strategic business architecture for value throughout the strategy execution process to continually test and learn
- Being proactive rather than reactive, and opening dialog with stakeholders
- Communicating in a language that stakeholders understand
- Calibrating value measurement efforts with key stakeholders

The Role of Strategic Business Architecture in Design

In addition to strategy formulation and execution, strategic business architecture and strategic business architects play a central role in the formulation of the design of different aspects of the enterprise. In fact, leveraging strategic business architecture to design and redesign an organization is one of the primary value propositions beyond its important role in strategy to execution. As Figure 2.1, the strategic business architecture ecosystem, depicts, there are many enterprise perspectives, tools, and approaches in the strategic business architecture toolkit. These perspectives and approaches combine to present holistic, multidimensional views of the organization.

These views of the organization and the enterprise-wide understanding they enable are critical components of design thinking. Design thinking, pioneered by the Hasso Plattner Institute of Design at Stanford University (known as the d.school), is a structured approach to leap forward to finding creative solutions to customer problems that are not linear or incremental but are innovative leapfrogs.

Tim Brown, the CEO of IDEO, one of the most successful practitioners of design thinking and business design, defines the practice this way:

> *"Design thinking is a human-centered approach to innovation that draws from the designer's toolkit to integrate the needs of people, the possibilities of technology, and the requirements for business success."*[4]

The first stage of the process is to empathically understand the problem from the perspective of the end user. In this stage, immersion, observation, and interviews can help gather information and understand the user's problem, need, and behavior. The define stage will help designers to analyze the information gathered during the empathize stage and define the core problem as a problem statement in a user-centered manner. During the ideate stage, designers start to generate ideas and look for alternative ways of viewing and solving the problem. There are many ideation tools to use, such as brainstorming, mind mapping, doodling, and other techniques. The objective is not to find the right answer but to generate as many ideas as possible.

During the third stage of the design thinking process, designers pick several ideas and build simple prototypes. The objective at this stage is to quickly and cheaply produce some prototypes to test in the real world and possibly identify the best solution. At the last stage, designers test the complete product from the prototype stage. The goal is to get feedback from failures, make adjustments, and improve the prototype. Iteration is a fundamental part of design thinking. The process of ideate, prototype, and test is repeated until the prototype meets the needs of the end user.

The idea of business design owes its existence to a collaboration between corporate America and academia. Roger Martin, former dean of the Rotman School of Management; David Kelley, the founder of Stanford's d.school; and Patrick Whitney, dean at Illinois Institute of Technology, together created a structured approach to innovation making design an integral part of the strategy, experience, business models, and the like.

In their approach, business design involves three core elements:

- **Empathy:** What are our customers' unmet needs?
- **Prototyping:** How might we better meet these needs?
- **Strategy:** How might we create competitive advantage?

Business design is a collaborative user-centric approach that perfectly blends design and management to help businesses craft, strategize, and deliver a viable business model based on user research, market analysis, strategy, and user experience.

Strategic business architects bring a needed perspective and skill set to the design thinking process and many aspects of design overall. They combine their enterprise-wide understanding and perspective with strategic, conceptual, financial modeling, and design thinking skills. Strategic business architecture facilitates the four general types of design:

- **Business design** defines how an organization creates, delivers, and captures value. Strategic business architecture provides the modeling approaches to represent, analyze, and innovate an organization's business design to maximize effectiveness. Strategic business architecture also helps to assess the cross-organizational impacts of making changes to its business design.
- **Enterprise design** elaborates the architecture and elements needed for value creation across the enterprise. Using enterprise design, we can identify intersections of opportunity, friction, and value creation. Strategic business architecture provides the enterprise-wide view to understand and connect these dots across the entire business and technology environment.
- **Product design,** the common perception of design, articulates a deliverable-marketable tool. Products (including goods as well as services and technologies) serve a purpose for particular stakeholders. Strategic business architecture provides the

ecosystem level understanding needed to understand market trends and stakeholder needs and value. It also helps to assess the organizational impact of offering new products or making changes to existing ones, including whether the organization has the necessary capabilities in place to support them.

- **Execution design** refers to the flow of activities, ideas, and engagements necessary for the production of a product or service or to make a change to the organization. Execution typically takes the form of projects and project portfolios. Strategic business architecture helps to ensure that we're doing the right projects that support the current business strategy. It also helps to ensure that projects are scoped and sequenced in the most logical way at a macro level.

The Role of Strategic Business Architecture in Agile Enterprise Transformation

The concept of a *composable business* is the creation of an organization from interchangeable "building blocks." Composable business enables an organization to maximize the design and delivery of the resilience and agility needed to rapidly respond to market opportunities and challenges. The foundation for a composable business is the business architecture, with capabilities at the center. Strategic business architecture provides the modular business building blocks with which an organization can be designed. A composable business architecture enables an enterprise to react faster to large-scale organizational transformations. Strategic business architecture enables the business model design to be analyzed to see if value creation and the associated business architecture components, such as value streams and capabilities, are modularly designed. Most aspects of the organization are composable. The main aspects that are analyzed for composability include strategy, customer, technology, workforce, operations, products, and stakeholder value.

For decades, organizations have been heavily focused on efficiency. The COVID-19 pandemic and other global disruptions have shown us that organizations need to be able to pivot quickly and that efficiency alone is not enough to ensure long-term survival. Organizations that are more modular can pivot faster to rapidly changing conditions. This modular approach allows an organization to restructure and deliver new products and value as needed and as internal or external conditions change. This type of organizational perspective and thinking enables the organization to not only survive but prosper in challenging and disruptive times.

Strategic business architecture enables the four basic principles of composable business:

- More speed through discovery
- Greater agility through modularity
- Better leadership through orchestration
- Resilience through autonomy

Composable strategic business architecture ensures that an organization (including its supporting technology infrastructure) is designed and built to maximize flexibility and resiliency. Organizations that implement the building blocks and principles of composable business are more successful at leveraging digital investments and ensuring that they are making the right investments at the right time.

The many business tools and perspectives that comprise the strategic business architecture ecosystem and toolkit combine to provide the enterprise-wide understanding needed to create a truly composable organization that is capable of agile transformation.

The Role of Strategic Business Architecture in Innovation Facilitation

Strategic business architecture can be leveraged throughout the entire innovation life cycle and makes innovation more impactful, effective, and embedded into all aspects of an organization. In fact, strategic business architecture practices are often a hub for internal innovation because of the unique, enterprise-wide understanding and perspective that a well-functioning strategic business architecture practice possesses. Strategic business architects are typically very well connected in the organization and have identified critical subject matter experts and strategic thinkers within the organization. They are often the people that are the "clearinghouse" for ideas and are in a unique position to connect dots for internal innovation opportunities. For example, business architects can help to generate or facilitate sharing of innovation ideas and identify focus areas where innovation is needed, either resulting from business priorities or known areas of improvement. These opportunities can be framed around defined aspects of the strategic business architecture.

Strategic business architects also provide the tools to analyze opportunities for value to the organization and potential associated risks. They can assess the viability and impact of innovation ideas on an ongoing basis and provide a perspective on how those ideas fit within the bigger-picture strategy and priorities of the organization.

The Role of Strategic Business Architecture in Value Measurement

Value measurement is consistently cited as a top area of importance in many organizations but also consistently cited as one of the areas of lowest maturity. According to the maxim often (incorrectly) attributed to Peter Drucker, "What gets measured gets managed." The next question is then, "What do you want to get managed?" Do you want your organization to be viewed as a cost to be managed (and maybe outsourced), or do you want your organization to be viewed as a strategic resource, a resource that informs strategy development and is a facilitator of strategy execution? The path that your organization takes is in large part dependent on what you measure and how effectively you communicate the strategic value of the efforts and contributions of your team to the larger organization.

In Chapter 7, we will explore a process for determining what you should measure to demonstrate the value of your team's contributions to the organization to the broadest possible set of key stakeholders in your organization. We will also discuss value measurement and communication as a primary means to "getting a seat at the strategic planning table" and developing a "strategic plan" as a foundation for your value measurement program. Value measurement should not be thought of solely as a means to demonstrate value to the organization but also as a means to create a strategic ongoing dialogue with key strategic stakeholders. The effective measurement and communication of the right strategic metrics *and* an ongoing dialogue with key strategic stakeholders to understand their critical issues and how they are measured will help you better identify strategic opportunities for improvement that will make you an invaluable strategic resource over time—it's a marathon, not a sprint.

Next Steps

We have outlined a robust set of possible roles for strategic business architecture in the organization as a critical enabler of strategy execution, design, transformation, innovation, and value measurement. These are the primary areas of strategic business architecture focus that bring maximum strategic value to the organization.

An effective strategic business architecture practice can be the critical (and often missing) component needed for successful strategy execution. As people begin to use strategic business architecture, its holistic nature and views help to shift their mindsets and behaviors over time. In the beginning, it may start with aha moments as people gain new understanding of where others in the organization are doing similar things or how what they do fits into the bigger picture of delivering value to the customer. This may evolve into asking new and hard questions, such as why certain projects are being pursued when they do not have strong strategic alignment or why a seemingly duplicate solution is being considered. With time and experience in leveraging strategic business architecture, organizations may make more significant changes.

For example, organizations have reoriented business ownership and investment around the cross-organizational view of capabilities and value streams, and they have designed an intentional, cohesive method for all teams to work together from strategy to execution, with a focus on value delivery.

A strategic business architecture perspective and practice can bring many benefits to the strategy execution process, such as the ability to:

- **Act with an enterprise consciousness that puts what is best for customers and the enterprise first, balanced with the needs of organizational and product silos.** Strategic business architecture not only reflects the full enterprise view, but also provides an *objective* view. This is particularly helpful to inform decisions around prioritization and investment. Strategic business architecture cuts through complexity, detail, and politics with a data-based view, such as to illuminate where projects or solutions are not aligned with the organization's strategy or are contributing to a fragmented customer experience.
- **Operate with a cohesive, end-to-end strategy execution process, with clearly defined integration across all teams, and transparency and accountability for the results.** It takes many different teams to successfully turn business direction into action. While strategic business architecture is just one of those teams with its own role to inform and translate strategy, strategic business architecture also provides an important connectivity across all other teams. Strategic business architecture provides the documented traceability from strategy to value streams and capabilities to projects—as well as all the linkages to perspectives from other teams, such as customer journeys, processes, system applications, and requirements. This traceability in the strategic business architecture knowledge base provides ongoing visibility and accountability for the results

that are delivered, ensuring that it does not get lost in disparate documentation.

- **Articulate and decompose business direction into an agreed-upon, clearly defined, and differentiated set of focal points (for example, goals, objectives, metrics, courses of action).** Strategic business architecture not only keeps business direction visible in the knowledge base, as mentioned earlier, but the very act of translating it into concrete impacts to value streams and capabilities helps to further refine that direction. The iterative process of translating strategy into changes to people, processes, information, and technology inevitably uncovers new questions and gaps that can help to further clarify the business model direction. Strategic business architecture helps the organization to dynamically sense and respond to the environment and adjust strategies and goals when internal and external conditions change and to dynamically replan work when strategies and goal change. Over time, this iterative process can lead to enhancements in how strategy is articulated for the organization.
- **Effectively communicate strategic direction throughout an entire organization, across all areas and all levels of people to create clarity, provide personal context, and mobilize action.** Strategy diffusion can be a significant challenge for organizations, which happens when the understanding of a strategy becomes less understood as it filters down through the various layers of an organization. Strategic business architecture can help in two ways.
  - It makes the strategy information available to everyone (as applicable) through the business architecture knowledge base, described through clear, consistent strategic focal points.
  - The translation of strategy into capability-framed changes to people, processes, information, and technology provides business context and relevance to help each person understand how they are impacted and what needs to change.

- **Enable decision-making and traceability for the end-to-end strategy execution process with an objective, business-focused view of the enterprise (that is, a business architecture knowledge base) that is friendly and accessible for anyone to use.** The knowledge base should be accessible to all roles for data-based decision-making throughout strategy execution. The knowledge base is particularly powerful because it *aggregates information across strategies, initiatives, portfolios, and projects.* This makes it possible to identify potential challenges or conflicts around resource usage, priorities, and the comprehensive outcomes and solutions being delivered to customers and other business stakeholders. It also enables the ongoing alignment of strategies, architecture, projects, and solutions across all areas and levels of the organization. In addition, the knowledge base supports the measurement of project and solution outcomes against the original business objectives.
- **Build, mature, and own strategic capabilities and shape the projects that will deliver enhancements to those capabilities.** In contrast to typical approaches where projects are planned and delivered in silos, capabilities provide a framework for planning, collaboration, and accountability across organizational and product silos. Over time, this approach helps organizations shift from *delivering projects* (that may or may not add up to the achievement of a strategy) to *building strategic business capabilities* (that will support the organization today and in the future).
- **Synergize business and technology solution investment and design around capabilities to ensure modularity, reuse, and consistency.** Capabilities and value streams provide the fundamental building blocks to ensure that solutions are not only reusable, but also consistent where necessary. For example, if a customer is interacting with various product areas of an organization, consistent solutions and experiences provide a simple and unified front.

- **Deliver capabilities (enabled by people, process, information, and technology) within the context of seamless, end-to-end journeys and value streams for customers, partners, and employees.** Journeys and value streams orchestrate the use of capabilities. In fact, business ownership can even be oriented around the structures of value streams and capabilities to drive consistent business direction and prioritization. For example, certain leaders may be responsible for delivering sets of capabilities that meet the needs of all journeys and value streams, while others may be responsible for ensuring unified experiences and value streams are delivered across all products, business units, and channels.

A new vision and mindset for strategy execution, enabled by strategic business architecture, can deliver dramatic results. A few measurable examples include the following:

- **Exceptional, integrated, and consistent experiences for customers/constituents, partners, and employees:** Strategic business architecture operationalizes journeys and experiences across silos, and ensures the organization is streamlined to provide consistent, integrated experiences.
- **Decreased complexity of the business environment and decreased complexity and technical debt of the IT environment:** Strategic business architecture ensures that, where applicable, business and technology solutions can be built once and reused. Strategic business architecture also identifies areas for business and technology simplification, such as redundant processes or applications.
- **Decreased time and cost to develop and maintain solutions:** As mentioned earlier, strategic business architecture ensures reusable solutions, which saves not only the up-front cost, but also the ongoing maintenance cost.
- **Decreased business risk and potential for noncompliance:** Strategic business architecture can be leveraged to aggregate and reflect risk within a shared enterprise business

context. It also creates traceability from external regulations and internal policies to the capabilities involved, along with traceability to business units, processes, and system applications. Strategic business architecture also helps to simplify the enterprise, further helping to reduce risk.

- **Decreased brand and reputational risks:** Strategic business architecture helps to design customer/constituent and partner solutions more effectively and holistically, so risks related to compliance, quality, ethics, security, or other concerns are lowered.
- **Better quality in products and services, as well as operations:** As mentioned earlier, strategic business architecture plays a key role in informing all types of design and ensuring better integration, execution, and transparency.
- **Better ability for stakeholders to consume the changes implemented:** Strategic business architecture quantifies the collective impact on stakeholders, oriented around capabilities and value streams. This is invaluable to inform organization change management and project planning so that stakeholders, impacts can be communicated and changes rolled out at the appropriate time.
- **Increased organizational agility and faster time to market for implementing strategies, products, and business changes:** Leveraging strategic business architecture ultimately results in an organization's ability to deliver on its mission and remain competitive. This is due to the common business vocabulary and mental model that strategic business architecture provides, along with a streamlined environment and an effective end-to-end strategy execution approach that can continually react to change.

This vision and set of possible roles for strategic business architecture as a central component of effective strategy execution rely on establishing, staffing, positioning, and growing a strategic business architecture practice that can effectively play these strategic roles—this is not easy. The remainder of this book will focus on the necessary components that will help you not only complete but win the marathon.

STRATEGY EXECUTION ORGANIZATIONAL ASSESSMENT

Reflect on the following questions to assess how well strategy execution is working in your organization based on the concepts from Chapter 2. Please refer to the scoring guidance provided in Chapter 1.

1. Our organization is aware of the concept of strategic business architecture and its value to strategy execution.
2. Our strategic planning function effectively leverages strategic business architecture for strategy development and strategy execution.
3. Strategic business architecture has a clear role and is embedded into our organization's defined, comprehensive end-to-end approach from strategy development through strategy execution.
4. Our organization utilizes some of the concepts that comprise strategic business architecture in at least pockets or parts of the organization.
5. Our organization recognizes the design concept of composable business and leverages capabilities as the foundation.

Chapter 3

The Strategic Business Architecture Toolkit

There is no perspective or set of views quite like strategic business architecture. Countless views exist, but they often represent just a single aspect or fragment of an organization. What makes strategic business architecture unique and invaluable is its holistic and multidimensional view of an entire organization.

There is tremendous power and efficiency in shared mental models. Imagine if we did not have a map of the world. How difficult would it be to plan a trip without understanding where you are, where you are going, or the best way to get there? Imagine if we did not have blueprints for buildings. How difficult would it be to communicate a common vision of what we are building or remodeling and activate all the workers in a coordinated way to achieve it?

Strategic business architecture *is* the shared mental model for an entire organization. It describes what an organization does and how it is structured to deliver value to its customers and support its operations. From a strategy and transformation perspective, it informs where an organization is today, where it is going in the future, and how it will get there. Strategic business architecture also provides a framework for macro-level design and redesign.

Beyond this, though, strategic business architecture facilitates a shift in mindsets and behaviors as people use it over time. Its holistic nature encourages people to think about the big picture, to focus on the customer and value delivery, to embrace cross-organization collaboration, and to design the organization with intent for today and tomorrow.

We will now take a deeper dive into what strategic business architecture is and how it represents an organization in order to create the enterprise-wide understanding needed for strategy execution.

Defining Qualities of Strategic Business Architecture

Regardless of what aspect of the strategic business architecture we look at, they all share some important qualities. Strategic business architecture is *fit for purpose* and designed to provide the holistic perspective that is required for moving from strategy to execution.

Strategic business architecture is:

- **Owned by strategic planning:** Strategic business architecture is entirely business focused, describing the scope of what a business does, in the language of that business. It should be created through cross-organizational representation and collaboration. Strategic business architecture is not an information technology (IT) view. However, it can be connected to an organization's IT architecture to reflect how the business is supported by applications and services, data and data deployments, and infrastructure.
- **Represented at a high level of detail:** A strategic business architecture is described from a higher elevation. It can be connected to the operating model details such as roles, processes, data, and systems, but the business perspectives that

are represented through a strategic business architecture are intentionally described at a higher level of detail.

- **Inclusive of the entire scope of an organization:** A strategic business architecture represents the entire scope of what an organization does and the business ecosystem in which it operates. It provides one shared view that is unified and abstracted across organizational structures, products, and geographies. There is one strategic business architecture for an organization (unless it is a conglomerate or other structure that would dictate separation). In addition, a strategic business architecture is oriented around the customer (or constituent) and value delivery as its North Star.
- **Reusable:** Strategic business architecture is a reusable set of information and views that are created, consolidated, and maintained over time and can be accessed by anyone in an organization. In contrast, strategic business architecture is not simply a set of one-time tools and deliverables that are created and archived. Having a shared understanding of the current state readily available accelerates the assessment and translation of strategic change, because it does not need to be rediscovered again and again.

The Scope of Strategic Business Architecture

Strategic business architecture is a holistic view of an organization that is composed of multiple business perspectives. Figure 3.1 shows the perspectives included in the scope of strategic business architecture according to one industry organization, though this book offers a broader, more comprehensive, viewpoint on the strategy execution–related aspects of this evolving discipline. This source defines four core domains of business architecture (in the center circle) and six extended domains (in the outer circle) to which they connect. Additionally, strategic business architecture can connect to domains from other related disciplines such as journeys from experience design, business processes from business

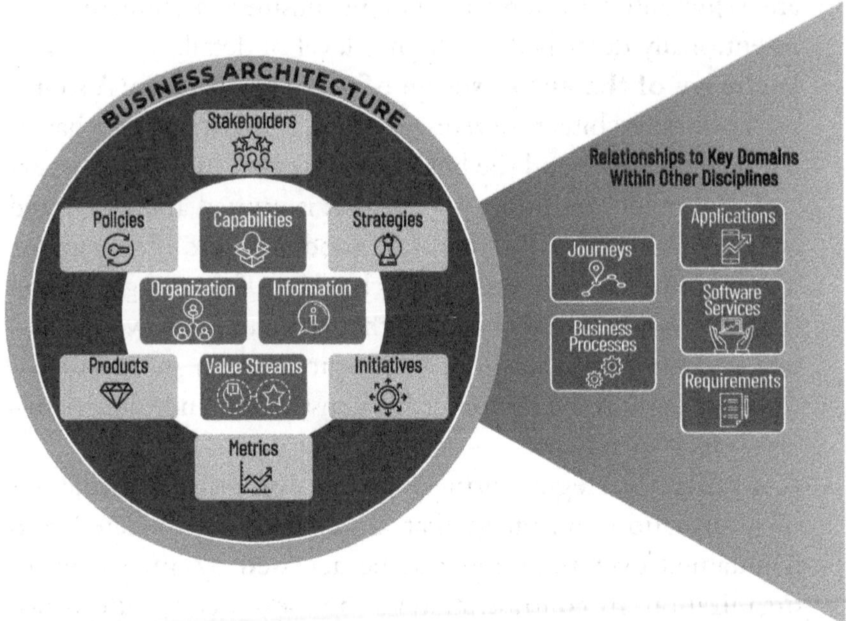

Figure 3.1 Strategic business architecture perspectives and relationships to other disciplines.[1]

process management, requirements from business analysis, or applications and services from the IT architecture.

Each of these business perspectives is used together seamlessly to align strategy and execution and design an organization. The individual domains provide for clear definition and ownership, as well as robust analysis and decision-making.

The Core Domains of Strategic Business Architecture

At the core, strategic business architecture includes the following:

- **Capabilities:** Capabilities are the unique abilities that an organization performs to deliver value and support its operations. They can be thought of as reusable building blocks of the business, and they produce concrete outcomes. Capabilities define *what* an organization does, not how.

- **Value streams:** Value streams represent how value is delivered from end to end to the key stakeholders of an organization, including customers, partners, and employees. Value streams define reusable building blocks of value delivery that can be leveraged many times along with capabilities.
- **Information concepts:** Information concepts are an abstract level of data defined from a business perspective that are absent of technical or data management constraints. Information concepts create a common business vocabulary by defining terms such as *customer, product, partner,* or *asset*. Information concepts are linked to capabilities and underpin the entire strategic business architecture.
- **Organization:** The organization represents business units, which may be internal business units or even external partners. Business units are related to capabilities, to establish clarity about which business unit has which abilities.

Of the four core domains, capabilities and value streams are of particular importance to strategy execution and require additional explanation. Capabilities are the nexus of the strategic business architecture. They are the one domain that connects to every other one. This makes capabilities invaluable for connecting strategy to execution and informing business decision-making. For example, for a given capability, we can readily understand how it is leveraged for value, the stakeholders who are impacted by it, and the products it enables. We can also understand the business units that deliver the capability, the information it uses, the processes that implement it, the systems that automate it, the strategies and initiatives that are currently impacting it, the policies that guide it, and more.

Value streams also play a critical role. Together with capabilities, they form the foundation of a strategic business architecture. Value streams provide the business value delivery context in which capabilities are used. A capability can enable many different value streams. Value streams and capabilities work together to help translate strategy into a coordinated set of actions, and together they provide the building blocks for macro-level design and optimization of an organization.

Value Streams and Business Processes

At this point, we would like to highlight a key point of clarification. To many people, value streams and business processes are interchangeable. Within a strategy execution context, what is most important is that capabilities have some sort of flow-based and value-based construct to provide context for their usage. This construct should be (1) described at a high level of abstraction, (2) oriented around value delivery, and (3) defined to be modular and reusable. In this book, we will leverage value streams as this construct. However, some organizations prefer to leverage high-level business processes as this construct instead. If this is the case for your organization, you may interpret the references to value streams as equivalent to your high-level business processes.

Whether an organization leverages value streams and/or business processes, for strategy execution to succeed, it is critical that change can be implemented seamlessly from the high-level perspective down to the details. Depending on the organization, this could include any of the following scenarios:

1. Value streams (high-level) aligned with more detailed processes
2. Value streams (high-level) aligned with high-level processes, which align with more detailed processes
3. High-level processes aligned with more detailed processes

This book generally focuses on the first two scenarios. (If the third scenario applies to your organization, simply interpret the concept of value streams as your high-level business processes.)

For context, here is how we differentiate value streams and processes. Value streams (and all of strategic business architecture) enable an organization to realize its business model. Business processes enable an organization to realize its operating model. (***Note:*** While an organization's *business model* describes the strategic perspective of how an organization creates, delivers, and captures value, an organization's *operating model* describes the operational aspects necessary to achieve that value and implement the business model. These concepts will be further defined later in this chapter.) Both value streams and business processes are equally important and necessary for effective strategy execution. Value streams are a domain of strategic business architecture, and business processes are a domain of business process management. Value streams provide a modular, macro-level view of an organization, whereas processes often provide a more detailed view of the work and how it flows (though high-level business processes may also be defined as mentioned).

Value streams and business processes are suited for different purposes and focuses. Value streams design and streamline work at a high level of abstraction across organizational silos. As it pertains to strategy execution, together with capabilities, value streams also frame where changes are needed to business processes and other aspects of the operating model. On the other hand, business processes are how the actual day-to-day work is carried out within an organization, and they are a focal point for continuous improvement to increase the efficiency of the internal operating environment. Business processes can and should be aligned to value streams, and together they are even more valuable to create cohesive experiences for people and ensure effective operations.

The Extended Domains of Strategic Business Architecture

The extended domains provide additional information about an organization that can be connected to the core domains, especially capabilities and value streams, to provide a richer set of insights for decision-making.

Strategies capture various aspects of business direction (including goals and objectives) along with **metrics,** which measure the performance of the organization. **Products** represent the goods and services that an organization offers to its customers. **Stakeholders** represent the external or internal players that participate in value streams to receive and/or contribute value. **Policies** guide the organization and may include external regulations or other directives, as well as internal policies. Finally, **initiatives** can be used to capture any current or planned scope of work to implement change at any level (***Note:*** This references one viewpoint on the discipline,[2] but this book provides a broader and clearer definition of the terms *project, program, portfolio,* and *initiative,* as defined in Chapter 1.)

It may seem like there is a substantial amount of information to be captured within the strategic business architecture. However, consider that the information is captured at a high level of granularity. Most important, a practical approach can and should be taken to build a strategic business architecture. This begins with defining and relating capabilities and value streams, based on defined information concepts. However, once this baseline is in place, the rest of the strategic business architecture can be built over time and is often developed as needed to support business usage and needs. More is discussed at the end of this chapter.

Leveraging Strategic Business Architecture for Decision-Making

While our focus is primarily on strategy execution, considering all the perspectives that comprise the holistic, multidimensional representation of strategic business architecture, its value can extend to other types of business decision-making. For example, connecting risks or policies to capabilities can provide an enterprise-level view on where potential risk and compliance issues are most concentrated and of the highest priority to address. Connecting products to capabilities can inform strategic decision-making around the introduction of new product offerings based on the organization's ability to deliver on them and the holistic impact to the rest of the organization.

Strategic business architecture is also ideal to inform structural changes such as mergers, acquisitions, and divestitures. It provides a readily available framework to compare what two organizations do, along with their business models and direction, in support of due diligence and integration activities. Strategic business architecture also helps to assess the impact of a potential divestiture and provides an organized set of actions to move forward.

Finally, the high-level, business-focused framework that strategic business architecture provides can be used to aggregate and analyze business performance from a variety of perspectives. For example, the various types of costs can be aggregated by capability to reflect a fresh and objective understanding of the spend and how it can be reduced in a way that makes the best sense for the enterprise. Or, metrics can be captured for capabilities to understand their level of business performance, or more specific measurements such as sustainability performance, in order to identify a targeted set of actions for improvement.

The Strategic Business Architecture Knowledge Base and Views

While the business architecture domains capture the information we need, we interpret and interact with that information through business blueprints or views. As shown in Figure 3.2, the *strategic business architecture knowledge base* is a repository of information

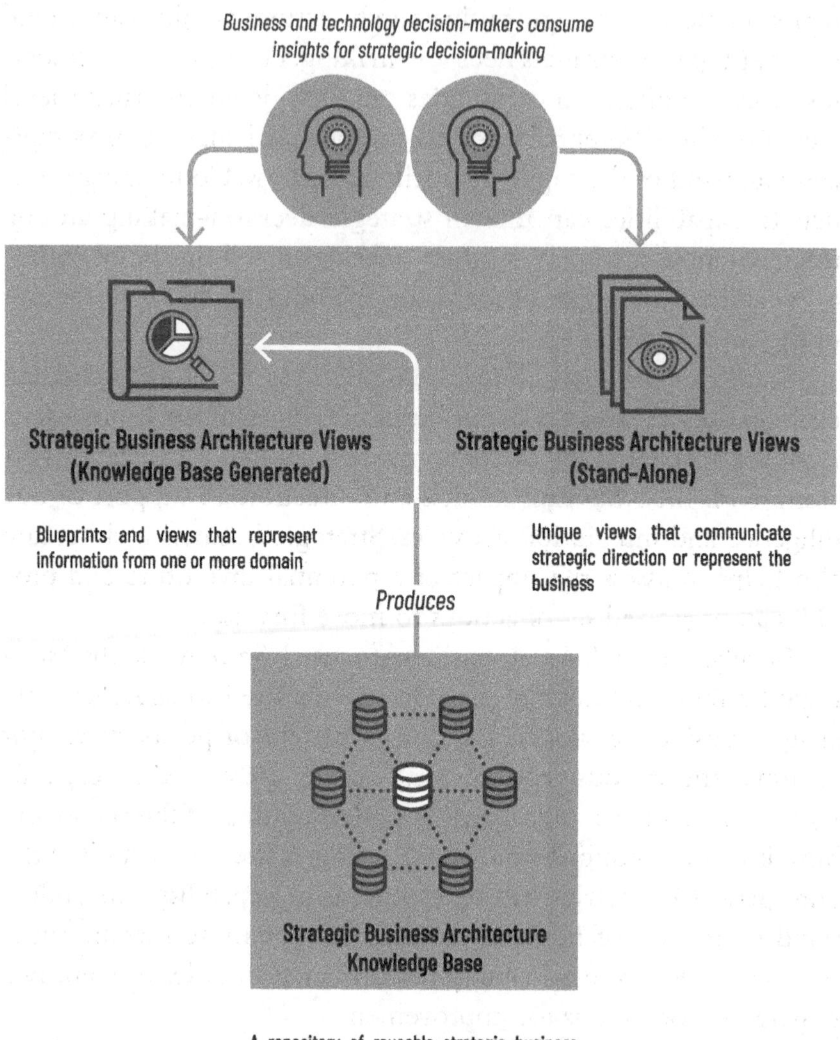

Figure 3.2 The strategic business architecture knowledge base and views.

for all strategic business architecture domains, including their relationships to each other and to other disciplines. For example, the knowledge base would include information about all of an organization's capabilities and their relationships to value streams, business units, business processes, and so forth. The knowledge base would also include aggregated information that is essential for strategy execution, including strategies, goals, objectives, metrics, and courses of action, along with their related value streams, capabilities, and initiatives. We will revisit this in Chapter 4.

Furthermore, as shown in Figure 3.2, countless *strategic business architecture views (knowledge base generated)* may be produced from the knowledge base. These views may include one or more or many different domains. For example, a capability map (also referred to as a *business capability model*) is a standard business blueprint that organizes capabilities into certain tiers and levels. Value stream/capability cross-mappings and value stream/business process cross-mappings are examples of common views to understand how key information relates across more than one domain.

Additionally, Figure 3.2 reflects that there are unique and important *strategic business architecture views (stand-alone)* that communicate strategic direction or represent the organization but are not generated directly from the formal strategic business architecture domains in the knowledge base. However, they are conceptually related. Examples here include value networks, value chains, the value proposition canvas, the business model canvas, and the operating model canvas.

While Figure 3.2 represents the long-term intent, and having an automated tool in place is essential for effectiveness and scalability, organizations often take a practical approach to achieving this over time. For example, in the beginning, when there is no knowledge base, the various views may be created on their own. Later, when a knowledge base is in place, where applicable, the relevant data from those views can be added. For example, organizations often build and begin using their capability maps, value streams, and business processes with Microsoft Visio, Excel, and PowerPoint (VEP) and then later import them into an automated repository.

Key Strategic Business Architecture Views from Strategy to Execution

Now we will focus on the most important strategic business architecture components and views that are involved in developing, informing, and translating strategy into execution, and ensuring alignment over time. Figure 3.3 shows the strategic business architecture ecosystem along with a categorization of each component by its most important contribution as informing or communicating strategic direction, representing the business and informing strategy execution, and/or implementing strategy execution. The conceptual relationships between components are shown as well.

At the end of this chapter, we will further explore the level of applicability of each of these components across the five stages from strategy to execution.

As Figure 3.3 highlights, capabilities are not only the nexus of the strategic business architecture, but also the nexus of strategy execution. This is reflected in the positioning of capabilities between strategy and execution, as well as how many components relate to them. Value streams are also a focal point with a number of relationships, though in many cases they are used in conjunction with capabilities and business processes. For example, projects deliver changes to capabilities *within a value stream context,* even though two separate arrows are shown.

Strategic portfolio management is also a key focal point in the process. This is where the strategy is actually implemented through projects that deliver on the changes needed to people, process, and technology, as framed through the strategic business architecture capabilities and value streams.

As shown in Figure 3.4, capabilities play a central role in bridging strategy and execution:

- **Strategy development/refinement,** to define the specific capabilities that need to be developed and/or modified
- **Portfolio management,** to ensure that the right projects and investments are made based on alignment with business strategy

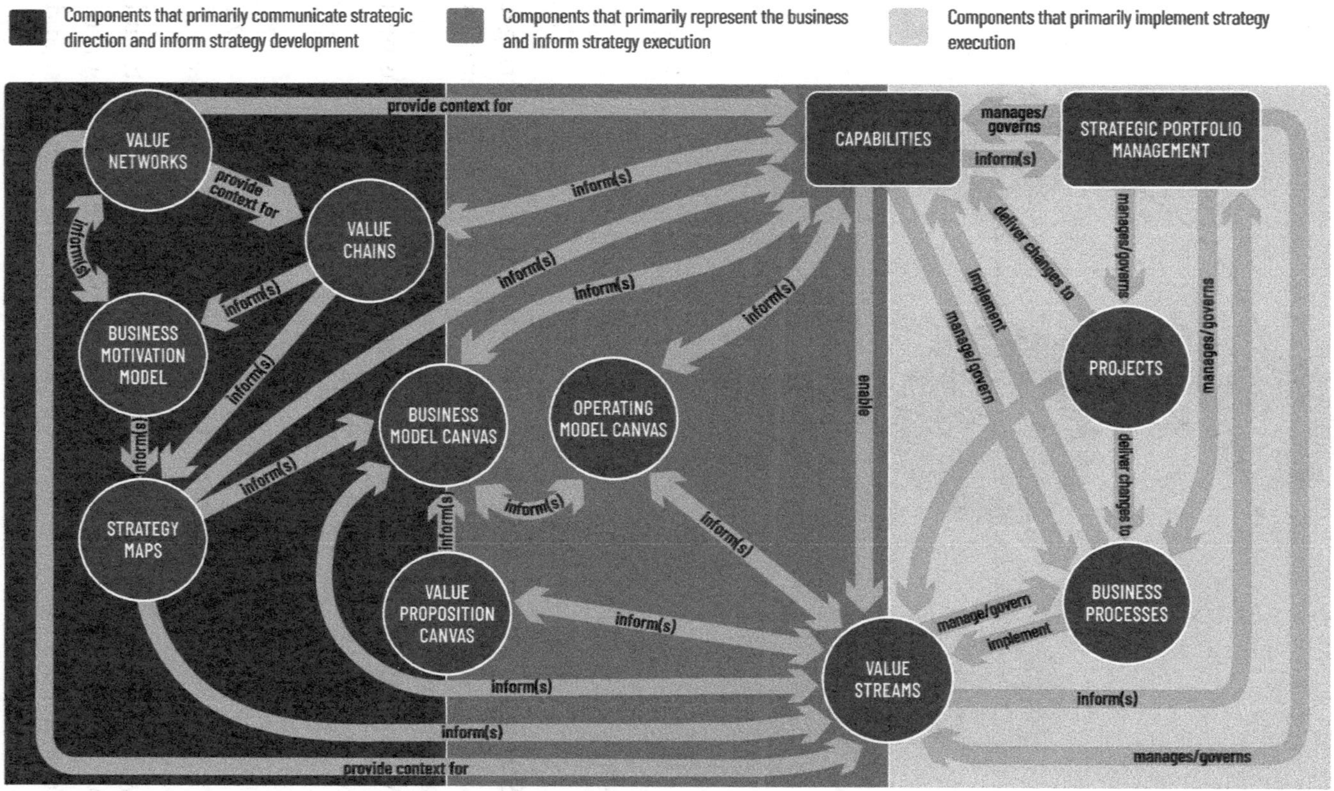

Figure 3.3 The strategic business architecture ecosystem.

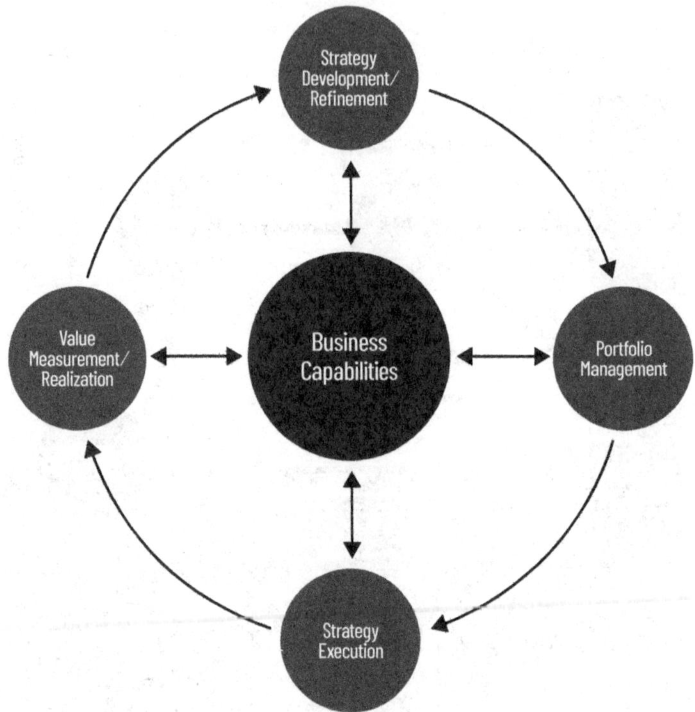

Figure 3.4 Capabilities are the nexus of strategy execution.

- **Strategy execution,** to ensure that the right projects get done in the most effective manner and that this work remains aligned with changes in strategy
- **Value measurement/realization,** to ensure that business value is understood and delivered

A Closer Look at Key Strategic Business Architecture Views

Now we will take a closer look at each of the components and views within the strategic business architecture ecosystem to understand briefly *what* each component is, *why* it matters, and *how* it is defined and related to the others.

To help illustrate each technique, we show an example of it in use for a hypothetical global apparel company that manufactures clothing, footwear, and accessories. The company sells apparel through its own retail stores and channels, as well as through partner retail stores and channels throughout the world. The company has a family of individual brands that function independently and pursue separate growth initiatives while leveraging the company's centralized supply chain management, information technology, and other supporting functions.

Value Network

What It Is

A *value network* is a representation of the various legal entities that make up and interact with an organization along with the value exchanged between them. A value network generates economic and societal value through complex dynamic exchanges between one or more enterprises, customers, suppliers, strategic partners, and the community. A value network represents an organization's business ecosystem.

Business Ecosystem

A business ecosystem is an economic community supported by a foundation of interacting organizations and individuals that work together toward a shared purpose, to create greater value for customers, society, and themselves beyond what they can do individually. The business ecosystem produces goods and services of value to customers, who are themselves members of the ecosystem.

Each of the strategic business architecture components and views can scale to reflect the ecosystem view and includes both internal and external stakeholders. For example, a business model can be created to reflect a joint venture between two organizations, or the scope of a value stream can be extended to reflect the end-to-end value of multiple organizations working together.

Why It Matters

Value networks are valuable to:

- Create a common understanding about the scope of entities that an organization interacts with and the nature of those interactions
- Inform the scope of an organization's strategic business architecture
- Analyze an organization's business ecosystem for strategic opportunities, including enabling political, economic, socio-cultural, and technological (PEST) analysis
- Perform and represent impact assessment for strategic and business change

How It Is Defined

The approach to representing business ecosystems is based on the Value Network Analysis (VNA) methodology by Verna Allee. As Figure 3.5 shows, a value network is composed of entities and transactions. *Entities* can include individuals (for example, funder, sponsor, lawyer), groups (for example, marketing team, engineering department, corporate lawyers, project managers), providers (for example, vendors, contractors, suppliers), customers (for example, end users, clients, resellers), and other organizations (for example, industry analysts, media outlets, governmental bodies). *Transactions* are exchanges between entities in an ecosystem and can include tangible deliverables (for example, payments, documents, contracts) or intangible deliverables (for example, feedback, insights, knowledge).

Value networks belong to the realm of strategy and strategic business architecture. They are typically created in partnership with a cross-functional group of business representatives, the strategy team, and the strategic business architecture team.

Orders
Materials & Components
Strategic Design Partners
Product Designs & Innovations
Design Trends & Insights
Revenue
Suppliers
Revenue
Material Components
Orders
Supply & Innovation Insights
Technical Knowledge
Orders
Manufacturing Partners
Finished Apparel
Revenue
Global Apparel Company
Materials, Components
Finished Apparel
Revenue
Finished Apparel
Manufacturing Partners
Finished Apparel
Revenue
Inventory Data
Consumers
Sense of Community
Product Ideas
Logistic Partners
Finished Apparel
Revenue
Orders
Finished Apparel
Inventory Data
Marketing Insights
Consumer Insights
Co-Branding Opp.
Revenue
Orders
Finished Apparel
Inventory Data
Transportation, Storage
Distributors
Partner Retail Stores, Department Stores, National Chains, Mass Merchants, E-Commerce Platforms

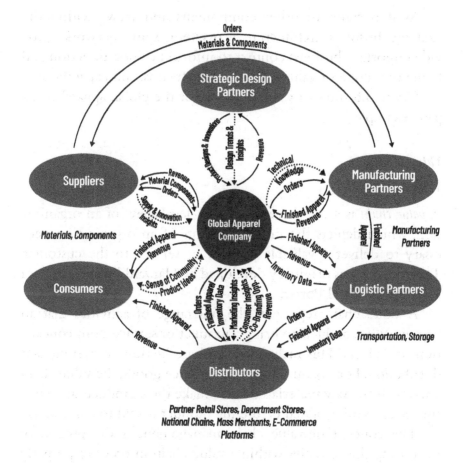

Note: This diagram represents a partial view of the organization's full value network.

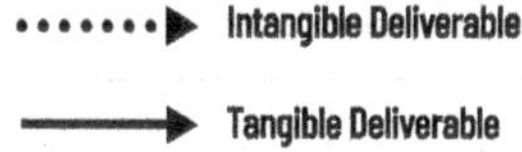

Partner Retail Stores, Department Stores, National Chains, Mass Merchants, E-Commerce Platforms

Figure 3.5 A value network example.

As it pertains to other components and views within the strategic business architecture ecosystem, value networks provide important business context to inform business direction and frame the scope of value chains, value streams, and capabilities.

Figure 3.5 shows a value network for the global apparel company example.

Value Chain

What It Is

A *value chain* is a one-page, enterprise-level view of an organization, which depicts the major segments of an organization necessary to deliver a valuable product or service to the customer. The concept was originally developed by Harvard Business School Professor Michael Porter.

A value chain represents the full range of activities that an organization conducts to bring a product or service from conception to delivery. This includes design, production, marketing, and distribution. For organizations that produce goods, the value chain starts with the raw materials used to make their products and consists of everything added before the product is sold to consumers.

The concept of value chain management is the process of organizing the activities within a value chain in order to properly analyze them. The goal is to establish communication between the leaders of each stage and ensure the product is placed in the customers' hands as seamlessly as possible.

Value Chain versus Supply Chain

A supply chain and a value chain are similar, but the value chain takes a few more things into consideration. The supply chain generally looks at the parts or materials that go into a product, where a product is manufactured, and the transportation logistics of getting it from the factory to the store.

> The value chain takes additional contributions into consideration such as product design, research and development, advertising and other marketing, and even the work of support resources such as lawyers, bankers, accountants, and technology experts.

Why It Matters

There are two primary ways to look at value chain analysis depending on how an organization is trying to edge out the competition:

- **Cost advantage analysis:** Attracting customers with low prices
- **Differentiation advantage analysis:** Attracting customers with unique benefits

Value chains are valuable for strategic decision-making to:

- Analyze how an organization achieves advantage.
- Identify opportunities for transforming that advantage, which may include shifting to more integration or modularity within the value chain.

How It Is Defined

A value chain is composed of primary activities and support activities. The primary activities often include inbound logistics, operation outbound logistics, marketing and sales, and service. The secondary or support activities often include firm infrastructure, human resource management, and procurement. However, each organization needs to adapt or expand these activities to reflect their organization's structure, language, and strategy.

Value chains again belong to the realm of strategy and strategic business architecture and are created in partnership with a cross-functional group of business representatives, the strategy team, and the strategic business architecture team.

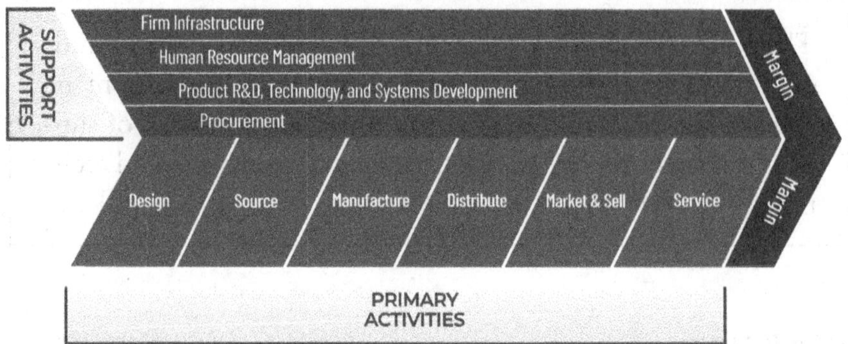

Figure 3.6 A value chain example.

As it pertains to other components and views within the strategic business architecture ecosystem, value chains provide the overall context for how an organization creates value as input to business direction. Conceptually, value chains can also inform the capabilities and value streams that are necessary for an organization to have.

Figure 3.6 shows a value chain for the global apparel company example.

Business Motivation Model

What It Is

A *business motivation model* (BMM) is a means to understand, represent, and analyze the motivations behind business decisions and actions. It formalizes the link between measurable objectives and courses of action.

Why It Matters

The BMM is valuable for two main purposes:

- To make decisions that are visible to all decision-makers and explain the rationale for making them. Leaders can also improve their decision-making ability by reflecting on the experience and learning.

- To assess the impact of decisions on business operations. This may include changes to roles, responsibilities, or processes.

How It Is Defined

As Figure 3.7 shows, a BMM is composed of the following core concepts:

- **Ends:** What the business wants to accomplish. Goals and objectives are commonly referenced.
- **Means:** How the business intends to accomplish the ends. The means may be a particular strategy, tactic, or mission.
- **Influencer:** Any factor an organization believes may affect it. This includes internal influencers (infrastructure, resource quality) and external influencers (customers, regulation, competition).
- **Assessment:** The risk and reward associated with an influence causing a significant impact on the organization. The assessment often involves a strengths, weaknesses, opportunities, and threats (SWOT) analysis to assess internal and external factors.

Figure 3.7 shows the components that comprise the BMM.

Conceptually the relationship between the ends, means, and influences helps answer two fundamental questions:

- **What is needed to achieve what the organization desires to achieve?** Here, decision-makers need to identify the means necessary to achieve the desired ends.
- **Why does each element of the business plan exist?** In other words, which end does each mean serve? What are the influences that provide the foundation for each choice?

BMMs belong to the realms of strategy and strategic business architecture. They include strategy-related information but also connect to additional business concepts. Ideally, the information within a BMM is first captured in the strategic business architecture knowledge base from which views can be created, as reflected in Figure 3.7. This allows for a much larger set of information

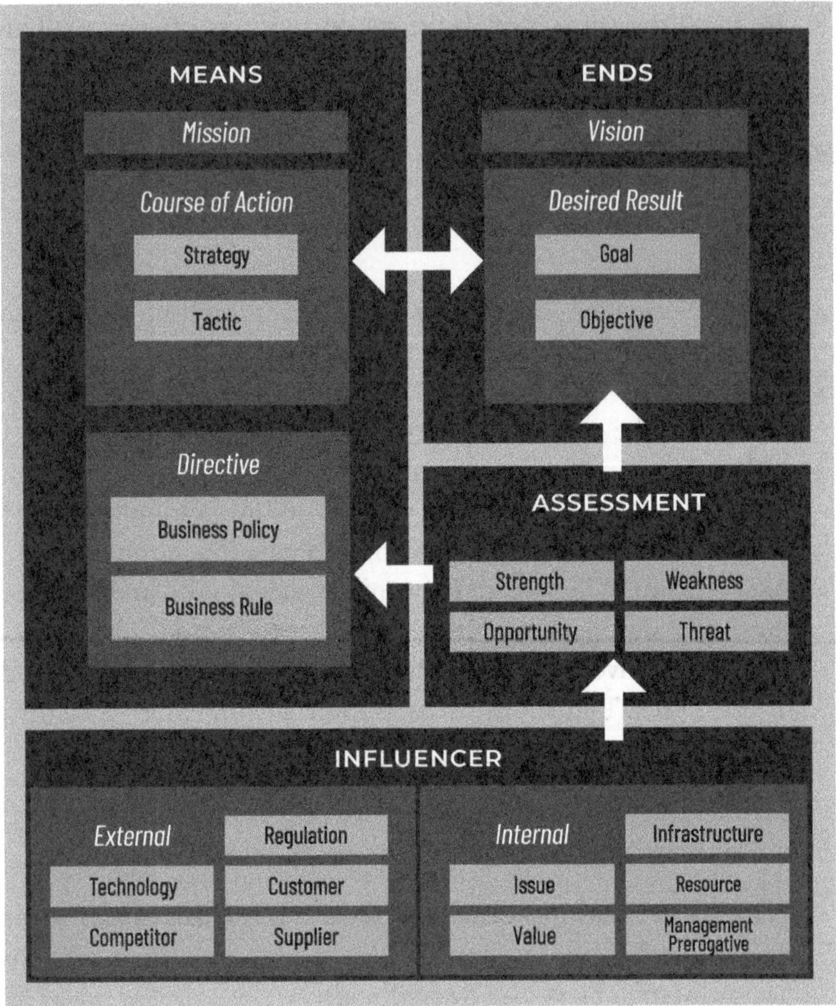

Figure 3.7 The BMM structure.

Source: OMG Business Motivation Model (https://www.omg.org/spec/BMM/1.3/About-BMM)

to be aggregated and analyzed to align strategy with execution. For this reason, the BMM is typically stewarded by the strategic business architecture team. Of course, the information is provided and validated by the appropriate business leaders along with the strategy team.

The BMM is an Object Management Group (OMG) standard for representing strategy. However, a contemporary and more comprehensive business architecture metamodel (components and relationships) defined by the Business Architecture Guild® has become a formal, adopted standard through OMG. This metamodel includes an updated set of strategy focal points and relationships to other business perspectives that can be leveraged to underpin the entire strategic business architecture knowledge base.[3]

As it pertains to other components and views within the strategic business architecture ecosystem, the BMM helps to inform strategy maps and provides the overall business direction to drive the changes to be executed, framed by value streams and capabilities.

We will explore how the information contained within the BMM can be used to translate strategy, with an example for our apparel company, in Chapter 4.

Strategy Map

What It Is

A *strategy map* is a diagram used to document the primary strategic goals being pursued by an organization or management team. It is an element of the documentation associated with the Kaplan Norton Balanced Scorecard and in particular is characteristic of the second generation of Balanced Scorecard designs that first appeared during the mid-1990s.

Why It Matters

Strategy maps are valuable to:

- Create a shared, visual representation of organizational strategy on a single page.
- Clarify the strategy and communicate it in a way that is meaningful and actionable to all employees.
- Understand the causal relationships between objectives and align efforts across the organization to achieve those objectives.

How It Is Defined

A strategy map is composed of four strategic perspectives:

- **Financial perspective:** Outlines the tangible outcomes of the organizational strategy
- **Customer perspective:** Describes the value proposition for the customers
- **Internal process perspective:** Specifies the essential internal processes that will have the greatest impact on the strategy
- **Learning and growth perspective:** Identifies the intangible assets important to the strategy

Each of these perspectives is shown as individual rows on the strategy map, and each contains objectives pertaining to them. The objectives are then linked together to convey the cause-and-effect relationship between them.

Strategy maps belong to the realm of strategy. They are typically created by the appropriate business leaders along with the strategy team. However, the business objectives contained on the strategy map should also be captured within the strategic business architecture knowledge base so that they can be related to other business perspectives such as capabilities for strategy execution and alignment. Strategic business architects can also be valuable partners to assist with the creation of strategy maps.

As it pertains to other components and views within the strategic business architecture ecosystem, strategy maps provide the business direction to drive the changes to be executed, framed by value streams and capabilities. They may also inform the business model canvas.

Figure 3.8 shows a strategy map for the global apparel company example.

Value Proposition Canvas

What It Is

A *value proposition canvas* defines the needs and value proposition for a specific customer segment and helps ensure an organization's

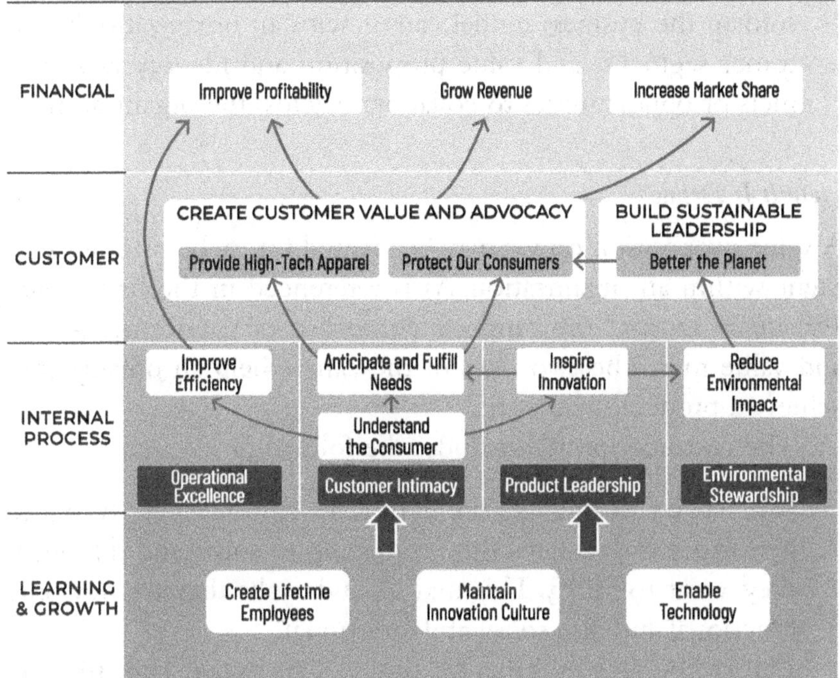

Figure 3.8 A strategy map example.

Source: Based on the canvases created by Norton and Kaplan, *Strategy Maps: Converting Intangible Assets into Tangible Outcomes*. Harvard Business Review, 2004.

product or service is positioned around customers' values and needs. It focuses on understanding customers' problems and producing products and services that solve them. The value proposition canvas was created by Alexander Osterwalder, Yves Pigneur, and Alan Smith. It can be used when there is a need to refine an existing product or service offering or when a new offering is being developed.

Why It Matters

The value proposition canvas is valuable to:

- Identify the fit between customers' values and needs and an organization's products and services.
- Uncover unmet needs and new opportunities to serve customers with new products and services.

- Inform the business model canvas with an organization's customer segments and value proposition and identify any conflicts or opportunities to collaborate across the organization.

How It Is Defined

A value proposition canvas may be created for each customer segment within an organization. As is referenced in the book *Value Proposition Design*,[4] the canvas is composed of a customer profile and value map. The two sides of the canvas help an organization achieve a product–market fit.

The customer profile includes the following:

- **Jobs to be done:** The different tasks customers are trying to perform, the problems they are trying to solve, and the needs they want to satisfy. This may include jobs that are not only functional, but also social and emotional.
- **Pains:** The problems that frustrate the customer while they are performing their jobs, which may include negative experiences and emotions, challenges, risks, financial costs, and other pains.
- **Gains:** The benefits the customer expects or wishes, or something that would surprise and delight them to make their life easier or more successful.

The value map includes the following:

- **Products and services:** The products, services, and features an organization offers.
- **Pain relievers:** The ways in which an organization's product or service removes a current frustration for the customer, which may include time or cost savings, resolving challenges, eliminating risks, and so forth.
- **Gain creators:** The ways in which an organization's product or service offers added value and brings additional benefits, which may include producing results beyond the customer's expectation, making the customer's tasks or life easier, creating positive social consequences, and so forth.

The value proposition canvas also belongs to the realm of both strategy and strategic business architecture. Canvases may be stewarded by the strategy team or the strategic business architecture team and are best created and facilitated together in partnership with the right business leaders.

There is a direct tie between the value proposition canvas and the business model canvas. For a given organization, there are typically multiple value proposition canvases representing different customer segments that are directly input into its business model canvas, specifically within the customer segments and value proposition building blocks.

As it pertains to other components and views within the strategic business architecture ecosystem, the value proposition canvas also informs the products listed within the product domain of strategic business architecture. The canvas also defines the value that needs to be delivered to customers through one or more value streams.

Figure 3.9 shows a value proposition canvas for the global apparel company example, describing the outdoor consumer segment.

Business Model Canvas

What It Is

A *business model canvas* demonstrates how an organization creates, delivers, and captures value.[5] An organization may have more than one business model to fit different customers or industries. The business model canvas was created by Alexander Osterwalder and Yves Pigneur.

In traditional terms, a *business model* refers to a company's plan for making a profit. It identifies the products or services the business plans to sell, its identified target market, and any anticipated expenses. The concept of a business model applies to organizations within any sector, though, including governmental, nongovernmental, and nonprofit organizations. The business model canvas can be adapted to represent these types of organizations.

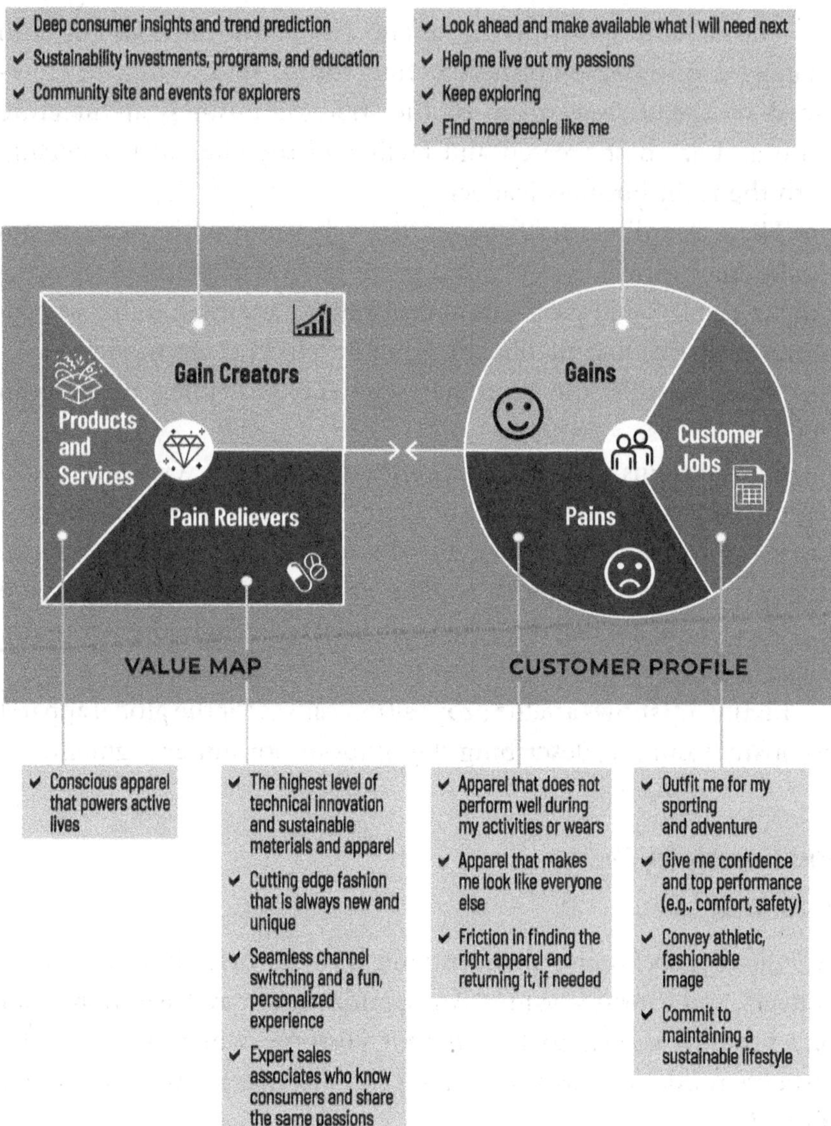
✔ Deep consumer insights and trend prediction
✔ Sustainability investments, programs, and education
✔ Community site and events for explorers
✔ Look ahead and make available what I will need next
✔ Help me live out my passions
✔ Keep exploring
✔ Find more people like me
Gain Creators
Products and Services
Pain Relievers
Gains
Customer Jobs
Pains
VALUE MAP
CUSTOMER PROFILE
✔ Conscious apparel that powers active lives
✔ The highest level of technical innovation and sustainable materials and apparel
✔ Cutting edge fashion that is always new and unique
✔ Seamless channel switching and a fun, personalized experience
✔ Expert sales associates who know consumers and share the same passions
✔ Apparel that does not perform well during my activities or wears
✔ Apparel that makes me look like everyone else
✔ Friction in finding the right apparel and returning it, if needed
✔ Outfit me for my sporting and adventure
✔ Give me confidence and top performance (e.g., comfort, safety)
✔ Convey athletic, fashionable image
✔ Commit to maintaining a sustainable lifestyle

Figure 3.9 A value proposition canvas example.

Source: Based on the canvases created by Strategyzer (www.strategyzer.com).

There are many different types and combinations of business models (for example, product, subscription, freemium, multisided platform, and so on).

Why It Matters

The business model canvas is valuable to:

- Create a shared mental model encompassing what an organization does to deliver value to customers or constituents on a single page.
- Define and communicate the business model for a new organization (for example, a start-up or new legal entity related to an existing organization).
- Identify opportunities for new value delivery or business model innovation, which may include business model transformation (for example, from a product to a platform business model) or diversification (for example, by creating an additional business model).
- Identify opportunities for improvement such as to address business model conflicts or weaknesses.
- Identify and communicate changes resulting from business model shifts, strategies, transformation, acquisitions, or other major business changes.

How It Is Defined

The business model canvas is composed of nine building blocks, which are defined in the book *Business Model Generation.*[6] The right side of the canvas focuses on value and includes building blocks for the following:

- **Customer segments:** The different groups of people or organizations that an organization aims to serve. Customer segments may be based on specific demographics, geographic locations, behavior patterns, or other characteristics.

- **Customer relationships:** The types of relationships an organization establishes and maintains with its customers, which range from personal assistance and dedicated support to self-service interactions.
- **Customer channels:** The different ways through which an organization reaches and interacts with its customers to deliver its value proposition, which may include sales forces, online platforms, distribution networks, physical stores, or other means of communication and distribution.
- **Revenue streams:** The various sources of income generated by an organization as a result of the value propositions offered to customers, which may be from direct sales, subscription fees, licensing, advertising, or other revenue models.

The left side of the canvas focuses on business enablement and includes building blocks for:

- **Partners:** The external entities, organizations, or suppliers that an organization collaborates with to leverage their resources, reduce risk, or gain access to new markets and capabilities.
- **Key activities:** The most important tasks and processes that a business needs to carry out to make its business model work, which are directly linked to the delivery of the value proposition and the fulfillment of the organization's purpose.
- **Key resources:** The critical assets, capabilities, or factors required to deliver the value proposition, reach customers, and operate the business effectively. Key resources may include physical resources such as infrastructure, intellectual property, human resources, or financial resources.
- **Cost structures:** The costs and expenses associated with running the business.

Both sides come together with *Value Proposition* in the center of the canvas, which defines the unique value that an organization offers to its customers.

The business model canvas also belongs to the realms of strategy and strategic business architecture and reflects aspects of both equally. The business model canvas may be stewarded by the strategy team or the strategic business architecture team and is best created and facilitated together in partnership with the right business leaders. In fact, strategists, business leaders, and strategic business architects should work together to bring their unique perspectives to the activities of not only creating, but also assessing, innovating, and communicating changes to the business model.

As mentioned earlier, there is a direct tie between the value proposition canvas and the business model canvas. There is also a close relationship between the business model canvas and the operating model canvas, discussed in the next section. The business model canvas informs key elements of the operating model including people, processes, information, systems, customers, and suppliers.

As it pertains to other components and views within the strategic business architecture ecosystem, the business model canvas informs the value streams and capabilities necessary to implement it. An organization's business model drives what its strategic business architecture needs to be, as well as any changes needed to the architecture over time. This involves every domain of the strategic business architecture beyond value streams and capabilities, including stakeholders, business units, products, policies, information, and more.

Figure 3.10 shows a business model canvas for the global apparel company example.

What It Is

While an organization's *business model* describes the strategic perspective of how an organization creates, delivers, and captures value, an organization's *operating model* describes the operational aspects necessary to achieve that value and implement the business model. There is not a consistent definition of an operating model or the elements it contains, but operating models frequently include

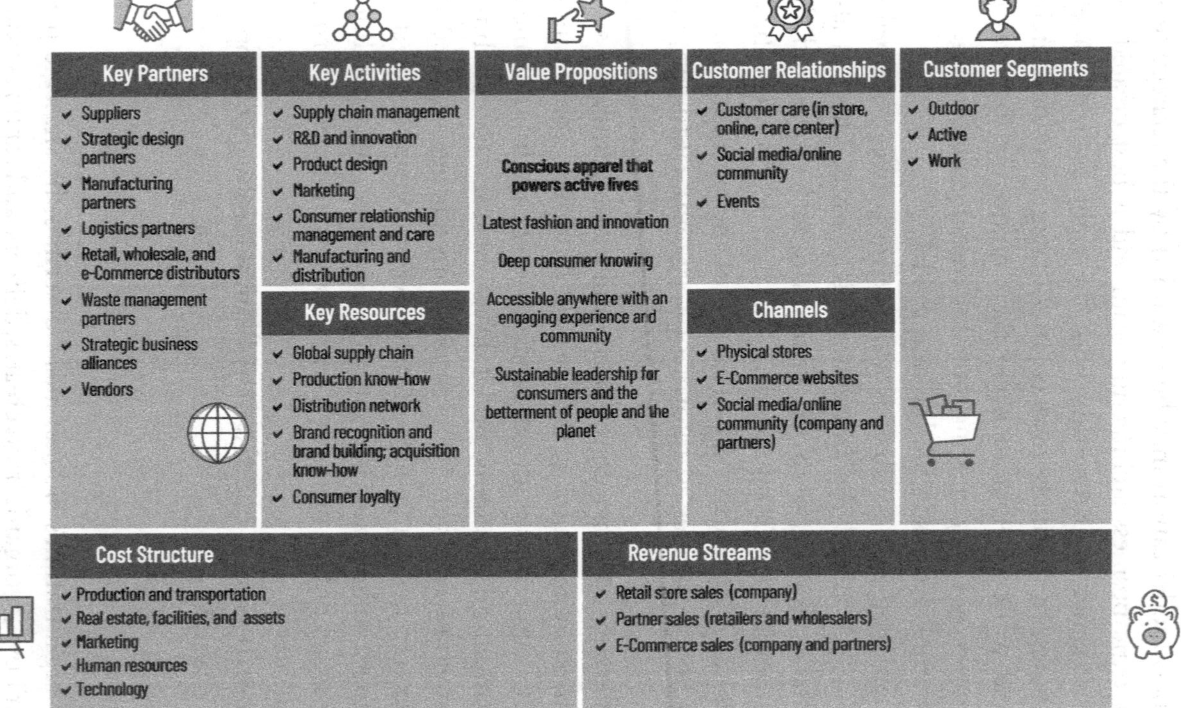

Key Partners
Suppliers
Strategic design partners
Manufacturing partners
Logistics partners
Retail, wholesale, and e-Commerce distributors
Waste management partners
Strategic business alliances
Vendors
Key Activities
Supply chain management
R&D and innovation
Product design
Marketing
Consumer relationship management and care
Manufacturing and distribution
Key Resources
Global supply chain
Production know-how
Distribution network
Brand recognition and brand building; acquisition know-how
Consumer loyalty
Value Propositions
Conscious apparel that powers active lives
Latest fashion and innovation
Deep consumer knowing
Accessible anywhere with an engaging experience and community
Sustainable leadership for consumers and the betterment of people and the planet
Customer Relationships
Customer care (in store, online, care center)
Social media/online community
Events
Channels
Physical stores
E-Commerce websites
Social media/online community (company and partners)
Customer Segments
Outdoor
Active
Work
Cost Structure
Production and transportation
Real estate, facilities, and assets
Marketing
Human resources
Technology
Revenue Streams
Retail store sales (company)
Partner sales (retailers and wholesalers)
E-Commerce sales (company and partners)

Figure 3.10 A business model canvas example.

Source: Based on the canvases created by Strategyzer (www.strategyzer.com).Operating Model Canvas

people, processes, technology, assets, and locations. An operating model is more than a sum of its parts—it defines how the elements successfully combine to deliver an organization's purpose and value.

In the book *Operating Model Canvas,* Andrew Campbell, Mikel Gutierrez, and Mark Lancelott define an operating model as:

> *". . . a* **visual** *representation (i.e., a model)*
>
> *. . . in the form of a* **diagram or map or chart** *or collection of diagrams, maps, tables, and charts*
>
> *. . . that show the* **elements of the organization,** *such as activities, people, decision processes, information systems, suppliers, locations, and assets,*
>
> *. . . that are important for delivering the organization's* **value proposition(s)**
>
> *. . . and how these elements* **combine** *to successfully deliver the value proposition(s)"*[7]

Why It Matters

The operating model canvas is valuable to:

- Create a shared mental model of an organization's operations on a single page.
- Inform the design of operating model details, such as processes, information, decision structures, job descriptions, incentives, people policies, offices, factory space, and more.
- Identify opportunities for improving operational inefficiencies.
- Identify and communicate changes to the operating model as a result of strategic shifts or other major business changes.

How It Is Defined

As is defined in the book *Operating Model Canvas,* the canvas is composed of six elements, including the following:

- **Value chain:** The work that needs to be done to deliver the value proposition

- **Organization:** The people who do the work and how they are organized
- **Locations:** Where people are located and the assets they need to help them
- **Information:** What information systems the people need to help them
- **Suppliers:** The suppliers who support the work
- **Management system:** The management system used to run the organization

The operating model canvas belongs to the realm of strategic business architecture. Strategic business architects play a critical role in facilitating discussions across business leaders, strategists, business subject matter experts, and designers from other disciplines to design the operating model at a macro level (for example, as reflected through the operating model canvas). Strategic business architecture is an important bridge to ensure that the operating model is designed and evolved as necessary to achieve the organization's overall value proposition, as well as carry out its business strategy.

Figure 3.11 shows an operating model canvas for the global apparel company example.

As mentioned earlier, there is a direct tie between the operating model canvas and the business model canvas. As the book *Operating Model Canvas* states, the six elements of the operating model canvas can provide a more powerful backend for the left side of the business model canvas (replacing the three building blocks of key partners, key activities, and key resources).[8] Figure 3.12 shows the integration of these two canvases for the global apparel company example, with the operating model canvas elements on the left integrating into the rest of the business model canvas.

Importantly, an organization's operating model should be framed by the scope of its strategic business architecture, and any changes to the operating model details resulting from organizational strategies or business model changes should be translated

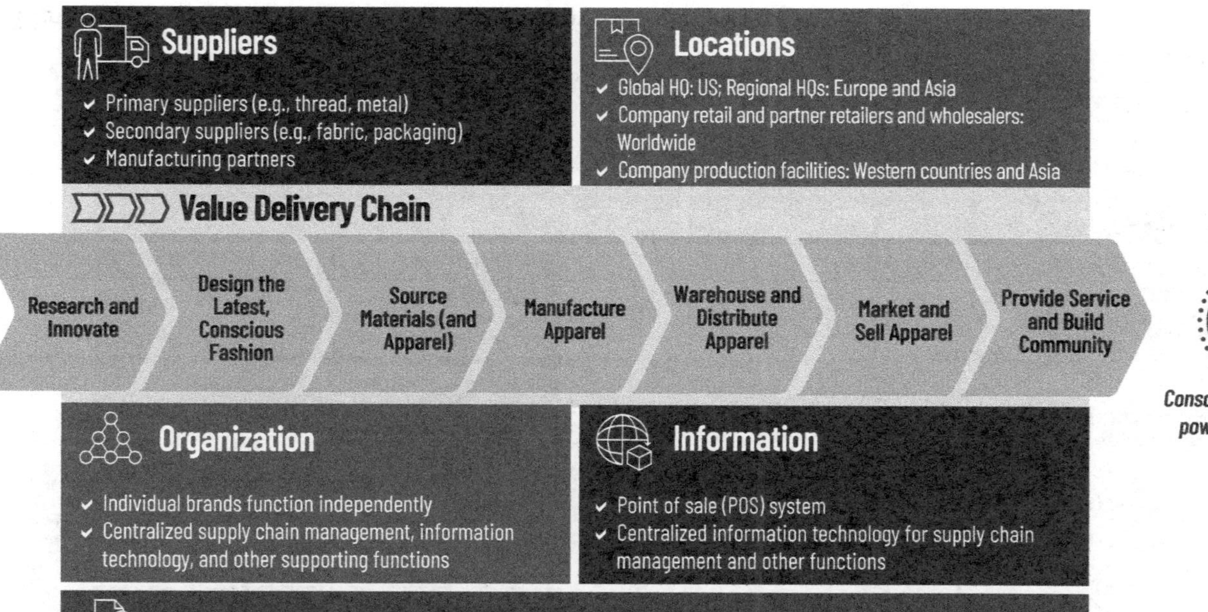

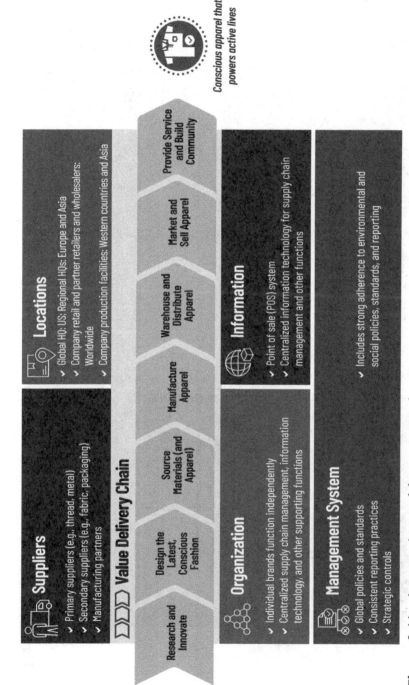

Figure 3.11 An operating model canvas example.

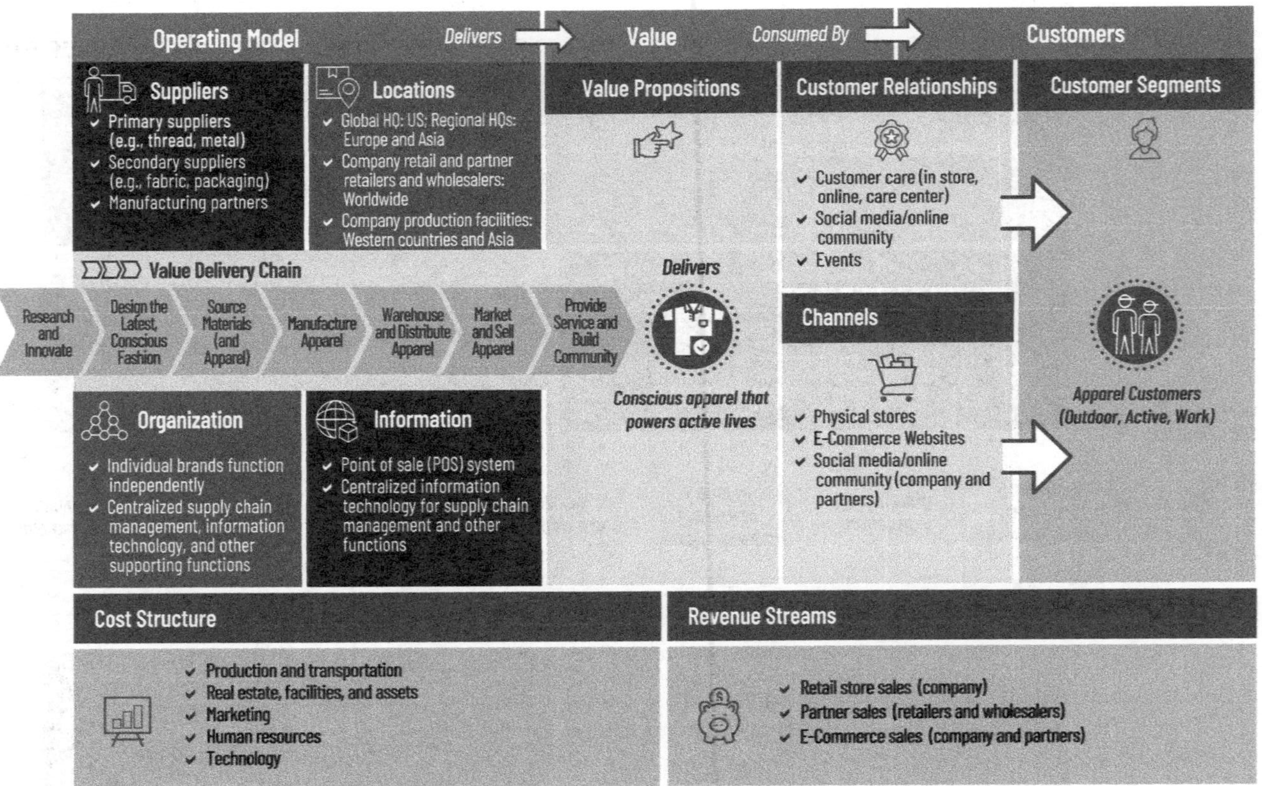

Figure 3.12 An integrated business model canvas and operating model canvas example.

through the strategic business architecture. On the other hand, the operating model canvas provides an important feedback loop to inform changes needed to value streams, capabilities, and other strategic business architecture perspectives.

Value Streams

What They Are

Value streams represent how value is delivered from end to end to the key stakeholders of an organization, including customers, partners, and employees. As mentioned earlier, value streams define reusable building blocks of value delivery that can be leveraged many times along with capabilities.

In addition to adhering to the overall qualities of strategic business architecture (business-focused and business-owned, high-level, enterprise scope, reusable), value streams have a unique set of characteristics that define and distinguish them.

Value streams are:

- **Business unit and product agnostic:** Strategic business architecture value streams are typically oriented around an information concept (for example, Acquire Product, Manufacture Product, Settle Claim, Trade Financial Instrument, Settle Payment). Due to their level of abstraction, value streams almost always involve more than one business unit, and they transcend product specifics.
- **Focused on value delivery:** Value streams are scoped with the specific intention to deliver value in the eye of the triggering stakeholder.
- **Encompassing of all scenarios:** Value streams are abstracted to represent the superset of any number of possible scenarios for which they could be used.
- **Not processes or workflows:** Value streams do not represent process or workflow details, though they may be cross-mapped to processes or event models to make the connection to the operating model.

Why They Matter

A value stream is valuable to:

- Create a shared mental model of the activities an organization performs to deliver value.
- Shift mindsets by focusing on what creates value and looking at what the organization does from the perspective of its stakeholders.
- Provide an enterprise-wide framework for macro-level design, streamlining, and project definition and strategic alignment.
- Orchestrate the automation of capabilities.

How They Are Defined

The business architecture body of knowledge, the *BIZBOK® Guide,* is a source that provides a comprehensive set of principles that can help ensure an organization's value streams are defined in a consistent way that will also achieve the expected benefits. Every organization generally has around 25+ value streams. However, there can certainly be more, especially if an organization has a complex business model and does many diverse things that deliver distinct value.

A value stream is triggered by a triggering stakeholder who may be external (such as a customer, partner, or regulator) or internal (such as a hiring manager, a product manager, or a finance officer). A value stream produces a value proposition at the end that provides value to the triggering stakeholder. Value streams are composed of stages. Each stage includes a description, a list of participating stakeholders, entrance criteria and exit criteria, and value item(s).[9]

Stakeholders are the key players within value streams and are also rationalized, defined, and associated to other business perspectives as part of the strategic business architecture.

Value streams (and their associated stakeholders) belong to the realm of strategic business architecture. They're typically defined and governed by a cross-functional group of business representatives and are stewarded by the strategic business architecture team.

Value streams are a central component and the foundation of the strategic business architecture ecosystem, together with capabilities. Value streams provide input to the value proposition canvas and business model canvas on how value is currently being delivered to customers. Value streams directly inform the value delivery chain(s) and value proposition components of the operating model canvas. Together with capabilities, value streams frame the changes and investments necessary to inform strategic portfolio management. Finally, value streams work in concert with business processes. For example, value streams may be used as an organizing construct for business processes, and they provide the overall context to help target business process improvements and investments. (Please see the aside "Value Streams and Business Processes," earlier in this chapter, for more information on how these two important components work together.)

Different Types of Value Streams

Strategic business architecture value streams are principle based and distinctly different from other types of value streams, such as *Lean* value streams or *SAFe* value streams. Each type of value stream is fit for purpose and differs in why they are created, how they are created, and who creates them.

Strategic Business Architecture and Lean Value Streams

Lean value streams are a part of the Lean discipline that focuses on removing or reducing waste within an organization. Lean value streams are used to help design and increase the efficiency of the internal operating environment. Where an organization typically has only 25+ high-level strategic business architecture value streams, which are relatively static, it may have many Lean

(*continued*)

(continued)

value streams to represent the necessary granularity. Lean value streams are more likely to evolve as the business evolves and because of targeted improvement activities.

Strategic business architecture value streams do not have a required notation and are typically represented simply as boxes and arrows. On the other hand, Lean value streams use a specific notation that helps to highlight and analyze key attributes such as how long an activity takes or the wait time between activities. Finally, the scope of strategic business architecture and Lean value streams often differs because strategic business architecture value streams have a requirement to deliver end-to-end stakeholder value.

Strategic business architecture value streams and Lean value streams work well in conjunction with each other. The activities within a Lean value stream may be cross-mapped to the applicable stages within a value stream. Strategic business architecture can be used as an organizing framework for Lean value streams and help to identify areas for alignment and best practice sharing, as well as inform Lean work priorities. Lean value streams can help inform strategic business architecture with a more detailed understanding of the current state.

Strategic Business Architecture and SAFe Value Streams

Within the Scaled Agile Framework®, SAFe value streams are a primary construct used to organize and deliver value. SAFe defines operational value streams and development value streams. Operational value streams are closer to strategic business architecture value streams. However, SAFe value streams are based on guidelines that are widely interpreted in practice and are often scoped to represent entire life cycles.

This means that multiple strategic business architecture value streams may apply across one SAFe value stream.

It is possible and ideal for principle-based, reusable strategic business architecture value streams to be used within SAFe for an organization's operational value streams. However, this is not always feasible depending upon the size and needs of an organization. Regardless, strategic business architecture value streams should be used as input to the definition of SAFe operational value streams. In cases where both exist, strategic business architecture and SAFe value streams can be cross-mapped together to provide context and understanding, as well as traceability.

Value Chains versus Value Streams

Value chains can be confused with value streams, but in reality, they are very different. In many organizations, there is typically one value chain, but there are many different value streams.

A value chain is a stand-alone view and an organizational strategic decision support tool. Value streams are defined sets of end-to-end activities that deliver value to internal or external stakeholders. Unlike value chains, which exist only as a view, value streams are a formal strategic business architecture domain that is related to other strategic business architecture perspectives such as capabilities and stakeholders.

The relationship between value chains and value streams is conceptual. For example, value streams do not cleanly map to or decompose from activities within the value chain.

Figure 3.13 shows a value stream for the global apparel company example.

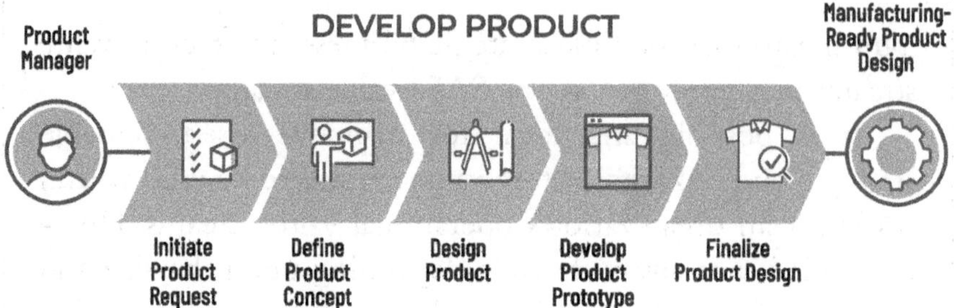

Figure 3.13 A value stream example.[10]

Source: BIZBOK® Guide Manufacturing Reference Model, with minor adaptations (https://www.businessarchitectureguild.org/page/INDREF)

Capabilities

What They Are

Capabilities are the unique abilities that an organization performs to deliver value and support its operations. They can be thought of as the reusable building blocks of a business, and they produce concrete outcomes. Capabilities define *what* an organization does, not how it does things.

In addition to adhering to the overall qualities of strategic business architecture, capabilities have a unique set of characteristics that define and distinguish them. These characteristics also ensure that capabilities can serve as the central component to translate strategy and inform decision-making.

Capabilities are:

- **Nonredundant:** Capabilities are unique and independent from each other. Capabilities are defined once for an organization, regardless of who performs them or how they are used.
- **Comprehensive:** Capabilities represent an organization comprehensively. A capability map should encompass everything an organization does, leveled consistently.
- **Not organization or process:** Capabilities are abstracted from the organizational model and process flows. A capability

map represents categorized abilities (capabilities), not a cohesive business process flow or the organizational structure.
- **Stable:** Capabilities are relatively stable, because they represent the whats not the hows (which change more frequently).

Why They Matter

Capabilities are valuable to:

- Create a shared mental model of what an entire organization does along with a shared vocabulary.
- Provide an enterprise-wide framework for macro-level design, streamlining, and project definition and strategic alignment.
- Provide a foundation for business ownership and investment that crosses organizational silos, especially beneficial for enterprise-wide ambitions such as customer experience or sustainability improvement.

How They Are Defined

The *BIZBOK Guide* defines a set of principles that can help ensure an organization's capabilities are defined in a consistent way that will also achieve the expected benefits.

As mentioned earlier, capabilities are typically represented in a conceptual model, a capability map, which contains all of an organization's capabilities. Building a capability map can be a thought-provoking exercise in introspective analysis and decomposition.

There are two key structural aspects of a capability map:

- **Tiers:** Capabilities are organized into three different tiers (typically represented as rows). Tiers provide additional business context and make the capability map more consumable with an organizing construct.
  - The **Strategic tier** contains capabilities that have more bearing on the direction of an organization (for example, Business Entity Management or Market Management).

- The **Customer-Facing/Core tier** contains capabilities that are customer-facing or foundational to what the organization does (for example, Customer Management, Channel Management, and industry-specific capabilities such as Shipment Management for a transportation company or Financial Instrument Management for a financial services company).
- The **Supporting tier** contains capabilities that are necessary to operate (for example, Human Resource Management or Finance Management).

A little-known fact is that these three tiers were originally inspired by the Porter Value Chain, discussed earlier in this chapter.

- **Levels:** Capabilities start at level 1 and break down into increasingly detailed capabilities, typically no further than level 6. For example, a level 1 capability breaks down into multiple level 2 capabilities, each level 2 capability breaks down into multiple level 3 capabilities, and so forth. For the purposes of high-level planning and analysis, level 3 capabilities are typically sufficient.

In addition to tiers and levels, capabilities can also be *attributed* to create a richer foundation for strategy translation, planning, and business performance improvement. Essentially the idea is to capture unique metrics by capability to measure its strategic importance and effectiveness. A variety of metrics can be captured to define the importance of a capability, but of particular relevance to strategy execution is a categorization of each capability based on their strategic contribution. A capability may be categorized as one of the following:

- **Advantage/transform-the-business capabilities:** Directly contribute to the customer value proposition and have a high impact on company financials. These are often the research and development capabilities that create the next-generation products or services and are typically kept inside an organization and highly protected.

- **Strategic support/grow-the-business capabilities:** Have high contribution to the operations of the business. These are often the operational capabilities that set an organization apart from the competition and are rarely outsourced.
- **Essential/run-the-business capabilities:** Are essentially the "keep the lights on" capabilities that are necessary to run a business. These are typically the support functions and are often candidates for outsourcing.

There are also a variety of metrics that can be captured to define the effectiveness of a capability (for example, Business Effectiveness, Progress Toward Target State), which assess the quality and extent of enablement for each capability. This ultimately comes down to the people, process, information, and technology behind each capability and how effectively and completely they support the organization's strategic and operational needs. Capabilities help to frame where enhancements to people, process, information, and technology are necessary, along with the actions needed to achieve them. This provides a critical foundation for strategy translation and planning, which we will explore further in Chapter 4.

Finally, capabilities should be based upon defined business information concepts. For example, the capability of Customer Information Management should rely upon a clear and agreed upon definition of a customer. In fact, the process of building a capability map begins with an understanding of core information concepts. A capability map creates a powerful mental model, and when underpinned by a common business vocabulary, it ensures that every person in the organization shares the same picture in their mind to see and communicate about what the organization does.

Different Types of Capabilities

The term *capability* is used within different contexts that are often unknowingly conflated and can be a potential source of confusion. A higher-level concept of *capability* may be used in strategy formulation to bring strategic choices to life. (They are sometimes known as the *big C capabilities.*) For example, core capabilities defined during strategy formulation may include Understanding Consumers, Innovation, Brand Building, Go-to-Market Ability, or Global Scale.

However, to translate strategy into concrete actions, a more tangible and granular definition of a capability as a business building block is necessary. The latter type of capability is defined as part of an organization's strategic business architecture, which is our focus in this book. (They are sometimes known as the *small c capabilities.*)

Examples of strategic business architecture capabilities include Customer Information Management, Customer Analytics Management, Product Management, Order Management, and Payment Management.

Strategic capabilities are more conceptual and few in number, while strategic business architecture capabilities are concrete and more numerous. Strategic capabilities are enabled by many different strategic business architecture capabilities.

Capabilities (and information concepts) belong to the realm of strategic business architecture. They are typically defined and governed by a cross-functional group of business representatives and are stewarded by the strategic business architecture team.

Capabilities are *the* central component composing the foundation of the strategic business architecture ecosystem, together with value streams. Capabilities bring together the resources necessary to provide the abilities that value streams require to deliver value. Capabilities enable value stream stages and contribute to the value item(s) produced from each stage. The value items from each stage accrue to deliver the end value proposition for the triggering stakeholder at the end. A capability can enable many value stream stages (across many value streams), and a value stream stage can orchestrate many capabilities in the course of delivering value.

Capabilities provide input to value chains, the business model canvas, and the operating model canvas to define the abilities currently in place, which can help to identify potential gaps in capability support, as well as opportunities for leveraging existing capabilities for new value delivery. Capabilities inform strategy maps and strategic decision-making by defining what an organization's current capabilities are and how well they are working.

Together with value streams, capabilities frame the changes and investments necessary to inform strategic portfolio management. Finally, capabilities serve as a high-level focal point for business ownership and direction to help target business process improvements and investments.

Figure 3.14 shows a capability map for the global apparel company example. The capability map shows the highest level of detail, often referred to as a *level 1* view.

Figure 3.15 also shows an intersection between capabilities and the business model canvas. Capabilities enable products and services. Those products and services are delivered to specific customer segments, through defined relationships and channels.

Business Processes

What They Are

Business processes represent a series of logically related activities or tasks performed together to produce a defined set of

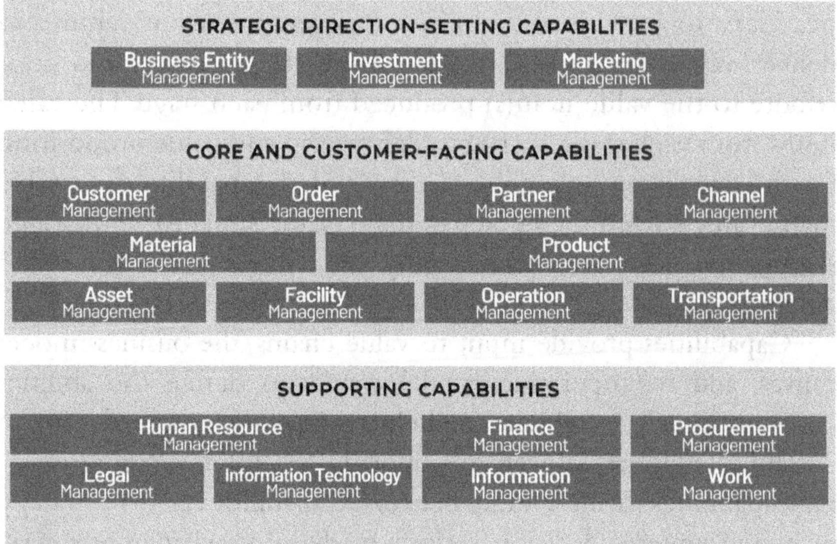

Figure 3.14 A level 1 capability map example.[11]

Source: Capability map is a hybrid created by the authors, with a combined information concept and functional orientation. This is partially aligned with the *BIZBOK® Guide* Manufacturing Reference Model.

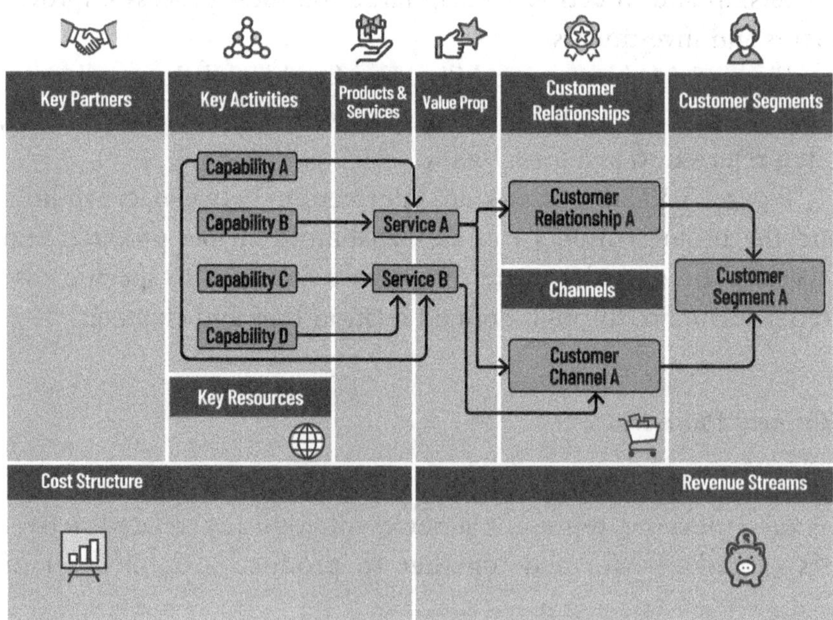

Figure 3.15 Capabilities and the business model canvas.

results.[12] Processes are part of the business process management (BPM) discipline that encompasses the identification, design, implementation, monitoring, and continuous improvement of business processes to enhance efficiency, effectiveness, and agility within an organization.

Why They Matter

Business processes are valuable to:

- Define how a business works at a more detailed level.
- Improve the efficiency and productivity of the organization, as well as identify opportunities to reduce costs, errors, and risks.

How They Are Defined

An organization's business process framework will define how processes are categorized, leveled within a defined hierarchy, and represented, including the modeling notation that will be used. A business process model is a graphical depiction of an individual process, which is minimally composed of activities or tasks, sequence flows (to connect activities), and roles.

Business processes belong to the realm of business process management. They are defined with the appropriate business representatives and are typically stewarded by the process team, though the strategic business architecture team typically helps to steward the relationships between processes and business architecture perspectives such as value streams and capabilities. There is close integration and partnership among the teams on an ongoing basis.

As it pertains to other components and views within the business architecture ecosystem, business processes relate the closest with value streams and capabilities. Processes implement value streams and capabilities. More specifically, processes are aligned to value stream stages, and they implement the capabilities that enable those stages.

Please see Chapter 6 for more information on business process management and its critical role as a strategy execution discipline.

Figure 3.16 shows a business process model for the global apparel company example.

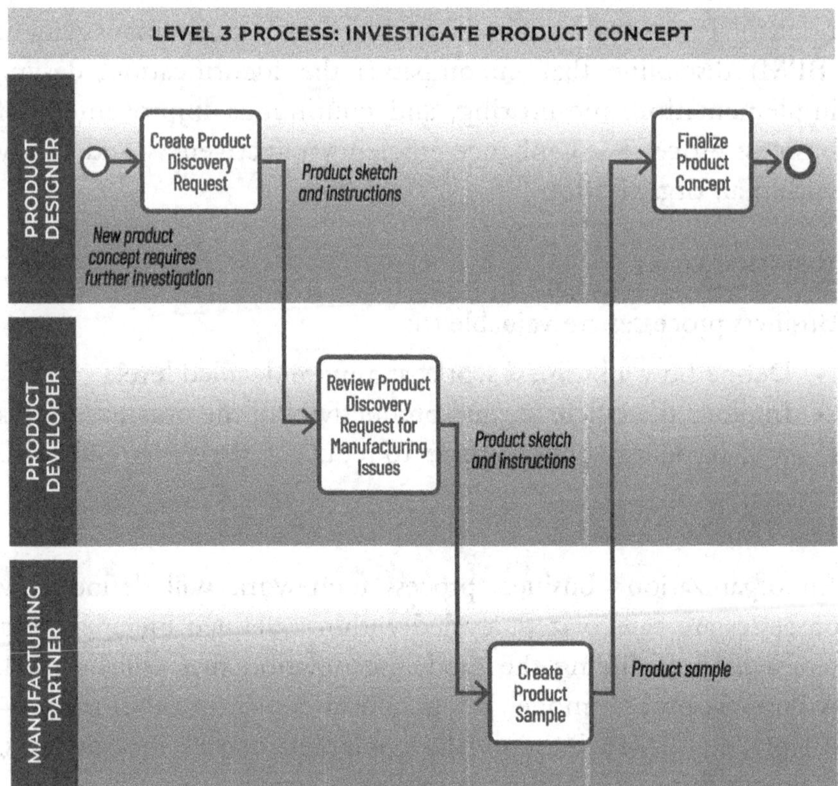

Figure 3.16 A business process model example.

Putting the Ideas Together: Capabilities, Value Streams, and Business Processes

Capabilities, value streams, and business processes together play a foundational role in strategy execution and business decision-making. They are sometimes confused, so we will take a short aside to further differentiate and define how they relate.

Capabilities define *what* is done, regardless of how, where, who, or how well it is performed. Value streams and business processes describe *how* things are done, at different levels of elevation as described earlier. Value streams describe *how* value is delivered to a stakeholder, and processes describe *how* something more specific is done.

Both value streams and business processes require capabilities and describe how those capabilities are used. As with any set of strategic business architecture domains or views, each has its purpose and place.

Figure 3.17 shows how these three components relate. The Develop Product value stream provides the overall organizing construct, and a sample of the enabling capabilities is shown below each stage. A sample of business processes that implement the value stream are shown across the specific stages to which they apply. As mentioned earlier, the process alignment to each of these value stream stages also indicates the capabilities that each process implements for those stages as well.

Strategic Portfolio Management and Projects

The components of strategic portfolio management and projects are key aspects of the strategic business architecture ecosystem to align strategy and execution. One of the most common forms of portfolio management is project portfolio management. We will discuss project portfolio management, as well as other types of portfolio management, in Chapter 5.

Please refer to Chapter 1 for clarity on the definitions of *project, program, project portfolio,* and *initiative.*

Bringing It All Together: Component Applicability across Strategy Execution

With a solid understanding of the components within the strategic business architecture ecosystem, we will now explore the level of applicability of each across the five stages from strategy to execution. Figure 3.18 lists each ecosystem component, along with an indication of high, medium, or low in terms of its usage within each stage.

Value networks, value chains, the value proposition canvas, and the business model canvas are more heavily used when developing

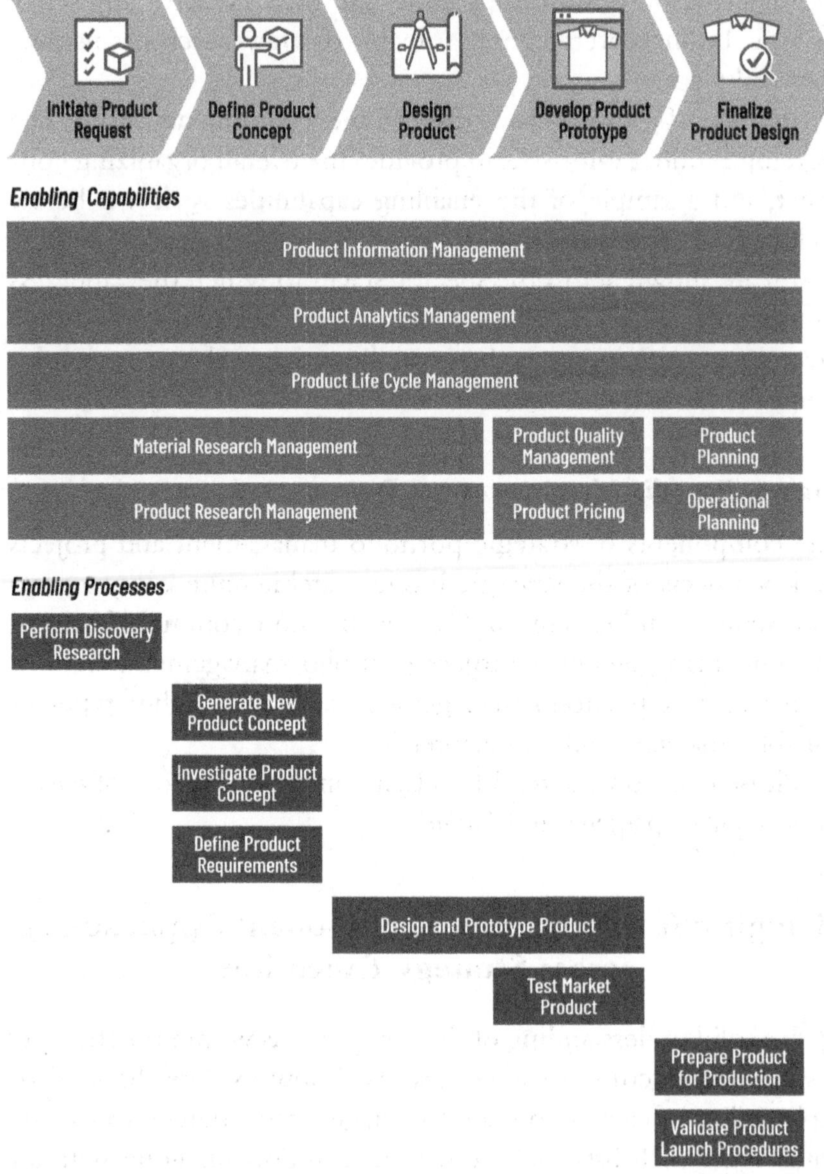

Figure 3.17 Alignment between value streams, capabilities, and processes.[13]

Source: Created by the authors. Value stream and capabilities are based on the *BIZBOK® Guide* Manufacturing Reference Model with minor adaptations. Processes are based on the APQC Consumer Products Process Classification Framework.

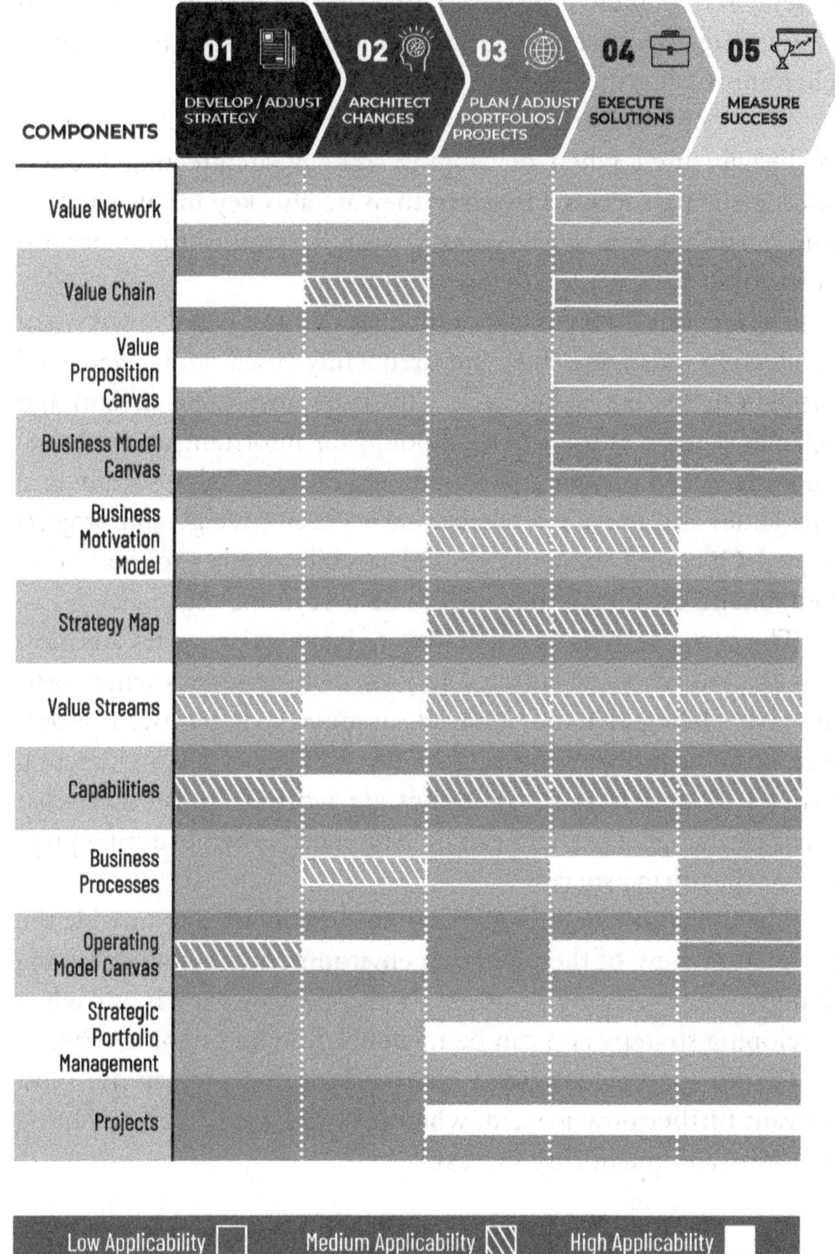

Figure 3.18 Component Applicability from Strategy to Execution.

strategy and architecting change, though they may be referred to at any time, especially while executing solutions or to reference when measuring success.

The BMM and strategy map provide business direction, so they are heavily used when developing strategy, architecting change, and measuring success. However, they are also key inputs to planning portfolios and projects and may be referred to frequently on an ongoing basis while executing solutions.

Though value streams and capabilities are most heavily used when architecting changes, they are frequently used and referenced throughout the entire life cycle. This is because value streams and capabilities serve as the key focal points for informing and translating strategy and planning portfolios and projects. Value streams and capabilities also provide a mechanism to keep strategy and projects aligned. Of course, value streams and capabilities relate to most other components as well, so they help to tie everything together.

The more granular perspectives of business processes are most heavily used when executing solutions, including cases where processes are being defined, evolved, improved, or removed. However, business processes are also highly valuable when architecting changes to understand how things are working today and what needs to change. They also can be referenced when planning projects or measuring success.

The operating model canvas is most heavily used to provide the big-picture view of the operating environment when architecting changes and executing solutions. It also provides key input when developing strategy and can be referenced on an ongoing basis.

Finally, strategic portfolio management and projects are most relevant further downstream, when planning initiatives, executing solutions, and measuring success.

Next Steps

We have explored the strategic business architecture toolkit, including each component and view within the strategic business architecture ecosystem and how they fit together. We have recognized how the enterprise-wide business views and data-driven approach of strategic business architecture can help to facilitate effective strategy execution and strategic decision-making. So, where do we go from here to build out the strategic business architecture for an organization?

As noted earlier in this chapter in the section "The Scope of Strategic Business Architecture," a practical approach should be taken to build out the strategic business architecture ecosystem. Stand-alone views such as a value network, value chain, value proposition canvas, or business model canvas can be created anytime. The best starting place is the view that is most relevant to addressing a current opportunity or challenge. For example, if your organization is looking to reimagine its business model, start with a business model canvas. On the other hand, if your organization is looking to expand and identify strategic opportunities within its business ecosystem, start with a value network.

Alongside these efforts, you may also want to begin building your strategic business architecture baseline. The baseline is composed of an enterprise-wide capability map (based on defined information concepts), a minimum set of value streams, and a cross-mapping between the two. As the strategic business architecture ecosystem reflects, capabilities and value streams are frequently leveraged, and together they form the foundation of the strategic business architecture. The strategic business architecture baseline should be created by a cross-functional group of business representatives. These efforts can be accelerated by leveraging industry reference models as a starting point. Various organizations provide starter models (often referred to as *reference models*) for capability maps, value streams, business processes, and other perspectives across a variety of industries.

Once the strategic business architecture baseline is in place, it can be expanded over time along with additional domains such as strategies, initiatives, products, or policies that can be captured *just enough just in time* as needed to support business decision-making and usage scenarios. Keeping a focus on business value is the key to making strategic business architecture practical and agile. Additional stand-alone views may be created over time as well. Expanding beyond the baseline will require a significant amount of partnership, as is expected. For example, strategies may come from leaders and the strategy team, products may come from product leaders, policies may come from compliance or human resources teams, and so forth.

An automated strategic business architecture knowledge base is ideal to contain all this information, but leverage views and templates in the beginning until investment in a tool is made. Gaining experience with the strategic business architecture toolkit to explore and demonstrate its value is most important and the rest of the pieces will fall into place over time.

In later chapters, we expand further upon this and discuss all the components necessary to build a successful and scalable strategic business architecture practice. Next, let's look at how the valuable perspectives from the strategic business architecture ecosystem help us to translate strategy into successful execution.

STRATEGY EXECUTION ORGANIZATIONAL ASSESSMENT

Reflect on the following questions to assess how well strategy execution is working in your organization based on the concepts from Chapter 3. Please refer to the scoring guidance provided in Chapter 1.

1. Our organization has a documented, business-owned strategic business architecture baseline (composed of an enterprise-wide capability map based on defined information concepts,

a minimum set of enterprise-wide value streams, and a cross-mapping between the two).

2. Rate the organization's maturity with capability mapping.
3. Rate the organization's maturity with value stream mapping.
4. Rate the organization's maturity with business process modeling.
5. Our strategic business architecture knowledge base is managed in an automated tool that meets our needs for maintenance, analysis, and visualization.
6. Our strategic business architecture knowledge base is continually kept current to reflect the business as it evolves and is expanded to provide new insights for business decision-making as needed.
7. Our organization has additional strategic business architecture views that are documented and business-owned (for example, value network, value chain, value proposition canvas, business model canvas) where relevant to support strategy development and execution and business decision-making.
8. All pertinent individuals (for example, leaders, strategists, strategic planners, strategic business architects, decision-makers) have access to our organization's strategic business architecture.

Chapter 4

Leveraging a Capability Perspective for Strategy Translation and Alignment

We have illuminated *the execution challenge*—a complex problem that organizations experience worldwide—which is rising to the top of the business agenda as a result of our fast-changing environments, with shorter strategy cycles and more change and uncertainty in most organizations. We articulated a vision for a more pragmatic, comprehensive approach to strategy execution to address that challenge, and we explored how strategic business architecture is a critical enabler from end to end. We then discussed the strategic business architecture toolkit, including each component and view within the strategic business architecture ecosystem, and how they fit together to create a shared understanding of an organization to help facilitate effective strategy execution and strategic decision-making.

So, how do we actually take business strategy and produce a set of coordinated and actionable results through the strategic business architecture? That is the question we will explore in this chapter, step-by-step, using the global apparel company example to illustrate the concepts where applicable.

As discussed earlier, capabilities are the nexus of strategic business architecture and strategy execution. Together with value streams, they serve as a focal point for informing and translating strategy into harmonized business changes; guiding program, project, and investment priorities; and providing a structure for holistic business ownership.

In this chapter, we will see how the strategic business architecture lens can lead to a new mindset and a new set of results for strategy execution. The outcome is not only the proactive translation of strategy into an aligned set of projects for execution, but also the reactive and continual ability to realign projects when the strategy and business environment change.

The Capability Perspective Closes the Gap between Strategy and Execution

Most organizations struggle with a disconnect between what the business strategy says and how the business will need to execute the strategy. This lack of shared understanding creates a gap between strategy and execution, as shown in Figure 4.1. For many organizations, this gap exists between the high-level, directional nature of strategy and the detailed, implementation focus of execution.

There is a natural dichotomy between strategy and execution in most organizations:

- Strategy sets direction; execution is a set of plans and tasks.
- Strategy is focused on the medium to long-term; execution is focused on the present.
- Strategy should be largely stable for the medium term; execution is volatile, based on internal and external changes.

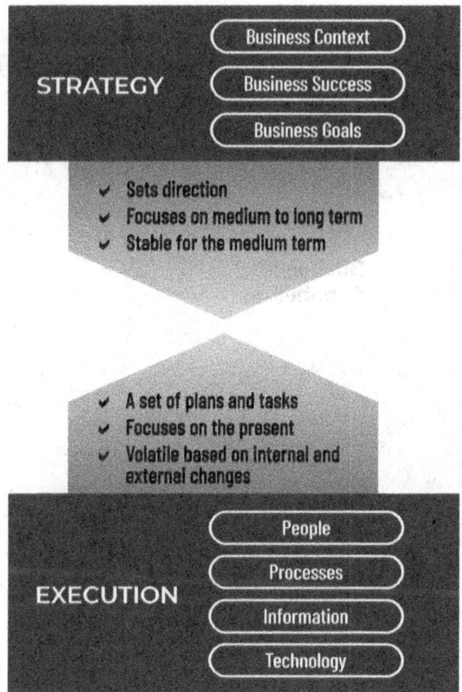

Figure 4.1 The gap in understanding between business strategy and execution.

This dichotomy leads to difficulties in translating strategy into execution, and a gap often forms between long-term enterprise goals and short-term plans and priorities.

The capability perspective helps close this gap by providing a simple, stable view of the organization and business model while creating a common language and understanding among organizational stakeholders of what the business must be able to do.

As shown in Figure 4.2, capabilities are used for translating, clarifying, extending, analyzing, and optimizing strategy and execution. The capability perspective facilitates strategy execution by:

- Translating high-level goals describing how the business will win into detailed opportunities and constraints involved in how the business needs to execute

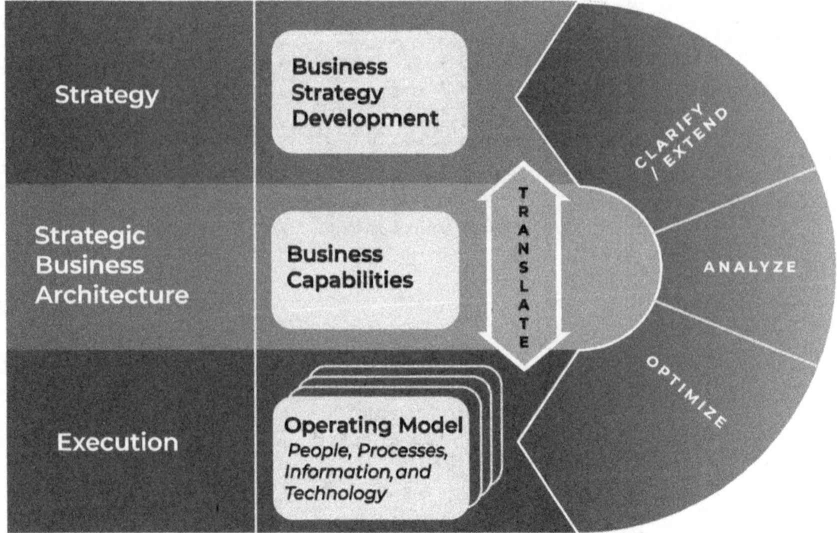

Figure 4.2 Capabilities close the gap between strategy and execution.

- Clarifying and extending the strategy when planning the business and the contribution of different parts of the organization
- Analyzing priorities and their impact when executing the business plan and strategy
- Optimizing the use of resources when reviewing the plan

The Role of Value Streams and Capabilities in Translating Strategy

Since value streams and capabilities are the key business building blocks and focal point for informing and translating strategy, it is worth reiterating some key points as a backdrop:

- Both value streams and capabilities are higher level in detail and represent an abstracted perspective that transcends organizational silos.
- Value streams and capabilities themselves typically do not "change," but rather one or more aspects of their *implementation* changes.

For example, an organization would always have a capability for customer (or constituent) information management, but how it is automated may change over time.

- A capability is implemented through people, process, information, and technology (the operating model).
- While capabilities connect to all business perspectives within strategic business architecture and other disciplines, value streams (and processes at a lower level of detail) provide context for where those capabilities are used.

As it pertains to translating strategy then, the role of value streams and capabilities is to provide context for, frame, and align the changes necessary to achieve a desired state.

Figure 4.3 illustrates these concepts.

Please refer to the aside "Value Streams and Business Processes" in Chapter 3. As it describes, some organizations prefer to leverage high-level business processes instead of value streams to provide the value context for capabilities. If this is the case for your organization, you may interpret the references to value streams as equivalent to your high-level business processes. Please refer to Chapter 3 for more information on how value streams and business processes work together.

Enhancing Strategy Execution Techniques with Strategic Business Architecture

Within the context of our comprehensive strategy execution perspective, when the first three stages are approached with an enterprise business lens, it can produce better business outcomes and prevent downstream execution challenges from ever occurring in the first place. As shown in Figure 4.4, there are seven key strategy execution techniques that can be enhanced through the holistic perspective of strategic business architecture.

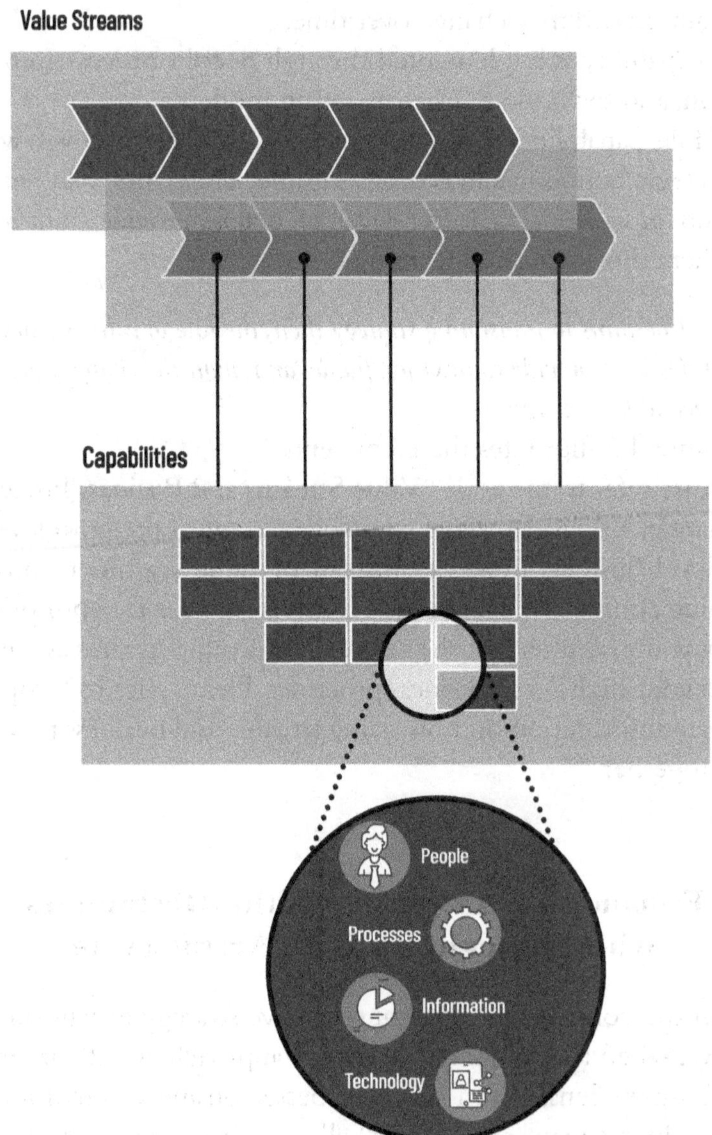

Figure 4.3 Value streams and capabilities frame and align changes.

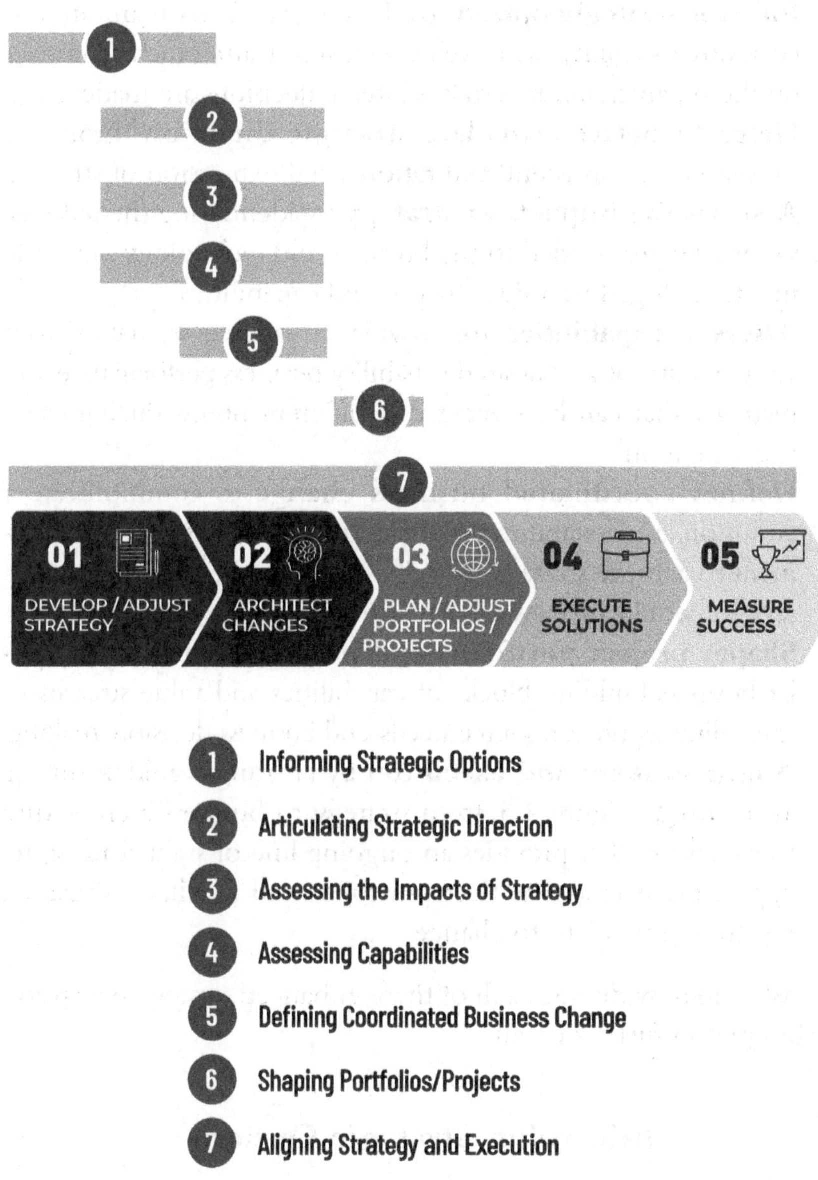

Figure 4.4 Strategy execution techniques enhanced with strategic business architecture.

In summary, strategic business architecture:

- **Informs strategic options** by defining what an organization is currently capability of, as well as communicating the full impact on the organization if certain strategic decisions are made
- **Helps to better articulate strategic direction** through a simple, clear, consistent, and rationalized expression of strategy
- **Assesses the impacts of strategy** by identifying the *collective* set of changes needed to the business and technology environment, cataloged by value streams and capabilities
- **Assesses capabilities** to provide an aggregate, data-driven view of current and desired capability business performance and maturity that can be leveraged at different points during strategy execution
- **Defines coordinated business change** to communicate a common understanding of the future-state business environment to achieve strategy, as well as the resulting changes necessary to people, process, information, and technology
- **Shapes project portfolios and projects** around the modular business building blocks of capabilities and value streams to streamline scoping, resource needs, and business decision-making
- **Aligns strategy and execution** by creating a golden thread, as shown in Figure 4.5, from strategy to business architecture to execution that provides an ongoing line of sight from strategy to projects and project portfolios and facilitates dynamic replanning to adapt to change

We will now discuss each of these enhanced strategy execution techniques in further detail.

Informing Strategic Options

"Strategy is the craft of figuring out which purposes are both worth pursuing and capable of being accomplished."[1] Importantly then, strategy builds upon *capabilities*.

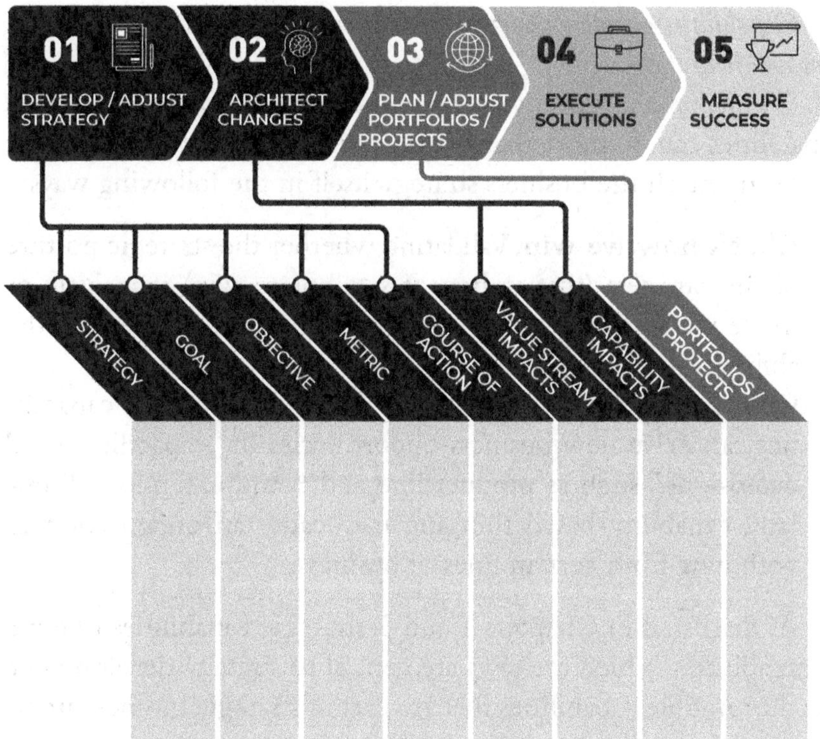

Figure 4.5 The golden thread: aligning strategy and execution.

Strategy is about choice and making specific bets on how to win in the marketplace, and then building an organization around those choices. This is where strategic business architecture comes in.

As it pertains to strategy development, strategic business architecture:

- Informs what an organization is currently capable of (for example, what capabilities are currently in place and how well they are working)
- Translates strategy into a set of actionable changes to help build up an organization's capabilities (or even build new ones) to achieve the strategy
- Ensures that an organization is intentionally designed to achieve its defined value proposition and strategy

Capabilities enable organizations to focus their resources on the things that will help them win.

When applied proactively during strategy formulation, business capabilities can do more than simply translate and guide execution; they can enrich the business strategy itself in the following ways:

- **Check how we win.** Validating whether the strategic posture of the business (that is, how it sets out to win) is realistic or needs modification, given current business capabilities and the ability to build new ones.
- **Change where we play.** Assessing where business capabilities can drive new business opportunities or "capability-based extensions," such as product line and brand extensions. Similarly, capability-based thinking may cause an organization to withdraw from certain lines of business.

As discussed in Chapters 1 and 3, strategic capabilities (the big C capabilities, which are few) are central to strategy development, but the tangible capabilities that are part of strategic business architecture (the small c capabilities, which are many) are necessary to deliver on those strategic capabilities. Since the strategic business architecture capabilities serve as a bridge between an organization's strategy and its ability to deliver on it, they are highly useful to inform strategy development and decision-making around strategic options.

For example, if an organization is considering offering a new product in a new market, its strategic business architecture will help people to understand:

- Do we have the capabilities needed to offer the new product?
  - If yes, are the capabilities working as they need to be? If not, what investments are required to mature the capabilities to the level necessary?
  - If no, does the organization want to build the capabilities or outsource them to a partner?
- What is the holistic impact on the organization of introducing the new product in a new market? For example, which

capabilities and value streams would be impacted? Which business units and partners would be impacted? Which processes and systems would be impacted? How much change would be introduced to stakeholders? Which regulations or internal policies need to be considered? Will any planned or current projects be impacted or require adjustments?

Benefits of the Enhanced Approach to Strategy Execution

As shown in Figure 4.6, when leveraged iteratively during the strategy development process, a strategic business architecture knowledge base can create a more streamlined path to selecting

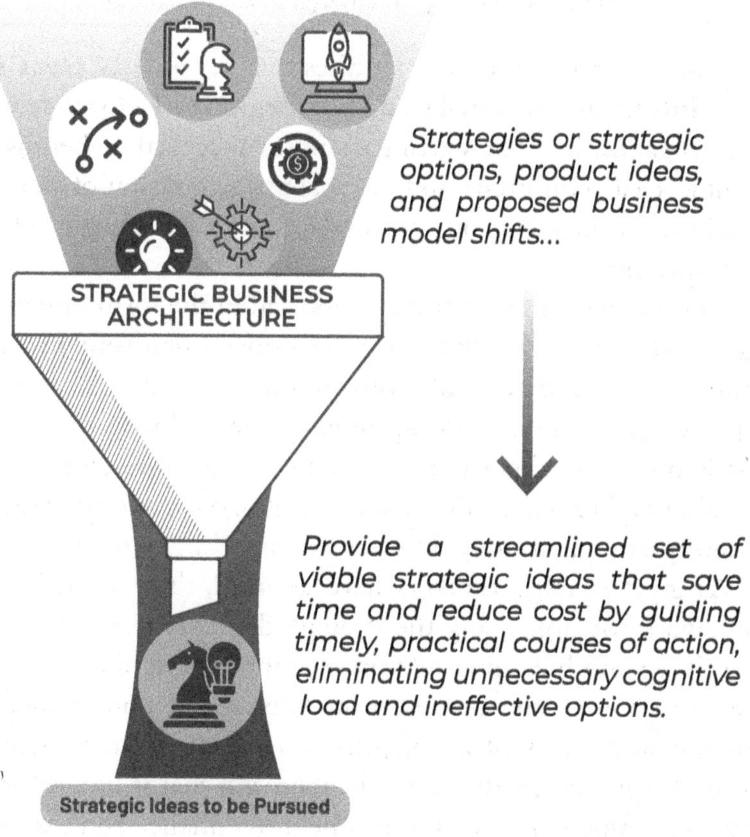

Strategies or strategic options, product ideas, and proposed business model shifts...
STRATEGIC BUSINESS ARCHITECTURE
Provide a streamlined set of viable strategic ideas that save time and reduce cost by guiding timely, practical courses of action, eliminating unnecessary cognitive load and ineffective options.
Strategic Ideas to be Pursued

Figure 4.6 Streamlining the path for strategic decision-making with strategic business architecture.

viable strategic ideas. This saves not only time and cost, but also mindshare because ineffective options can be eliminated sooner, and the best courses of action (for example, the decision to outsource) can be discovered up front.

In addition, an organization's strategic business architecture also provides a new source of innovation. For example, a business model canvas provides an ideal construct for evolving and innovating the ways in which an organization creates, delivers, and captures value. Or, value streams and capabilities can be leveraged in entirely new ways that draw upon their strength, such as to enable new products and services or value propositions.

Articulating Strategic Direction

Successful strategy execution requires two key aspects: **clear strategic intent** that is **translated into organized effort** across an entire organization. The starting point for success then begins with a simple, clear, consistent, and rationalized expression of strategy.

However, in many organizations, this clear strategic intent is often missing.

Bad strategy and non-strategy abound in the form of nebulous high-level statements, fluff, organizational improvements, plans, laundry lists of projects, solutions, and more. Strategies, goals, and objectives often do not add up or align across the corporate, business, and functional perspectives—and in some cases, may even be at odds. In addition, terms such as *strategies, goals,* and *objectives* may be interpreted in entirely different ways within an organization.

As great strategy thinkers have asserted, there needs to be a framework for organizing the strategy discussion, and it needs to be a living and breathing reference point for ongoing discussions that everyone in the organization knows and understands. The contents and views of an organization's strategy documentation should be guided by the strategic approach that it uses. However, strategic business architecture can help to enhance and extend the documentation of strategy.

As it pertains to articulating strategy direction, strategic business architecture:

- Uncovers new insights, gaps, and overlaps that can be input to strategy refinement
- Converts strategy documents (including the strategy map and business motivation model views mentioned previously) into an aggregated and distributable set of information that is connected with the rest of the organization (for example, products, capabilities, value streams, business units, projects, and so on) through the strategic business architecture knowledge base
- Adds the value stream and capability components into the strategy translation process, which helps to refine the strategic direction as well as define a coordinated response to it (which will be explored in the next section)

Figure 4.7 shows an example of the articulation of a small portion of strategy for the global apparel example introduced in Chapter 3. For context, consider that one of the organization's *strategic capabilities* includes sustainability leadership along with others, such as deep consumer understanding and connection, innovation, brand building, and globally optimized supply chain.

As you can see, the organization has expressed an overall aspiration or desire through one **goal** to "Reduce Greenhouse Gas Emissions." It has defined a specific measurable result through the **objective** to "Reduce Total Greenhouse Gas Emissions by 30% by 2030." There would be multiple cascading objectives that help to achieve this, such as those related to reducing transportation-related emissions and apparel waste. Our example will focus on the objective to "Reduce Apparel Waste by 40% by 2030." **Metrics** capture a specific number that measures an objective. In our example, we will track apparel waste by "Textiles Recycled (in Tons Per Year)." Tracking baseline and ongoing measurements is, of course, necessary to track the achievement of a specific objective.

The final strategic focal point shown here is the **course of action.** This describes a coherent action that helps to create a

GOAL	OBJECTIVE		METRIC	COURSE OF ACTION	•••
• Reduce Greenhouse Gas Emissions	• Reduce Total Greenhouse Gas Emissions by 30% by 2030	• Reduce Transportation-Related Greenhouse Gas Emissions by 25% by 2030	• Total CO_2 Emissions From Fleet Vehicles (Tons Per Year)	• Optimize Trips	
			• Average Efficiency of Fleet Vehicles (Average Actual Miles Per Gallon)	• Convert Fleet to Electric Vehicles	
		• Reduce Apparel Waste by 40% by 2030	• Textiles Recycled (Tons Per Year)	• Apparel Take-Back Program	

Symbol and dotted line denote *sustainability objective*

Figure 4.7 An example of articulating a clear and consistent expression of strategy.

cohesive response to achieve a specific objective. It does not describe implementation details. Following our example through, you can see that creating a new "Apparel Take-Back Program" is one major course of action the organization is taking to reduce apparel waste. Courses of action also provide a critical bridge to translate strategy into cohesive execution, along with value streams and capabilities, as described in the next section.

While Figure 4.7 shows just a portion of the strategy articulation, the strategic business architecture knowledge base can capture the full aggregate view. This includes decompositions (for example, an objective can cascade into more detailed objectives) and many-to-many relationships (for example, a course of action can enable many objectives, and an objective can be enabled by multiple different courses of action).

Again, while our example uses goals, objectives, metrics, and courses of action, each organization should leverage the naming, sequence, and definition of the focal points that are specified by their selected strategic management approach (which often differ across those discussed in Chapter 1). Most important is to ensure that that each strategic focal point is clearly defined, correctly interpreted, and consistently used across an organization.

The very process of unpacking strategic direction into these defined focal points creates clarity, shared understanding, and refinement. It should be a collaborative process with leaders, strategists, strategic business architects, and other roles as applicable working in close partnership. It should also be a highly iterative process with continual feedback loops between the first two stages of the strategy execution perspective.

Benefits of the Enhanced Approach to Strategy Execution

The use of strategic business architecture helps to improve the outcomes of articulating strategy by facilitating new insights, clarity, and conversations. This includes the following:

- Creating a clear, consistent, and actionable expression of strategy across an organization
- Identifying misalignment between the different levels of corporate, business, and/or functional strategy
- Identifying overlaps or gaps between strategy and the necessary courses of action required to achieve it
- Creating an aggregated and multidimensional view of strategy information that is connected to the rest of an organization's design and operations

The use of strategic business architecture can also help to improve the process of developing and communicating strategy over time. It surfaces opportunities for describing strategy in clearer ways and can inspire new approaches. For example, through this process, one strategy team realized that challenges were created when different business and function leaders and their teams developed their own courses of action separately. The strategy, goals, and objectives were created cohesively for the enterprise by the strategy team, but the courses of action became conflicting and ineffective as a result of being developed in business and functional silos. This discovery led the organization to change its process where the strategy team facilitated a shared set of courses of action together with all the business and function leaders.

Assessing the Impacts of Strategy

With clear strategic intent defined as a starting point, it can then be translated into organized effort across an organization. This is the juncture where other approaches skip ahead to the definition of projects and create the strategy-to-execution gap that will eventually lead to the downstream execution challenges. With a strategic business architecture, however, this additional step instead bridges that gap and creates the line of sight that will allow strategy and execution to stay connected and aligned continuously.

As it pertains to assessing the impacts of strategy, strategic business architecture:

- Catalogs the collective impact on an organization's value streams and capabilities as a result of all of the defined goals, objectives, and courses of action
- Quantifies and visualizes the collective impact of strategy on specific aspects of the business and technology environment (for example, stakeholders, business units, products, journeys, processes, systems, and so on)

Figure 4.8 shows the value stream and capability impacts that would result from the global apparel company's objective to reduce apparel waste and the course of action to create an apparel take-back program. The Acquire Material value stream and Material

GOAL	OBJECTIVE		METRIC	COURSE OF ACTION
• Reduce Greenhouse Gas Emissions	• Reduce Total Greenhouse Gas Emissions by 30% by 2030	• Reduce Apparel Waste by 40% by 2030	• Textiles Recycled (Tons. Per Year)	• Apparel Take-Back Program

VALUE STREAM IMPACTS	CAPABILITY IMPACTS	PORTFOLIOS / PROJECTS
• Acquire Material	• Material Management	
• Acquire Product	• Customer Loyalty	
• Return Product	• Information Management	
	• Customer Information Management	
	• Customer Analytics Management	
• Send Shipment	• Shipment Management	

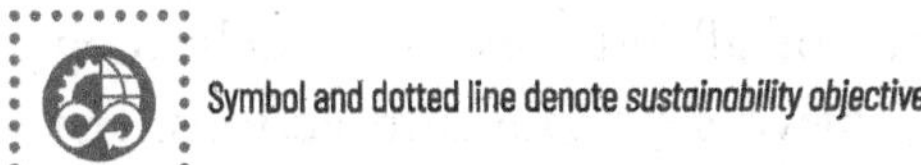
Symbol and dotted line denote *sustainability objective*

Figure 4.8 An example of assessing the impacts of strategy on value streams and capabilities.

Management capabilities will be impacted as used apparel becomes a new source of input for materials. In addition, the Acquire Product and Return Product value streams and the Customer Loyalty Information Management, Customer Information Management, and Customer Analytics Management capabilities will be impacted as customers return used apparel and receive loyalty rewards and then purchase new apparel and apply those rewards. Finally, the Send Shipment value stream and the Shipment Management capabilities will be impacted to allow for used apparel to be picked up at stores and delivered to waste management partners for sorting and processing.

While not shown in the figure, these same value streams and capabilities would be impacted by many other objectives and courses of action being pursued by the organization. Value streams and capabilities can be used to aggregate all changes for analysis and implementation, as we will explore later in this chapter.

Beyond the ability to catalog and rationalize impacts, value streams and capabilities can quickly and methodically identify the other aspects of the business and technology environment that will be impacted as well, through their connections in the knowledge base. Figure 4.9 shows an example of tracing the Customer Information Management capability (within the context of a customer returning a product) through to the stakeholders, business units and partners, products, information, policies, journeys, processes, applications, and in-flight portfolios/projects that would be impacted.

Benefits of the Enhanced Approach to Strategy Execution

Leveraging strategic business architecture to assess the impacts of strategy introduces an additional activity into strategy execution, which offers new perspectives and business outcomes. It creates a holistic understanding of all business and technology impacts up front to proactively drive decisions and actions. For example, this can help to ensure all stakeholders are involved, mitigate any impacts to the customer or constituent experience, address necessary compliance requirements, and establish collaboration with in-flight projects that are working in the same space.

In addition, the introduction of strategic business architecture also helps to communicate strategic direction in a more contextual and actionable way, which can help to reduce the effects of strategy diffusion throughout an organization.

Finally, the cataloging of strategy impacts organized around value streams and capabilities creates the foundation to organize work and business ownership in a more streamlined way during the Defining Coordinated Business Change step.

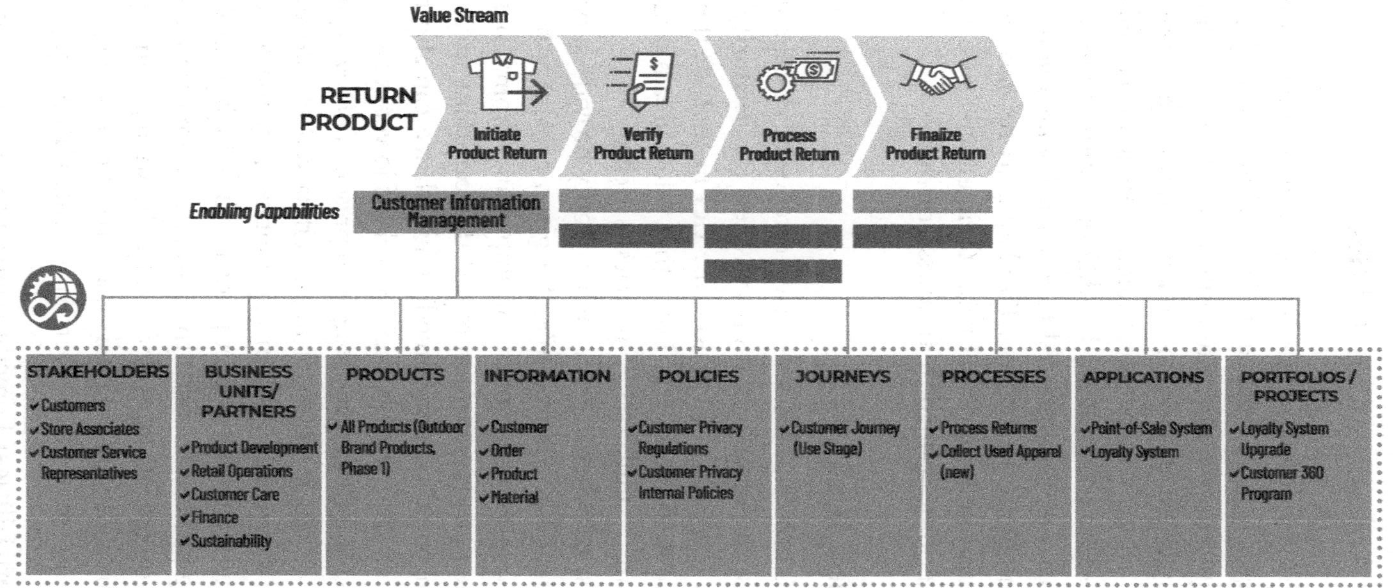
Value Stream
RETURN PRODUCT
Initiate Product Return
Verify Product Return
Process Product Return
Finalize Product Return
Enabling Capabilities
Customer Information Management
STAKEHOLDERS
Customers
Store Associates
Customer Service Representatives
BUSINESS UNITS/ PARTNERS
Product Development
Retail Operations
Customer Care
Finance
Sustainability
PRODUCTS
All Products (Outdoor Brand Products, Phase 1)
INFORMATION
Customer
Order
Product
Material
POLICIES
Customer Privacy Regulations
Customer Privacy Internal Policies
JOURNEYS
Customer Journey (Use Stage)
PROCESSES
Process Returns
Collect Used Apparel (new)
APPLICATIONS
Point-of-Sale System
Loyalty System
PORTFOLIOS / PROJECTS
Loyalty System Upgrade
Customer 360 Program
Symbol and dotted line denote sustainability objective

Figure 4.9 An example of holistic business impact analysis.

Assessing Capabilities

As discussed in Chapter 3, having a strategic business architecture baseline—composed of an enterprise-wide capability map (based on defined information concepts), a minimum set of value streams, and a cross-mapping between the two—is a prerequisite for strategy translation. (These efforts can be accelerated with industry reference models and various techniques.) In addition, capturing unique metrics on capabilities—often referred to as *capability assessments*—provides essential input to the process. The key is to be *intentional* about managing capabilities and maturing their effectiveness and implementation over time, guided by business priorities.

Capability Assessment Metrics

As introduced in Chapter 3, there are two categories of capability metrics: business importance and effectiveness (or "maturity"). Organizations can employ one or more metrics in each of these categories as Figure 4.10 illustrates. (Note that value stream stages may be assessed using a similar set of metrics as well.)

Assessing at least one metric from each category provides a balance for decision-making. For example, if a given capability has a low level of effectiveness but is not of top importance from a business perspective, the investment in improving that capability may be a lower priority (or could be outsourced). This balance can also be represented in the scoring criteria used as well. If lower scores for metrics in the business importance category represent a *higher importance,* and if lower scores for metrics in the effectiveness category represent *less effective performance,* then capabilities with the lowest aggregate scores illuminate the highest priorities in which to invest.

A good starting point is to assess the nature and importance of a capability to the organization, as defined by the strategic importance metric. As discussed in Chapter 3, a capability may be categorized as advantage, strategic support, or essential. To recap:

- **Advantage capabilities:** Directly contribute to the customer value proposition and have a high impact on company financials.

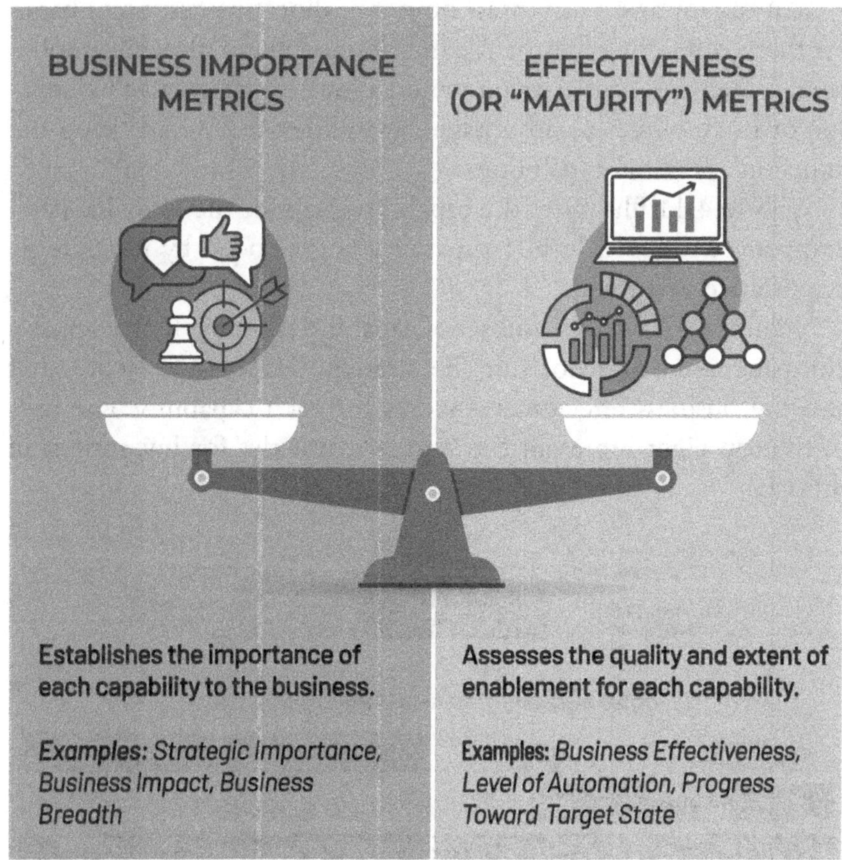

Figure 4.10 Two categories of capability assessment.

These are typically kept inside an organization and highly protected.

- **Strategic support capabilities:** Have high contribution in direct support of advantage capabilities. These are the operational capabilities that an organization performs on a daily basis and are rarely outsourced.
- **Essential capabilities:** May not be visible to the customer but contribute to an organization's business focus and have a big impact on the bottom line. These capabilities are a target for efficiency improvement, especially for high-volume work, and are often candidates for outsourcing.

An organization can assess how it is allocating resources based on these different types of capabilities and their strategic importance. Ideally, an organization would allocate a far greater percentage of its resources to advantage capabilities versus the "keep the lights on" essential capabilities.

Figure 4.11 illustrates the capability map for the global apparel company with each level 1 capability color-coded by its strategic importance category.

Figure 4.12 assesses a subset of capabilities for the global apparel company reflecting not just the strategic importance scores but also the business effectiveness scores for each capability. The cells in the top right represent the highest priorities for investment in this case.

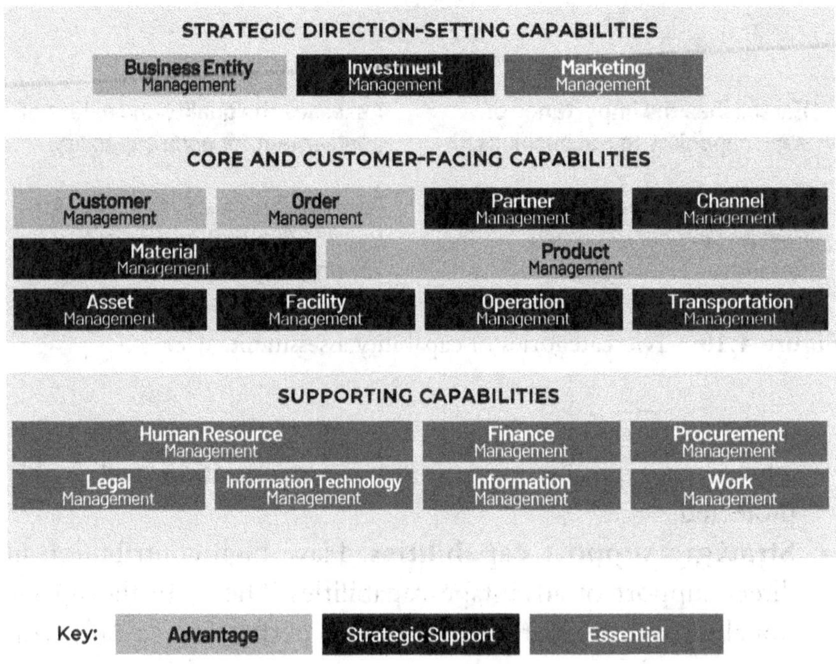

Figure 4.11 An example of assessing capabilities for strategic importance.

Source: Capability map is a hybrid created by the authors, with a combined information concept and functional orientation. This is partially aligned with the *BIZBOK® Guide* Manufacturing Reference Model.

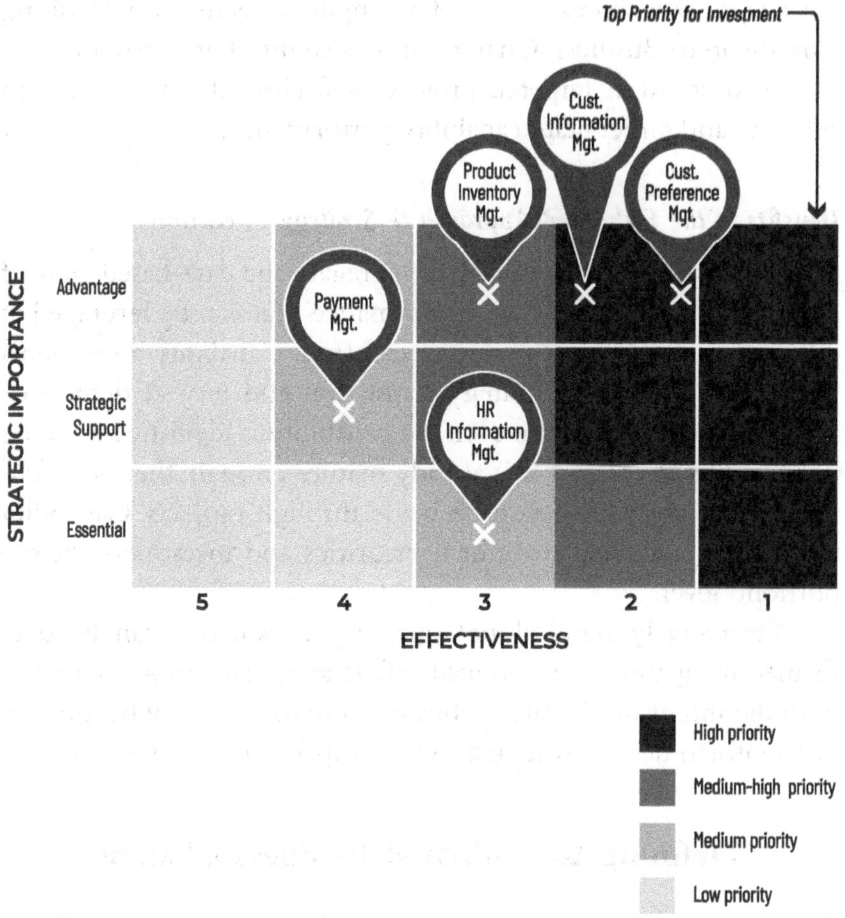

Figure 4.12 An example of assessing capabilities for strategic importance and effectiveness.

While some metrics are less subjective, most of the rating information for capability assessments is specified by business subject matter experts, either individually or together in collaborative conversations. The assessment information then becomes part of the reusable strategic business architecture knowledge base and must be kept up to date, such as to reflect improvements that have been delivered by projects.

Not only should capability metrics capture the current-state scores for a capability, but business leaders should also set the target-state scores as well. This inputs directly into Defining Coordinated Business Change and Shaping Portfolios/Projects (the next steps) as targeted projects will close the gaps between current- and target-state capability performance.

Benefits of the Enhanced Approach to Strategy Execution

Capability assessments provide an aggregate and data-based view of current and desired business performance that can be leveraged at different points during strategy execution. Capability assessments inform the process of strategy translation and project definition. This is important because even if a capability is identified as being impacted by strategy, if it is already mature enough, then it would not require any changes to be made through projects. Capability assessments also help to inform priorities and investments at the portfolio level.

Alternatively, stand-alone capability assessments can be performed at any time—even outside of a strategy execution context—with the intent of identifying business improvement opportunities or to inform decisions such as which capabilities to outsource.

Defining Coordinated Business Change

As mentioned earlier, capabilities enable organizations to focus their resources on the things that will help them win. At a more detailed level, they also help to harmonize and organize business change for implementation at scale.

As Figure 4.13 shows, without capabilities, strategies and other strategic direction translate into many individual actions, including projects and activities at all levels. Even with the best efforts at coordination, these many actions can often be redundant, misaligned, and lacking sequence and dependencies—and they create a significant cognitive load for the people involved. In contrast, when strategies and other strategic direction are translated through the capabilities, as described during Assessing the

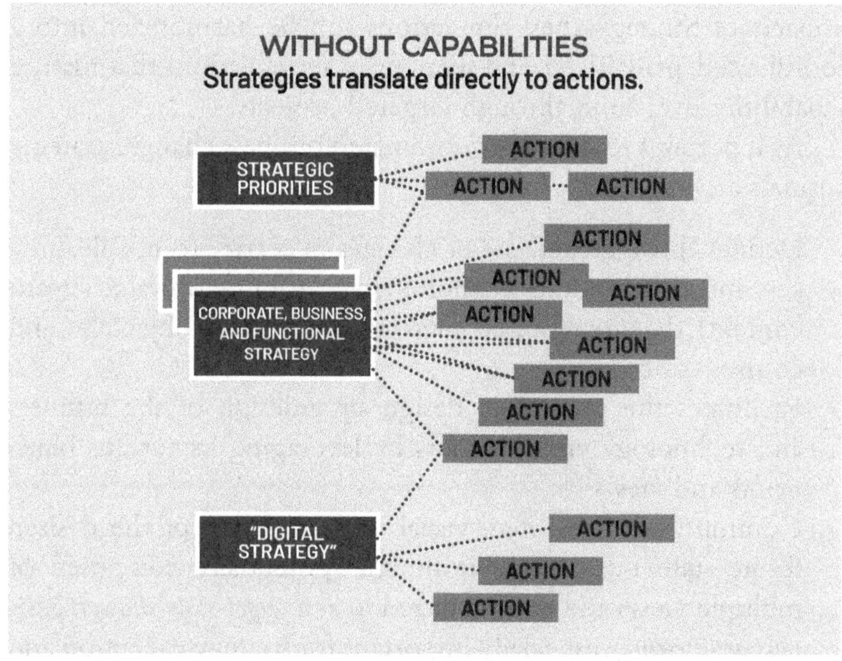

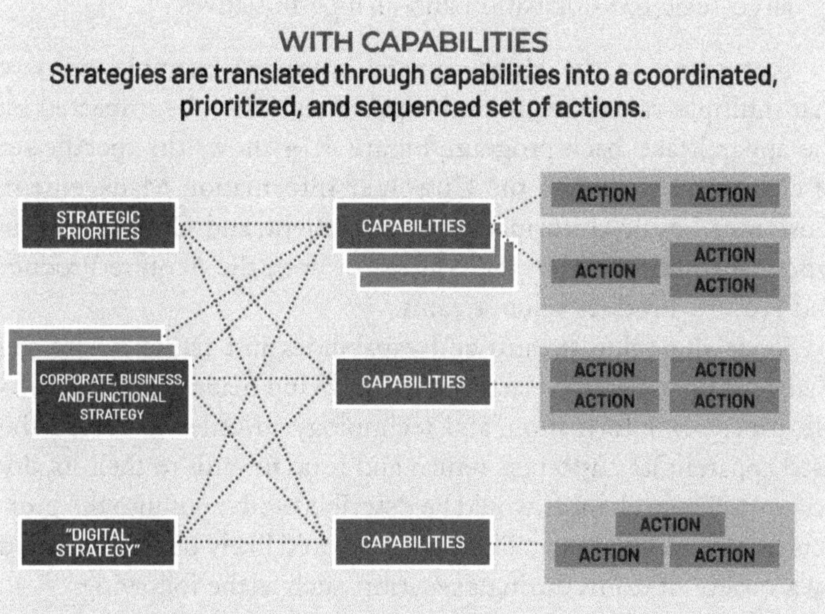

Figure 4.13 Capabilities coordinate changes.

Impacts of Strategy, then the actions can be harmonized into a coordinated, prioritized, and sequenced set of actions that mature capabilities over time, through targeted projects.

As it pertains to defining coordinated business change, strategic business architecture:

- Defines the aggregate set of changes necessary to people, process, information, and technology, by capability (in value stream context), that are required *across* strategies, goals, objectives, and courses of action
- Facilitates the process of design or redesign of the business and technology environments by leveraging its various blueprints and views
- Communicates a shared, visual understanding of the desired future-state business environment (potentially composed of multiple views and often referred to as a *target-state strategic business architecture*), especially important for strategy execution and large-scale transformation and change initiatives

Returning to the global apparel company example, we saw that multiple value streams and capabilities would be impacted by the apparel take-back program. Figure 4.14 shows the specific set of changes necessary to the Customer Information Management, Customer Loyalty Information Management, and Customer Analytics capabilities, within the context of both the Acquire Product and Return Product value streams.

Since the value streams and capabilities just frame where the change is happening, the actual changes being made are to the people, processes, information, and technology in order to record the used apparel that customers return and issue rewards to their loyalty accounts. These changes would be described and input into the projects that are defined next. The changes would likely be implemented by a variety of teams during execution, such as the following:

- The human resources team and/or the organization design team for the people changes
- The business process management team for the process changes

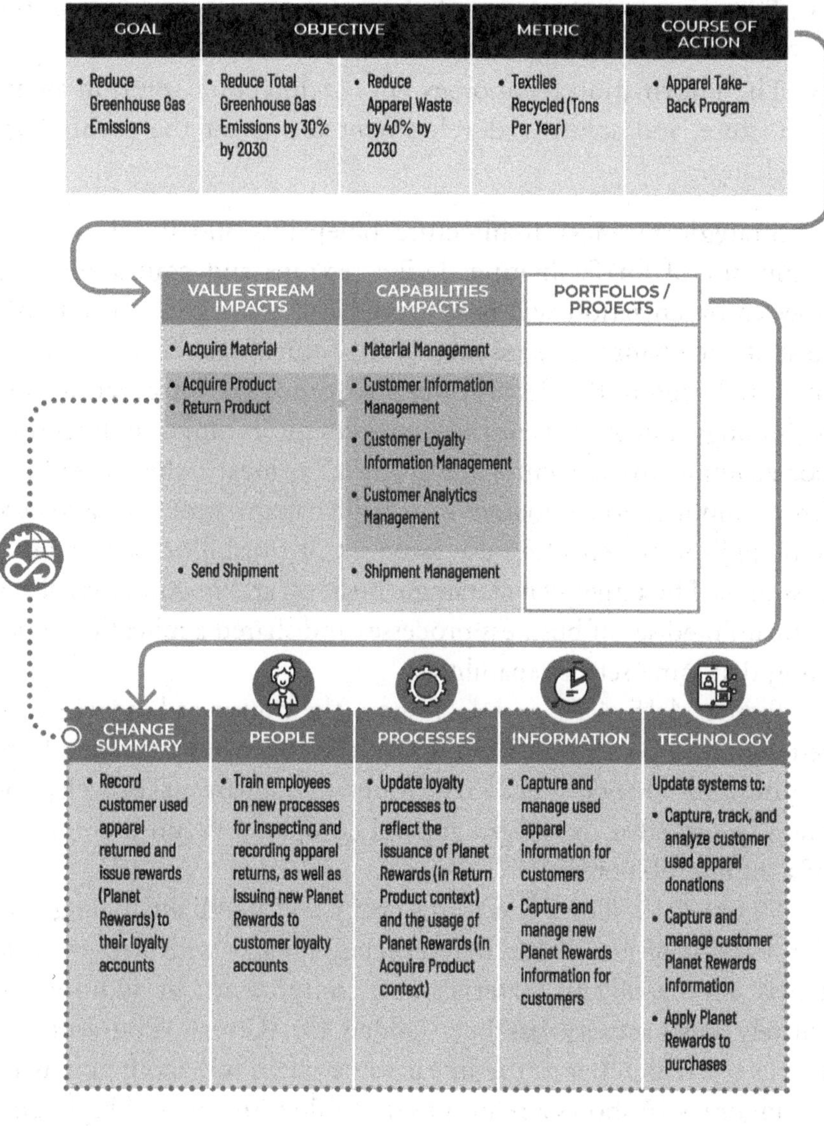

GOAL
OBJECTIVE
METRIC
COURSE OF ACTION
• Reduce Greenhouse Gas Emissions
• Reduce Total Greenhouse Gas Emissions by 30% by 2030
• Reduce Apparel Waste by 40% by 2030
• Textiles Recycled (Tons Per Year)
• Apparel Take-Back Program
VALUE STREAM IMPACTS
CAPABILITIES IMPACTS
PORTFOLIOS / PROJECTS
• Acquire Material
• Material Management
• Acquire Product
• Return Product
• Customer Information Management
• Customer Loyalty Information Management
• Customer Analytics Management
• Send Shipment
• Shipment Management
CHANGE SUMMARY
PEOPLE
PROCESSES
INFORMATION
TECHNOLOGY
• Record customer used apparel returned and issue rewards (Planet Rewards) to their loyalty accounts
• Train employees on new processes for inspecting and recording apparel returns, as well as issuing new Planet Rewards to customer loyalty accounts
• Update loyalty processes to reflect the issuance of Planet Rewards (in Return Product context) and the usage of Planet Rewards (in Acquire Product context)
• Capture and manage used apparel information for customers
• Capture and manage new Planet Rewards information for customers
Update systems to:
• Capture, track, and analyze customer used apparel donations
• Capture and manage customer Planet Rewards information
• Apply Planet Rewards to purchases
Symbol and dotted line denote sustainability objective

Figure 4.14 An example of translating strategy into a coordinated set of business changes.

- The data architecture and data management teams for the data changes
- The information technology (IT) architecture, solution architecture, and solution development teams for the technology changes

Strategic business architecture blueprints and views are also highly useful for facilitating design sessions and communicating how an organization will be changed and redesigned in response to strategic change. The essence of the future-state change is again often reflected in the details of people, processes, information, and technology, but it is *framed by* the strategic business architecture. For example, the current-state strategic business architecture for a large simplification initiative may depict many processes and system applications enabling the same set of capabilities across business units. The target-state strategic business architecture may show a streamlined set of business processes and shared applications enabling that same set of capabilities.

Figures 4.15, 4.16, and 4.17 show the power of blueprints for redesign and communication. Each one illustrates an example of the business changes necessary to put the apparel take-back program in place for the global apparel company, within the context of a different blueprint.

Figure 4.15 shows the value chain and highlights changes in the activity of Source, as the recycled apparel will now provide a new source of raw materials and components. In addition, an entirely new activity has been added for Reverse Logistics and Recovery, which bends the linear value chain to become circular.

Figure 4.16 shows a relevant set of value streams and highlights the four that are impacted by the creation of the apparel take-back program. In summary:

- The Acquire Product value stream will be enhanced to educate customers and allow them to use new types of loyalty rewards (Planet Rewards) when purchasing new apparel.
- The existing Return Product value stream can be reused, but in addition to customers returning new apparel, the value stream

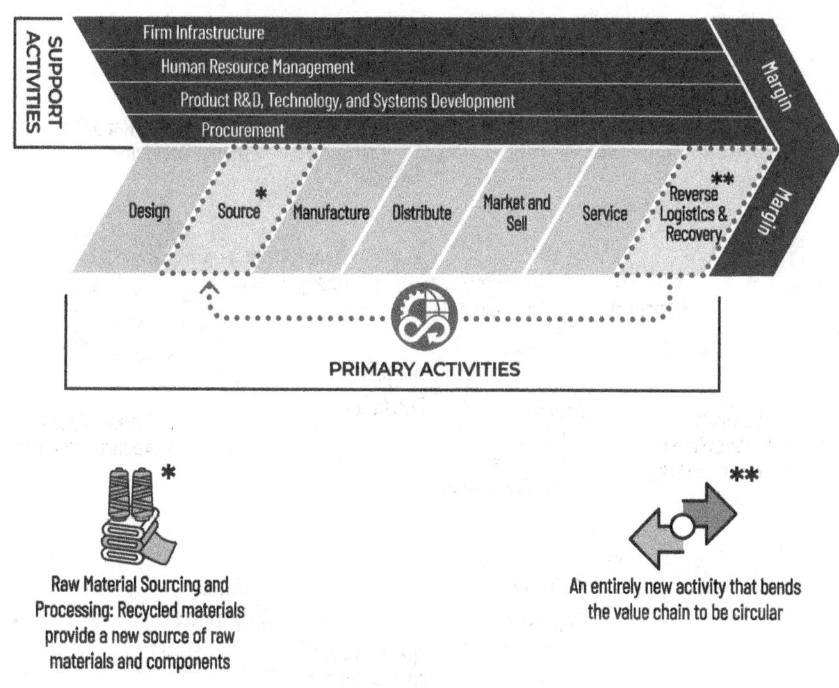

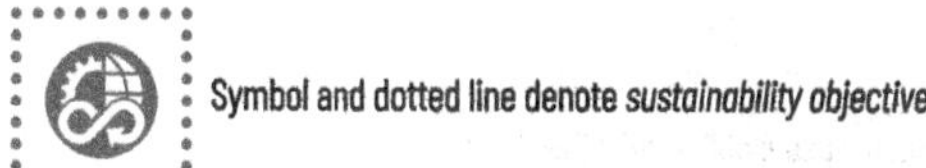

Figure 4.15 An example of value chain impact analysis.

will now handle an additional scenario to allow customers to return their used apparel and receive rewards for doing so.

- The Send Shipment value stream will be leveraged to move additional shipments when used apparel is picked up at stores and delivered to waste management partners for sorting and processing.
- The Acquire Material value stream will be modified to accept used apparel as a source of input for materials.

Changes to value streams will typically require changes to some of the corresponding capabilities and business processes.

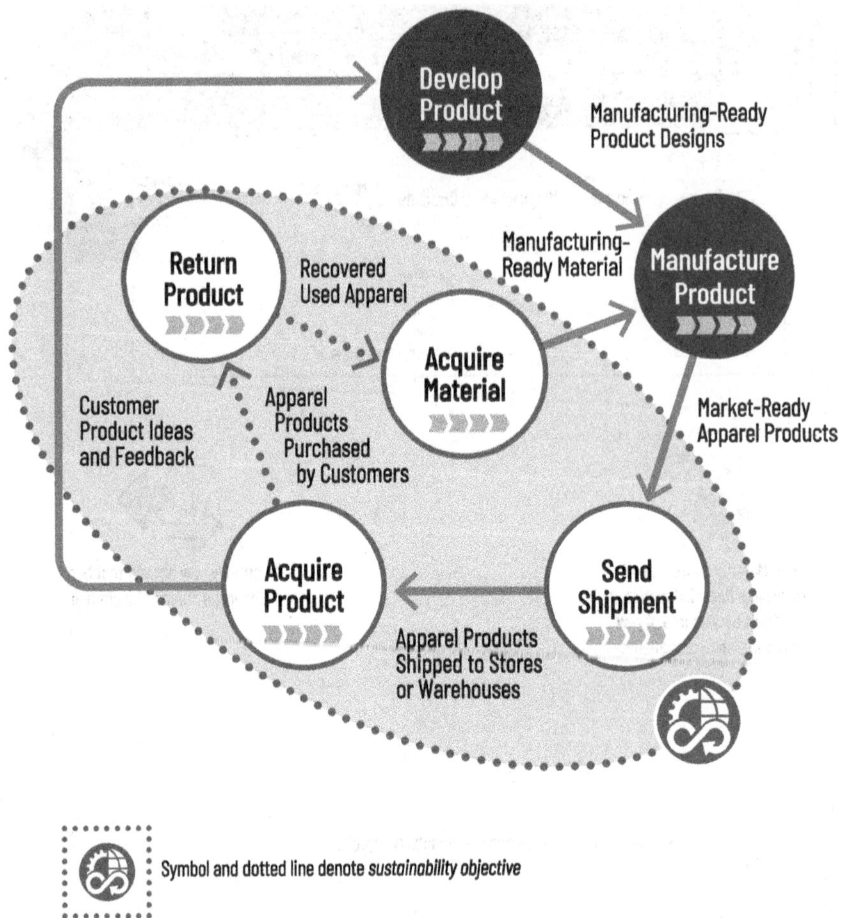

Figure 4.16 An example of value stream impact analysis.[2]

For example, Figure 4.17 highlights a set of key changes to capabilities and business processes within the context of the Return Product value stream.

Benefits of the Enhanced Approach to Strategy Execution

The use of strategic business architecture shifts the entire mindset for defining the business changes necessary to achieve strategy. It shifts the approach *from* delivering laundry lists of projects and solutions that are most often defined and prioritized in silos *to*

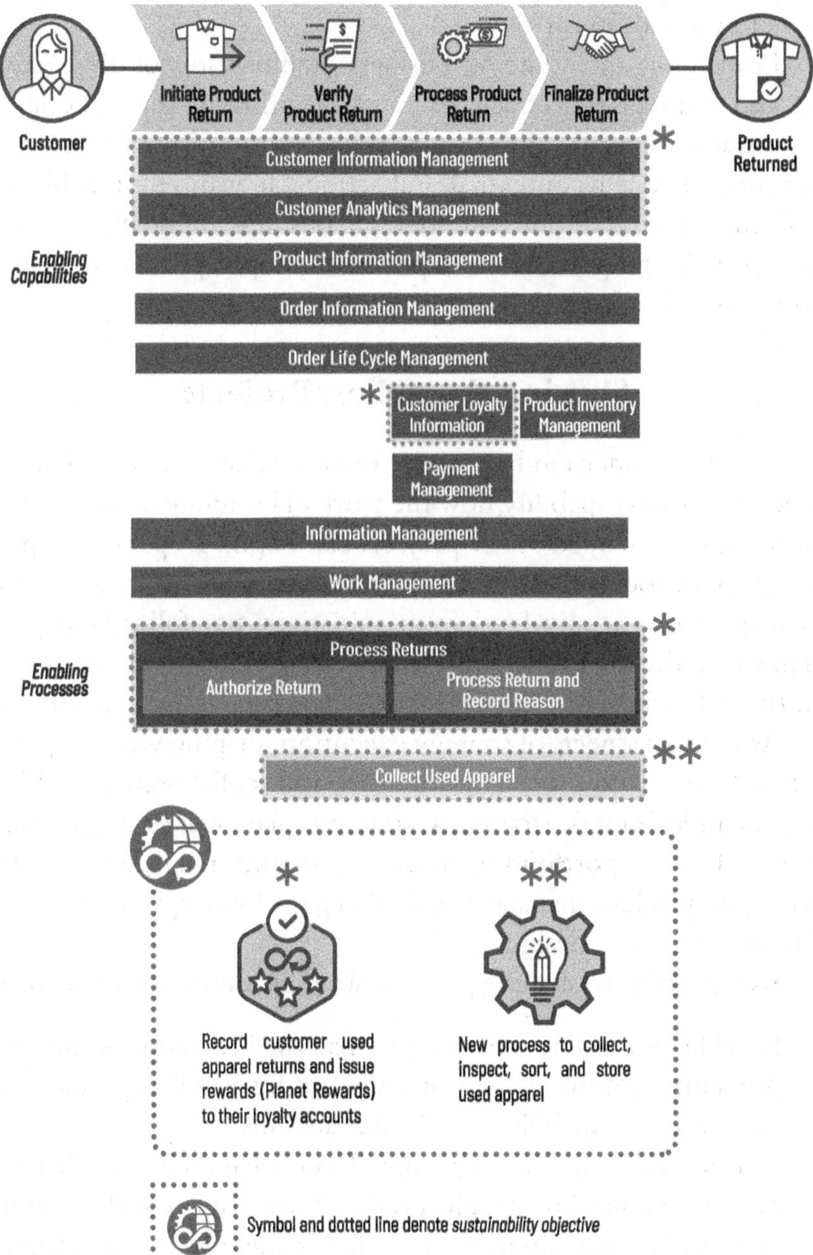
RETURN PRODUCT
Initiate Product Return
Verify Product Return
Process Product Return
Finalize Product Return
Customer
Product Returned
Customer Information Management
Customer Analytics Management
Enabling Capabilities
Product Information Management
Order Information Management
Order Life Cycle Management
Customer Loyalty Information
Product Inventory Management
Payment Management
Information Management
Work Management
Enabling Processes
Process Returns
Authorize Return
Process Return and Record Reason
Collect Used Apparel
Record customer used apparel returns and issue rewards (Planet Rewards) to their loyalty accounts
New process to collect, inspect, sort, and store used apparel
Symbol and dotted line denote sustainability objective

Figure 4.17 An example of value stream, capability, and process impact analysis.[3]

building strategic business capabilities that will support the enterprise today and tomorrow.

Leveraging the strategic business architecture for this activity also reduces the effects of strategy diffusion throughout an organization because direction can be communicated to people in a more detailed, contextual, and actionable way. This is achieved both through the future-state strategic business architecture views, as well as the pinpointed descriptions of people, process, information, and technology changes.

Shaping Portfolios/Projects

With a clear understanding of the high-level actions and changes needed for each capability, now the work of bundling them into the most logically scoped set of projects can begin. Depending upon the scope of focus, strategic business architecture can be leveraged to shape work at any level from initiatives, portfolios, and programs to individual projects. (Please refer to Chapter 1 for clarity on the definitions of *project, program, project portfolio,* and *initiative.*)

As with all aspects of strategy execution, shaping work requires a significant amount of partnership and collaboration, which may include leaders, strategists, strategic planners, strategic business architects, portfolio managers, program managers, project managers, product managers, and all types of enterprise and solution architects and designers.

As it pertains to shaping projects, strategic business architecture:

- Provides a scalable and logical structure to scope initiatives, programs, and projects around the modular building blocks of the business, capabilities, and value streams
- Defines each project at a high level, including the changes that are required to people, process, information, and technology, along with inputs such as key stakeholders and change impact, relevant reusable solutions, experience and compliance considerations, and collaboration points or dependencies with

other teams (***Note:*** information for the project definition may be provided through the Business Outcome Statement introduced in Chapter 2.)
- Creates the last part of the golden thread to create the traceability between strategy, architecture, and projects, which provides an ongoing line of sight for continual alignment

As shown in Figure 4.18, the approach is to scope work around capabilities in a value stream context. If multiple capabilities within a value stream stage need to be enhanced, then a project can be scoped around one or more stages. On the other hand, if a capability needs to be enhanced across multiple value stream stages, a project could be scoped around one or more capability. Of course, projects may be scoped using a hybrid of both the value stream stage and capability perspectives.

As Figure 4.18 shows for the global apparel example, the visualization of value stream stages and capabilities by their level of effectiveness or maturity through heatmapping can help to guide the analysis, scoping, and communication of projects.

Figure 4.19 illustrates the overall concept and thought process for capability-based planning. Capabilities are assessed to be at a current state of maturity. Desired improvement for effectiveness, along with changes introduced by strategies and other business direction, results in a set of defined capability enhancements. Enhancements to capabilities are delivered through projects over various time horizons, leading to the eventual achievement of the target-state level of maturity for a given capability.

Since an organization is continually changing, the maturity of a capability could achieve a desired target state and then return again to a lower level as new needs for it are defined. Capabilities provide a valuable construct to track and deliver on this continual change within an aggregate business context.

It is important to note that, depending on the scope of focus, work may initially be defined at a very macro level to establish an overall coordinated path of action. As planning continues

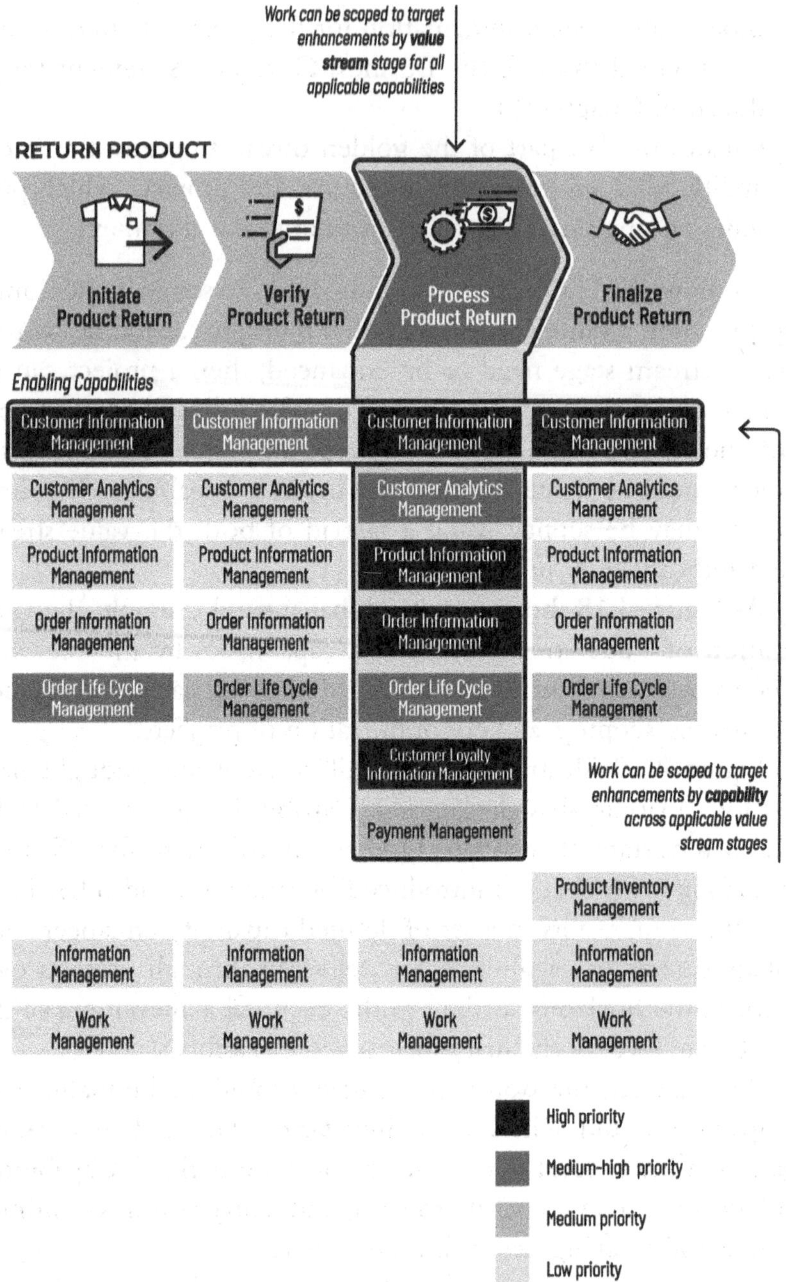

Figure 4.18 An example of defining work based on capabilities and value streams.[4]

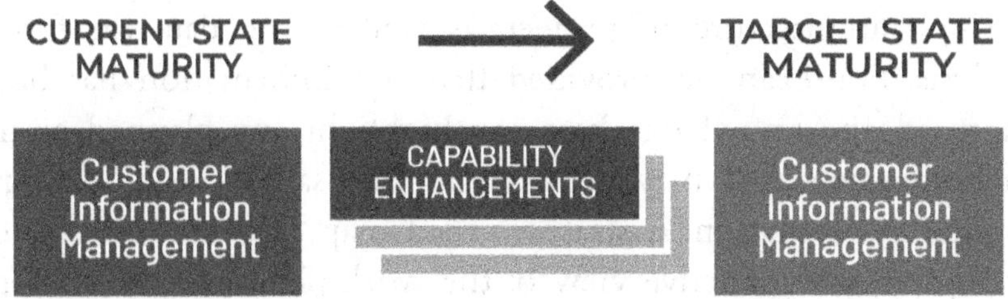

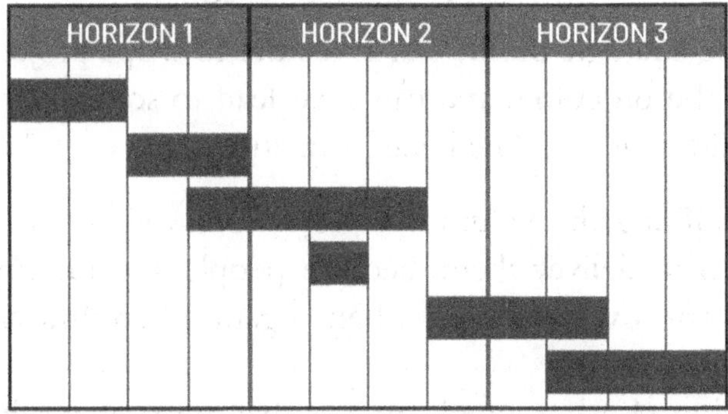

Figure 4.19 Capability enhancements are delivered through projects.

downstream, this will of course need to be further broken down into value stream– and capability-framed programs and projects, or within an agile context, units of work within the product backlog such as epics and features.

Any type of work can be framed by value streams, capabilities, and other strategic business architecture focal points. Not only does this ensure clarity of scope, but it also allows capabilities to become the Rosetta stone that creates connections across strategies, transformations, strategic initiatives, products, programs, projects, and operational efforts that may be targeting the same capabilities.

Project names can be captured in the strategic business architecture knowledge base and cross-mapped to the applicable business objectives, value streams, and capabilities. This is what creates the end-to-end traceability (the line of sight) from strategy to business architecture to project, as well as the data for future analysis. For example, provided that the information has been captured, the knowledge base can highlight any planned or in-flight projects that may be targeting the same capabilities and require coordination. A strategic road map may also be created to represent a collective view of the work planned for a strategy or large change initiative along with their sequence and a general notion of timing.

Benefits of the Enhanced Approach to Strategy Execution

Leveraging strategic business architecture to shape projects greatly improves the outcomes and can even lead to scoping work in an entirely different way. The benefits include:

- Streamlining the volume of projects, as well as the resources needed to deliver them, because people and funding can be more effectively focused when organized around capabilities and value streams
- Defining clearly scoped projects that are strategically aligned and of the highest priority that can feed into strategic portfolio management
- Heading off the downstream challenges that can occur as a result of siloed strategy translation and planning (for example, duplicate or fragmented solutions and experiences, everything is a priority, and so on)
- Identifying key aspects of projects—such as stakeholders, dependencies, collaboration opportunities, and compliance needs—up front so that delivery teams can hit the ground running
- Accelerating teams during the Execute Solutions stage with a view of the big-picture context, a clear scope of projects, a fully agreed-upon business vocabulary, and even a framework for identifying requirements
- Tracking and governing project progress in a relevant business context with corresponding business outcomes for executives and strategic planners, instead of within a system context

Aligning Strategy and Execution

As described in Chapter 1, there are two key aspects of strategic alignment that need to be continually assessed: (1) Is an organization structured and designed with intent to deliver on its strategy? And (2) Is there a continuous line of sight between strategy and the organization's project portfolio? Strategic business architecture is instrumental to answering both.

With projects defined and execution under way per the previous stages, progress can be compared to the original business objectives and defined future-state views on an ongoing basis, leveraging the end-to-end traceability of strategic business architecture. The traceability from strategy to business architecture to projects also facilitates dynamic replanning as well. For example, if the market shifts and a strategy is no longer a priority, the projects tied to it can be readily identified and paused to ensure that the portfolio of work stays relevant.

With the extreme speed and volume of change, strategy and execution are highly fluid and must be tightly linked and iterative. While the strategy execution perspective includes one final stage for Measure Success, the role of strategic business architecture and strategic business architects is to continuously:

- Provide insights on the alignment between strategy, the maturity of the capabilities delivering it, and the projects that are enhancing those capabilities
- Ensure that the business solutions developed align with the target-state strategic business architecture and design
- Ensure that the business outcomes delivered align with and measure up to the original business objectives

Even if an organization has not gone through the process of translating strategy through the steps described earlier, as long as the strategic focal points, capabilities, and projects are captured and linked within the knowledge base, new insights can be discovered. The strategic business architecture lens provides objective data that transcends silos and politics so people can make the hard decisions that are best for the *enterprise*. For example, new questions can be answered such as:

- Which projects do not align with strategic priorities and business objectives? Should we continue investing in them?
- Are there any business objectives that do not have a project delivering on them? Or are the current set of projects not delivering *enough* enhancements to the capabilities and value streams to achieve the objectives?
- Which projects are defined in a way that will deliver conflicting results? Should we pause and reconcile our direction first, regardless of the timelines we set for ourselves?
- Which projects have overlapping scopes or could benefit from creating shared business solutions?
- Which projects have opportunities for collaboration?
- Which projects should be reprioritized?
- Which projects should be resequenced?
- Which projects are not on track to deliver the expected results?

Benefits of the Enhanced Approach to Strategy Execution

So, what if we do all of this and enhance our approach to strategy execution? Not only will we design a complete and coherent response to realizing strategy and head off the execution challenges, but we create a clear line of sight between strategy and execution. Like a living organism responding to its environment, organizations have an end-to-end organizational agility to continually adapt to change with speed and scale. This is further accelerated by the modular and streamlined organization design that strategic business architecture facilitates.

Leading Change through Strategic Business Architecture

A leader's ability to set, guide, and align business direction is not isolated to just the strategy and strategic direction. Leaders can also set direction by guiding the future-state strategic business architecture blueprints and strategic road maps that translate that direction into changes to people, processes, information, and technology, which are delivered through projects. Additionally, leaders can steer the organization through the decisions that are made to these artifacts along the way.

Leveraging a value stream and capability perspective not only shifts people's mindsets toward enterprise ways of thinking and working but also can extend to business decision-making and accountability as well. Capabilities and value streams transcend organizational structures, products, and geographies, so they provide an ideal construct to bring leaders together to make decisions about business direction and investments. This is particularly valuable for aspirations that span across an organization such as delivering an exceptional customer/constituent experience, achieving sustainability goals, or integrating an acquisition.

Figure 4.20 shows the structure of an enterprise-wide transformation focused on customer experience. The rows on the left represent transformation teams responsible for delivering reusable, ready-to-consume capabilities across people, processes, information, and technology. The columns across the top represent transformation teams responsible for delivering value streams and customer experiences united across business units, products, and channels. The capabilities were consumed within the value streams. Each of the capability and value stream transformation teams was led by an executive, supported by a lead strategic business architect and lead IT architect. Each transformation team had a target-state strategic business architecture (that is, a common picture of the desired future-state business environment created using strategic business architecture views) and a strategic road map. Additionally, an integrated view of all target-state strategic business architectures and strategic road maps was created across the entire customer experience transformation. Finally, there was a committee of top executives from each of the customer-facing business units who together approved the direction and investment across the entire scope of customer-related value streams and capabilities on an ongoing basis.

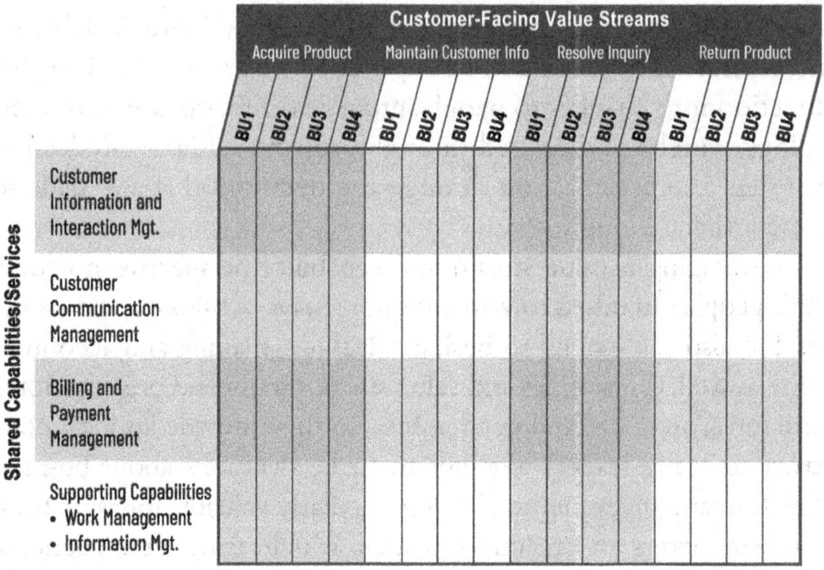

Customer-Facing Value Streams

Shared Capabilities/Services	Acquire Product				Maintain Customer Info				Resolve Inquiry				Return Product			
	BU1	BU2	BU3	BU4	BU1	BU2	BU3	BU4	BU1	BU2	BU3	BU4	BU1	BU2	BU3	BU4
Customer Information and Interaction Mgt.																
Customer Communication Management																
Billing and Payment Management																
Supporting Capabilities • Work Management • Information Mgt.																

Figure 4.20 Strategic business architecture provides structure for holistic business ownership.

The cube shown in Figure 4.20 is highly useful for scoping and structuring large transformation and strategic change initiatives, as well as providing an ongoing framework for governance and business decision-making around an enterprise perspective. Consider the apparel take-back program scenario for the global apparel company. If that same company were in the midst of an enterprise-wide customer experience transformation like the one described earlier, the defined value stream and capability enhancements needed for the take-back program could easily be compared. We would likely find that many of the same capabilities and value streams would be the focus for both the customer experience transformation and the creation of the take-back program.

Before any projects were created for the take-back program, the capability and value stream enhancements could first be reviewed to ensure that there were not any overlaps or conflicts in direction or sequence with those planned as part of the customer experience. In addition, new collaborations could be identified such as opportunities to combine or expand the scope of some projects to most effectively deliver on the capability enhancements necessary to achieve *both* goals.

Next Steps

We discussed how strategic business architecture can be leveraged to enhance strategy execution by informing strategic options, articulating strategic direction, assessing the impacts of strategy, assessing capabilities, and then defining coordinate business change and shaping it into projects that deliver upon it. We also discovered how the line of sight is created from strategy to business architecture to projects through the golden thread, and how important that is to keep strategy and execution aligned on a continual basis. Strategic business architecture brings an enterprise lens to strategy execution that can head off the execution challenges that typically occur downstream, and it introduces a new mindset that produces new results.

So, where do we start with implementing these ideas? Since we are ultimately changing the ways of thinking and working within an organization, this is always a human journey that takes time. However, there are two particularly good places to introduce new strategy execution thinking.

The first good starting place is to *translate one strategy from end to end*. Select a strategy, a strategy refresh, or another comprehensive set of business directions (for example, a response to a significant regulatory change or the integration of a new acquisition), and translate it into a coordinated set of projects using the techniques described in this chapter. This option is extremely valuable not only to experience and derive the benefits from, but because it provides a concrete example to illustrate the concepts from end to end, which can help to build buy-in among other people.

While translating one strategy from left to right as described above is ideal, it is often not a feasible starting point as many organizations begin their journey. However, the golden thread works equally well running backward from right to left. So, a second good starting place is to *bring a capability lens to investment decision-making* (described in Chapter 5) *or even a current set of in-flight projects.* In this scenario, take any set of projects (for example, investment requests, in-flight projects, and so on) and map them to the capabilities they're enhancing, as well as the business objectives they're enabling. Analyze and visualize the results to show how the planned/in-flight capability enhancements (described through the investment requests or projects) compare with the capabilities that are most critical to achieve the strategy. In addition, analyze and visualize the aggregate counts and amounts across all investment requests/projects.

This option is also extremely valuable as it often reveals a brand-new set of insights into misalignment between strategy and investments, as well as redundancy across investments that would otherwise not be discovered. The analysis can even be performed retroactively (for example, upon investment requests from a previous period of time) to demonstrate the potential value.

We will explore this topic further in Chapter 5, where we look at the role of portfolio management in strategy execution along with the additional perspectives that strategic business architecture can bring. Following that, in Chapter 6, we will explore the bigger picture of how different functions and disciplines work together to connect and deliver strategy execution from end to end.

STRATEGY EXECUTION ORGANIZATIONAL ASSESSMENT

Reflect on the following questions to assess how well strategy execution is working in your organization based on the concepts from Chapter 4. Please refer to the scoring guidance provided in Chapter 1.

1. Our organization uses capabilities to inform strategy development and strategic option decision-making (for example,

leveraging capability assessments to understand what the organization is capable of and how well capabilities are working).

2. Our organization uses capabilities and value streams and other applicable strategic business architecture perspectives and views to assess the impacts of strategy.
3. We understand and can quantify the collective impact of our strategy and all strategic business changes across the organization to people, process, information, and technology.
4. Our organization leverages capability assessments to inform investments in business performance and enhancements, guiding the definition, scoping, and prioritization of projects.
5. Our organization uses our strategic business architecture (in concert with other design disciplines and techniques) to represent the future state of the business based on strategy.
6. Our organization scopes and frames programs and projects around the delivery of enhancements to capabilities and value streams (capability-based planning).
7. Our organization synergizes investments and designs business solutions around modularity and reuse, leveraging capabilities as the foundation.
8. We understand and can quantify the collective impact of our projects across the organization to people, process, information, and technology.
9. Our organization maintains traceability between strategy focal points, value streams and capabilities, and projects within our strategic business architecture knowledge base (to formalize and maintain the line of sight and enable dynamic replanning).
10. Our organization measures the business outcomes for each project against the original business objectives and takes action to address any gaps.

Chapter 5

Strategic Portfolio Management and Effective Strategy Execution

This chapter will explore different types of portfolios that facilitate effective strategy execution. We will focus on understanding the two primary portfolios that need to be properly managed for effective strategy execution—the project portfolio and the business capability portfolio—though we will discuss other asset portfolios as well.

Traditionally, portfolio management was separated from strategy development and execution, but it is becoming clear that effective enterprise-wide business strategy execution requires an integration of business strategy development, strategic business architecture–related functions, and enterprise portfolio management. A solid strategy is no good if it can't be well executed.

According to Gartner, organizations that are highly effective at strategic portfolio management are twice as likely to achieve better business outcomes as those that aren't.[1] The focus on digital business and digital transformation means that the traditional, siloed, style of portfolio management is inadequate as siloed portfolios cannot work in isolation to provide the organization with a true picture of strategy execution and overall organizational performance. Integrated strategic portfolio management is needed for effective strategy execution and to optimize the value of all major organizational investments.

What Is Portfolio Management?

As discussed in Chapter 1, the concept of portfolio management is derived from financial portfolio management where we manage the assets of the organization (projects, business capabilities, processes, value streams, technology assets, human capital, and other assets) as investments for the organization. These organizational investments are allocated to investment strategies based on assumptions about future performance to maximize value/risk trade-offs in optimizing the organization's return on investment (ROI). Portfolio management attempts to optimize the mix of assets in the organization's portfolios.

It's useful to differentiate between projects, programs, and portfolios as sometimes these terms are used interchangeably. A *project* is managed with a clear end date in mind, according to a set scope and budget. A *program* is a collection of two or more projects sharing a common goal. A *portfolio* is a group of related initiatives, projects, and/or programs that attain wide-reaching benefits and impacts. Many organizations have project and program management skills and capabilities but often lack solid strategic portfolio management skills and capabilities.

The skills and perspectives needed to be effective at strategic portfolio management are very different from those needed to be effective at project or program management—success at managing projects and programs does not guarantee that a person will be successful at portfolio management. A much more diversified set of skills, as well as a broader strategic perspective, is required for effective portfolio management. As we've discussed, the goal of portfolio management is to ensure that the highest business value is achieved from the investment for the enterprise. Portfolio management is an optimal way to categorize, capture, and communicate value in business language. Value is achieved from the right balance of risk and reward.

Strategic portfolio management forges a critical link between the strategic planning process and the project execution process, enabling management to reach consensus on the best use of resources by focusing on projects strategically aligned with the goals of the organization. It also ensures that projects are aligned with each other and do not produce duplicative or conflicting business outcomes or solutions. Strategic portfolio management is much more than a set of projects. As shown in Figure 5.1, it comprises a set of managed portfolios typically consisting of technology assets; human capital assets; value stream, process, and capability assets; and project investment assets allocated to business strategies according to an optimal mix based on assumptions about future performance. Strategic portfolio management is an optimal way to categorize, capture, and communicate the business value of the organization's assets and asset-related investments. Value is achieved from the right balance of risk and reward decisions. Through this process, potential risks are identified, and the likelihood of occurrence and severity of consequences are determined. Identifying scenarios and evaluating risks leads to high-value portfolios.

Figure 5.1 Common enterprise portfolios.

The following are typical data elements tracked for each asset portfolio:

- Capabilities, value streams, and processes:
  - Purpose
  - Outcome
  - Cycle time
  - Resources involved
  - Performance indicators
- Human capital assets:
  - Demographics
  - Competencies
  - Compensation
  - Job class
  - Skills
- Technology assets
  - Cost (on the books)
  - Types/numbers/location

    - Position in life cycle
    - Life span
    - Conformance to standards
- Project investment assets
    - Budget/schedule
    - Skills required
    - Supporting technology
    - Risk mitigation plans and contingencies

Continuous Portfolio Management

Portfolio management is the continuous process of selecting and managing the optimum set of project-oriented initiatives to deliver maximum business value. Historically, this process consisted of an intensive point-in-time review, with the goals of determining the current state of strategic priorities and making recommendations for project portfolio changes. These endeavors are highly labor-intensive, and the results are extremely time sensitive. While valuable in terms of the information offered, this process typically produces static reports with relatively short shelf lives. It is also not conducive to the adaptation required in today's fast-changing environments.

A strategic portfolio management process consists of a continuous path of selecting and managing the optimum set of project-oriented investments that deliver maximum business value. Continuous portfolio management begins with the development of a plan outlining how broad and deep the portfolio should be (driven by business objectives), what measurable expectations exist, and the risk and reward boundaries. Precursors to these activities include determining the organization's readiness to develop and benefit from strategic portfolio management, understanding the organization's ability to successfully implement portfolio management, and the development of an overall organizational charter for the strategic use of portfolio management. As described in Chapter 4, without the information and enterprise perspectives provided by the strategic business architecture ecosystem, making sense of the current state of strategic priorities as part of a continuous process can be highly challenging in many organizations, and as a result, suboptimal portfolio decisions are often made.

Underlying strategic portfolio management is the fundamental belief that we should not necessarily consider information technology (IT) property (such as hardware, software, and data) and expenditures as costs or expenses; instead, we should view them as assets and investments with a unique value to yield measurable returns over time. In addition, portfolio management is both an analytical technique for evaluating investments and a managerial tool for prioritizing and allocating resources. We must prioritize our portfolios according to their ability to: (1) consider assets and investments for their efficiencies in supporting day-to-day operations, (2) consider assets and investments that support the expansion of the business by improving asset use or migrating to more effective/efficient processes and capabilities, and (3) consider assets and investments that seek new business opportunities. Once listing the investments, we can finalize the initial scope and depth of the portfolio management implementation.

For some, simply categorizing investments and using the portfolio as a communication tool is enough, whereas others elect to apply the detailed statistical and management process disciplines of portfolio management to their investments. Scale often drives the scope of portfolio management implementations: Smaller organizations may follow a simple portfolio management implementation; larger organizations will benefit from the rigor and discipline of a detailed process. In either case, using a formal implementation process will accelerate business value and provide the most effective basis for ensuring effective strategy execution.

The case is becoming clear for an integration of strategic business architecture and strategic portfolio management. The rationale is clear. If strategic business architecture provides an enterprise-wide set of information and is an enterprise-wide strategic function that informs strategy development and is integrated with strategic planning and facilitates strategy execution, then all parts of the strategy execution chain must report to the strategy execution group/component of the strategic planning function for successful and effective strategy execution. For example, in organizations where project portfolio management (PPM) does not report to the strategy execution function, we often see the project layer as the point where effective strategy execution breaks down. In these organizations, strategy execution functions, such as strategic business architecture, often have to use whatever influence mechanisms they possess to convince the PPM function to adjust the project portfolio to reflect the current strategic priorities and often fail (at least in part) to do so. Comprehensive and effective enterprise strategy execution cannot be fully achieved without having the execution management layer (portfolio management) report to the strategy execution function. This is not the case however in many organizations today, and this lack of reporting is a main contributor to the poor results of strategy execution discussed in Chapter 1.

Effective Strategic Portfolio Management Informs Changes in Strategy

The information flow from strategy development/refinement and PPM goes both ways, and the business architecture value streams and capabilities provide the bridge. Project teams should provide input on portfolio reprioritization decisions and provide customer insights that should be factored into strategy refinement decisions. Capabilities and value streams provide the shared business context for interpreting the input and insights, as well as their impacts on strategy or portfolio initiatives. The focus on autonomy in many organizations has made it difficult for some organizations to share feedback from distributed project teams with portfolio decision-makers. The involvement of project teams in portfolio decisions varies greatly in organizations.

Strategic portfolio management provides a process for selecting the highest-value initiatives and optimizing against budget, human resources, risk, and other constraints. Benefits of the strategic portfolio management discipline are numerous. It allows for unambiguous choices based on business impacts and measurable benefits. Strategic portfolio management is a valuable tool for tactical-level creation and maintenance of strategic alignment among strategy, core business capabilities, and project level execution.

Effective Strategic Portfolio Management Facilitates Organizational Communication and Understanding

The most basic use of strategic portfolio management is in the communication of the elements of asset portfolios in an enterprise investment communication framework. Enterprises starting strategic portfolio management often position the process as a communications tool. This perspective focuses on the initial scope and business dialogue needed to create a single repository of categorized investments. This inventory includes enterprise assets and projects categorized for business-appropriate dialogue. Project prioritization, business case justification, basic portfolio governance, and relationship management processes start to take shape as a result of the communication fostered by strategic portfolio management.

As portfolio management matures within the enterprise, active management of a portfolio where risk and reward are proactively balanced is practiced. The initial target is usually a relatively easy-to-understand sub-portfolio of assets and projects related to a certain part of the enterprise or certain strategic objective. Larger organizations will find it beneficial to appoint an overall portfolio manager to ensure coordination across portfolios. These groups typically combine relationship management (including change and problem management) services and product creation and delivery, along with planning and measurement.

After developing a comfort level and competencies utilizing strategic portfolio management with a sub-portfolio of assets and projects, strategic portfolio management typically advances across the entire organization. This level of portfolio management seeks to integrate all asset portfolios into one organization-wide investment portfolio. The process integration knowledge gained by assessing the deployment of strategic portfolio management at an individual sub-portfolio level can help prepare the portfolio management plan covering the entire organization. Organizational processes and governance must be mature and integrated for this level of strategic portfolio management to be successful.

Creating the Portfolio

The first step in implementing strategic portfolio management is to appropriately categorize investments. Portfolio management identifies potential risks and determines the likelihood of their occurrence and the severity of consequences. The items in a portfolio are typically classified by the level of risk versus expected benefits, the current fair value of the investment, and the expected investment life cycle.

Leading enterprises often employ a three-category model for asset and project categorization: operate the business, expand the business, and transform the business. It's crucial to adapt these categories to the particular context, taking into account risk tolerance and process maturity. Gray areas between each category will exist, and enterprises will need to manage them within any linked value management, portfolio management, project prioritization, and business case justification processes.

Let's consider some examples:

- **Operate-the-business investments** are needed to keep the business functioning. Spending in this category provides mission- and business-critical services. Common spending entities include electricity, lighting, heating/air-conditioning, telephone, network services, IT vendor support, and disaster recovery. Typical external influences that modify spending decisions here include business climate changes and corporate events or activities (for example, mergers and acquisitions [M&As] and divestitures).

- **Expand-the-business investments** are needed to increase the scope of products and services. Investments might include software upgrades, adding incremental capacity, or developing staff skills. Spending here affords new levels of process efficiency and effectiveness that the business perceives it will need and that the current assets cannot deliver. Assets in this category influence business performance through process agility (effectiveness) or through the ability to respond to new service requests in significantly less time than predecessors.
- **Transform-the-business investments** involve project-based spending that creates new products and/or services that broaden an enterprise's ability to enter new markets. Emphasis here is on the speed required to gain control of a new market via first-mover advantage. Sample investments include new business ventures, M&As, new products, major new business initiatives, and business process outsourcing.

Categorizing investments implies first listing the investments and then grouping them by business unit and by overall shared services/products. Consider implementing portfolio management in such an environment as business unit by business unit. As the portfolio management experience matures, grouping business unit portfolios together and managing them holistically is the natural evolution of applying the discipline of strategic portfolio management.

During the categorization process, it's vital to compile the information required to make portfolio categorization decisions. This information takes many forms and comes from various sources. Often, there's a list of currently active projects and another "wish list" of requested or proposed projects awaiting further review. Some of these projects will have detailed work plans, and many of the larger projects will have extensive scope and business case documentation that can be leveraged. Moreover, interviews and discussions with stakeholders will uncover information on otherwise "unknown projects" to complete the portfolio categorization process. Strategic business architecture is employed to ensure that projects in the portfolio are aligned with current business strategy and priorities.

Instead of focusing on detailed project schedules and task assignments, make sure any data collected is high level. Focus data collection on capturing information for use in the categorization process. Information gathered is both qualitative and quantitative and generally contains information about projects, schedule/cost estimates, budgets, dependencies, strategic initiatives, expected benefits, risks, relative priority, value, and ranking. The categorization process also captures information about available resources, roles, costs, skills, and important organizational or administrative information. Investment value is achieved from the right balance of risk and reward. Identifying potential risks, determining their likelihood of occurrence, and understanding the severity of consequences are essential parts of the portfolio creation process.

The appropriate mix of investment categories must be a dynamic business decision driven by market requirements, competition, internal requirements, business strategies, and so on. Believing that a proper mix exists is a dangerous assumption. The operate-expand-transform mix is neither a destination nor a primary performance indicator. Setting a good portfolio mix and managing toward it creates momentum and a performance culture that manages velocity metrics rather than a static portfolio mix.

When a high-performing organization makes a significant capital investment, its mix will typically shift significantly to the operate-the-business category. However, just because it spends more in this category, it does not cease being a high-performing organization. The operate-expand-transform mix is not an indicator of performance capability—it is only an indicator of current financial flexibility. For example, current spending on transformation does not equal transformation capabilities. That emphasis may be a last-minute, frantic attempt to avoid a catastrophe.

Assets are typically segmented into core, nondiscretionary, discretionary, strategic, and venture categories:

- **Core assets** are necessary expenses to enable operation of the organization (for example, power, facilities, maintenance).
- **Nondiscretionary assets** are typically forced expenditures caused by regulatory compliance, expansion, or the need to replace outmoded or worn-out assets. Spending activity in this category centers on expanding existing capacity to meet growth requirements, rather than introducing new products or services.
- **Discretionary assets** are required expenses to upgrade or replace existing assets (for example, platforms, versions). Spending in this category affords new levels of process efficiency and effectiveness that the business perceives it will need and that the current assets cannot deliver.
- **Strategic assets** are typically designed to support a growth or transformation business strategy (for example, customer relationship management [CRM], product life-cycle management, supplier relationship management). This category includes project-based spending that creates new products and services to deepen an enterprise's existing market penetration.
- **Venture assets** are typically used to incubate future business opportunities or experiment with the transformation of business models or product/service lines. This category includes project-based spending that creates new products and services to broaden an enterprise's reach to enter new, untapped markets.

Upon finalizing the categorization of projects, perform an analysis to understand how many core business capabilities are positively impacted by each project. Next, consider those projects with the potential to positively impact multiple core business capabilities for maximum strategic impact.

Managing the Portfolio

After establishing portfolio categories, it's important to place each investment in the appropriate category based on the risk and reward decisions made in the portfolio plan. A strong portfolio measurement process is valuable for assessing actual portfolio performance against targets set in the planning phase and outlining discrepancies. Furthermore, establishing monitoring triggers helps signal potential portfolio problems. Following a formal portfolio management process allows the enterprise to optimize the return on the overall investment portfolio and to maximize its use in creating business innovation.

The key disciplines of planning and strategy, future-state planning, and strategic portfolio management all overlap at the central core of the portfolio. The planning and strategy discipline enables innovation and manages the business related to the particular asset portfolio, while future-state planning designs the portfolio's evolution. The portfolio management process consists of two interrelated cycles: asset portfolio management and project portfolio management, both driven by business strategy. These, in turn, frame the enterprise prioritization process for the identification, creation, acquisition, or deployment of the assets.

The asset cycle continually seeks to optimize the value that the assets are able to generate by identifying improvement, optimization, creation/acquisition, and innovation opportunities. Optimal timing for asset disposal/retirement is understood and planned for up front at asset creation or acquisition. Any projects necessary for asset creation/acquisition/improvement are identified and passed to the PPM cycle. Monitoring asset usage ensures optimal ROI, and regularly assessing value generated drives the appropriate use/retirement/enhancement strategy.

The project cycle actualizes the prioritized business transformation opportunities identified in planning and asset improvement identification. New projects are added either as recently identified and prioritized opportunities or as previously developed scenarios whose triggering event has occurred. Project adjustments (for example, accelerate, slow down, retire) may also occur based on regular reviews of the projected value that the project will generate. Thus, enterprises should reevaluate the business cases for both ongoing and non-triggered projects and take appropriate action to optimize the portfolio's value. This reevaluation should occur on a regular basis, preferably quarterly. As projects enter the portfolio, managing their implementation and also measuring delivered projects' value against initial expectations is key, as is transferring any modified/created assets to the asset portfolio and managing them as previously described.

It's important to manage the portfolio with a life-cycle mindset, with stages such as portfolio goal setting, portfolio performance measurement, and cycle closing by adjusting and rebalancing the portfolio appropriately (that is, adding, accelerating, decelerating, and exiting portfolio components). Moreover, enterprises must embed asset and project portfolios and their management processes into the business ecosystem. Be aware that building robust portfolio management capabilities is a staged process, tied to business process maturity.

Portfolio Governance

Effective strategic portfolio risk management entails both top-down and bottom-up risk management practices. Top-down management addresses risk in a granular, synchronous fashion, supporting executive-level decisions around portfolio initiation, investment strategies, progress review, and value strategies. The focus is on understanding risks before plans are defined or operationalized. Conversely, bottom-up management concentrates on performing detailed, continuous assessment of risk and deals with day-to-day operational risks. Together, they provide a 360-degree, multidimensional view of risks that considers an enterprise as a whole.

The heart of strategic portfolio governance is the strong connection between principles, processes, people, and performance. Principles and processes, the backbone of governance and organizational culture, are fundamental to portfolio management. Strategic portfolio governance must establish enterprise-wide governing principles to articulate governance guidelines within which expected behaviors occur within the enterprise. The enterprise should create a governing body that includes senior business unit leaders. This group will develop appropriate principles for governing the enterprise.

The principle component of portfolio governance has two primary functions: principle development and principle compliance. A consistent set of principles must articulate the guidelines within which expected behaviors occur with the intent of directing the enterprise toward an acceptable level of commonality. Examples of portfolio principles include the decision that investments are classified as either assets or projects, the decision that investments will be divided into categories meaningful to the business and relevant to the organization (that is, operate the business, expand the business, transform the business), and the decision that the investment mix is to be defined by a portfolio steering committee, with balancing and tuning recommendations informed by the strategic business architecture.

A set of consistent, enterprise-wide processes must be defined to execute the governing principles. These processes can be broadly grouped into operational processes, administration processes, financial processes, logistics processes, and strategic processes. Effective portfolio governance requires governing bodies to ensure that the relevant principles and processes are developed, adhered to, and evolved over time. These groups include the strategic planning, executive steering committee, IT steering committee, and various centers of excellence. The most overlooked and ill-managed aspects of portfolio governance are the controlling of the performance (controls and checks) of the various governance processes and the monitoring of the compliance with established principles.

Effective portfolio governance mitigates conflict between long- and short-term goals. An enterprise can neither focus just on the tactical, day-to-day decisions to promote immediate revenue and profit, nor focus only on the strategic, future-oriented vision of the enterprise to promote long-term growth and persistence. To effectively transform, an enterprise must mitigate conflicts between these opposing forces. Good governance practices also create a climate of trust and increase agility and freedom of action. The enterprise, therefore, must foster individual trust, decision-making, and empowerment within the governance structure in order to achieve effective strategic portfolio governance.

Communicating the Portfolio

It is critically important that all stakeholders understand the portfolio plan and any changes made. This involves developing communication plans, delivering the messages to stakeholders, and measuring communication success. Communication is a particularly critical part of the initial adoption of portfolio management. As the portfolio management process evolves into a continuous cycle of analysis and fine-tuning, the portfolio changes become less significant, and the adjustment process becomes more efficient through standard practice. When implementing large changes to the portfolio, there is risk of pushing the enterprise into a long adjustment period of very low productivity. Clearly communicating the changes required to move to the newly optimized portfolio, as well as the logic behind the decisions, is critical to minimizing any downtime associated with a change in strategic direction.

Effective communication serves two objectives:

- **It clearly outlines the changes and unambiguously defines the new direction.** The new portfolio represents a top-down plan that sets direction and constraints to guide the bottom-up planning activities. The new direction and constraints, along with any assumptions, must be clearly conveyed to make the detail planning as efficient as possible.

- **It provides the rationale for project teams to make changes in support of the "bigger picture."** Ensuring project teams understand their role and their contribution to the value, balance, and alignment of the portfolio is important for building buy-in and support. Buy-in is not a black-and-white issue, but rather a matter of degrees. The more buy-in and support obtained, the more efficiently the changes will be implemented and sustained.

Agile Portfolio Management Has Now Become Part of the Mainstream

Agile is an iterative approach to project management and software development that helps teams deliver value to their customers faster and with fewer headaches. Instead of betting everything on a "big bang" launch, an agile team delivers work in small but consumable increments. Requirements, plans, and results are evaluated continuously so teams have a natural mechanism for responding to change quickly.

Ultimately, agile is a mindset informed by the agile manifesto's values and principles. Those values and principles provide guidance on how to create and respond to change and how to deal with uncertainty. Agile approaches to portfolio management continue to mature and grow, but many organizations have yet to clearly link project objectives to business strategy. Portfolio management only becomes strategic when organizations use it to help reach business goals.

An effective portfolio manager must combine the skills of a business architect, a financial manager, a program manager, and an entrepreneur. Often this person is not simply an effective project manager—successful strategic (and agile) portfolio management requires a much more broader skill set, perspective, and set of experiences. An adaptive culture is needed to ensure that resources can support changing strategic needs. We will discuss the skills needed for success in more detail in Chapter 7.

The use of agile portfolio management techniques and the evolving digital business and its requirements for greater productivity have created greater interest and emphasis on adaptive resource management. This involves monitoring projects, making decisions, and changing project resources in response to new information and changes in strategy. Adaptive resource management is enabled by strategic business architecture and the enterprise-wide information and perspectives it provides for such strategic decision-making.

Being adaptive in resource allocation requires a very different culture and mindset from simply planning resources for upcoming projects. It's about embracing the change associated with the introduction of new information from a change in strategy, as well as the potentially numerous associated resource and project changes. This is very different from the rigid planning practices typically associated with project management and requires a team that is flexible and embraces dynamic, complex environments. This is the type of portfolio management team needed for resilient and agile responses to dynamic market conditions.

Project Portfolio Management

Enterprises use projects to convert business strategies into new services, processes, and products needed for their success and viability. Organizational projects should be a reflection of the business strategy and should directly link to the components of that strategy. Selecting the right projects to meet business strategy is a critically important process. Yet, selecting projects that support strategy is often cited as an area of extreme weakness.

The strategic business architecture ecosystem diagram in Figure 5.2 depicts how the business capabilities (and changes to those capabilities) inform PPM. This is the heart of the strategy execution equation. For most organizations, PPM is the first and most crucial focus area of strategic portfolio management to get right. Management of other enterprise portfolios (capabilities,

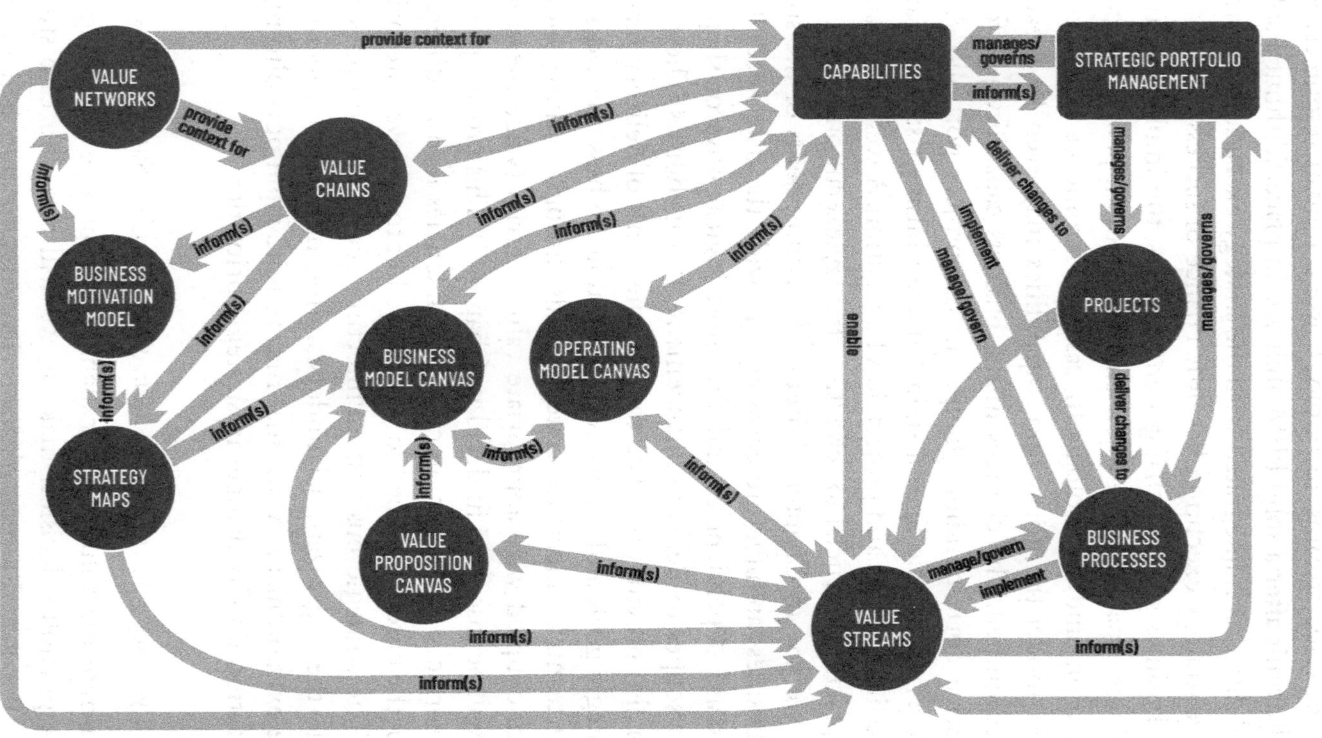

Figure 5.2 The strategic business architecture ecosystem.

processes, value streams, technology assets, human resources) are typically built after a solid PPM ability is in place. Without a solid PPM ability that is integrated with the strategy execution function, effective strategy execution has little chance of success.

As business strategy changes and evolves, the implementation of business capabilities are often changed through people, process, information, and technology. In cases of significant strategic or business model transformation, capabilities may even be created or discontinued. The changes in the business capability portfolio then drive corresponding changes in the project portfolio. At a high level, this is the line of sight between business strategy (and changes in strategy) and project-level execution. A well-integrated PPM practice is crucial for effective strategy execution.

As we saw in Chapters 3 and 4, the components of the strategic business architecture ecosystem provide the data needed to understand dependencies and the most logical ways of shaping project scopes to deliver enhancements to capabilities. The ecosystem also provides the data to trace the work of delivery teams to strategic goals and proactively communicate how the work of project teams connects to strategic goals through intuitive views that are coupled with appropriate value metrics (value measurement will be discussed in detail in Chapter 7). This process proactively surfaces and communicates dependencies in how different parts of the enterprise need to work together to achieve enterprise goals. The strategic business architecture ecosystem components provide the organizational understanding needed to effectively handle extraordinary events that may require rapid portfolio reprioritization due to changes in strategic priorities.

Capability-Based Project Portfolio Management: A Case Study

To illustrate the value that a capability perspective can bring to project portfolio decision-making, we will review a case study from a Fortune 500 organization. The organization had multiple project portfolios, each structured around a different product or function. One executive leader managed each portfolio and determined the investments for the next horizon. Together, the leaders formed a portfolio leadership committee representing the scope of investments for the enterprise. The portfolio leaders suspected that there may have been some misalignment of project investments both across the portfolios and back to the strategy. However, they did not have data to substantiate this. As a result, they requested an analysis of the project investment requests through an enterprise capability lens, both within and across the portfolios.

To perform the analysis, the strategic planning and strategic business architecture teams worked together to:

1. Align each project investment request back to the strategy and the specific business objectives that it was enabling.
2. Align each project investment request to one or more capabilities that were intended to be enhanced. (***Note:*** Value stream enhancements could also be included in the analysis, though they were not in this case.)
3. Aggregate the level of strategy enablement and planned investment by capability within and across portfolios and visualize as capability heatmaps. (***Note:*** Level 2 or 3 capabilities provide the ideal granularity for this type of decision-making.)
4. Synthesize the results as a set of key findings and recommendations to present to the portfolio leadership committee.

Figure 5.3 compares two key summary views from the analysis. The organization's level 2 capability map is shown in both views but aggregates different information. (***Note:*** The capability names have been removed from the boxes for confidentiality.)

The Organizational Strategy view shows the importance of each capability to the organization's strategy. The color scheme for heatmapping in this view would typically be:

- Red boxes indicate a capability of **high importance** to achieving the strategy.
- Yellow boxes indicate a capability of **medium importance** to achieving the strategy.

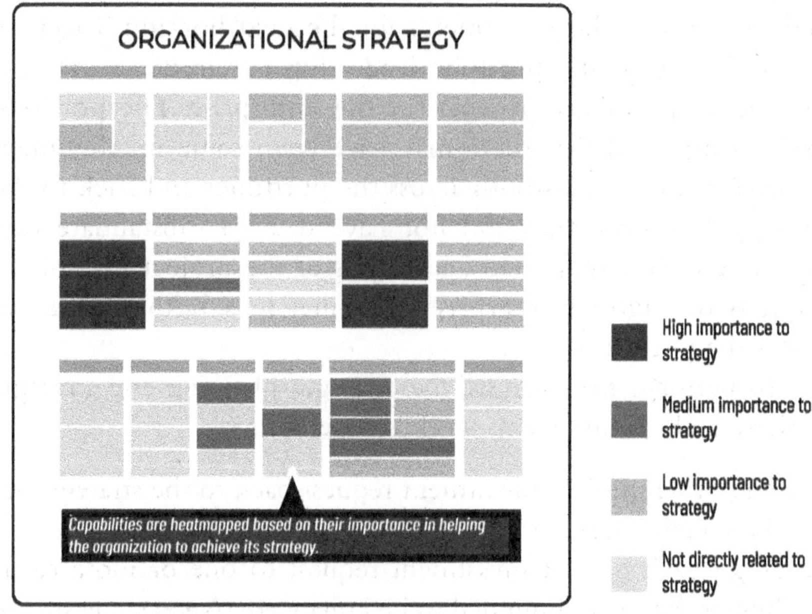

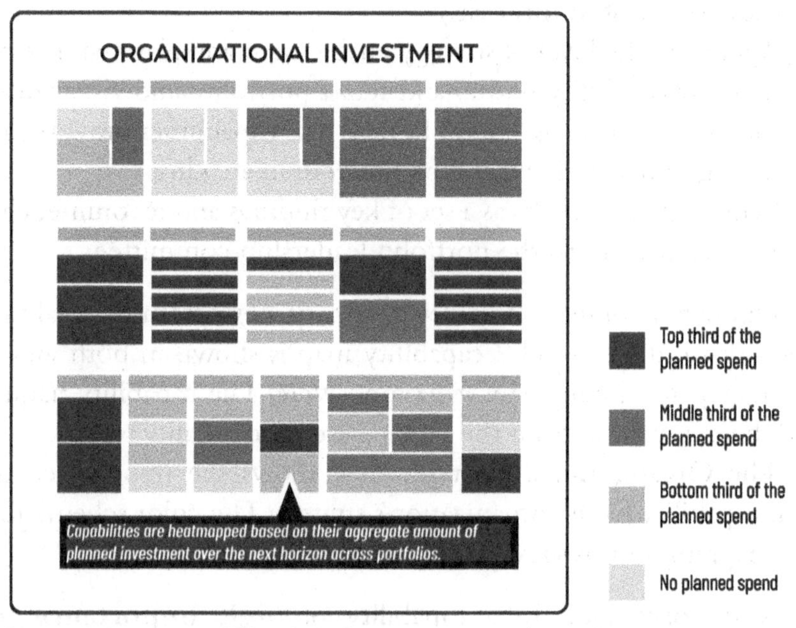

Figure 5.3 A capability-based investment analysis across project portfolios.

- Green boxes indicate a capability of **low importance** to achieving the strategy.
- Gray boxes indicate a capability that is **not directly related** to an organization's ability to achieve its strategy (though, of course, it would still be important to its successful operation).

On the other hand, the Organizational Investment view shows an aggregation of the planned spend for each capability across all the portfolios. (Individual views for each portfolio were created but are not shown.) The color scheme for heatmapping in this view would typically be as follows:

- Red boxes indicate a capability planned to be the **top third of the planned spend** for the next horizon (based on the aggregation from Step 3).
- Yellow boxes indicate a capability planned to be the **middle third of the planned spend** for the next horizon.
- Green boxes indicate a capability planned to be the **bottom third of the planned spend** for the next horizon.
- Gray boxes indicate a capability for which no project investment requests were submitted and, thus, there is **no planned spend** for the next horizon.

This objective, data-based analysis illuminated an entirely new set of insights for the portfolio leadership committee by taking an enterprise capability perspective. It highlighted:

- Misalignment between the organization's strategy and its planned investments. For example, the bottom-left two boxes in the Organizational Strategy view are not directly related to achieving the organization's strategy but were planned to be the top third of the investment per the Organizational Investment view.
- Redundant project investments across portfolios. For example, some of the same or similar solutions were being built in different product or functional areas, where shared solutions

could have been leveraged instead. Without a capability lens, this redundancy would not have been identified (and was not previously).

- Philosophical differences across the organization. For example, the product areas were approaching the delivery of customer experience with different philosophies, assumptions, and mindsets. This led to an inconsistent and fragmented experience for customers that had multiple products from the organization.

The enterprise perspective that capabilities brought to the PPM process not only shifted the investments that were made for the current horizon, but also influenced the entire process going forward. This included:

- Requiring the owners of each project investment request to indicate the capabilities being enhanced so that the aggregate heatmap views could be readily produced and analyzed
- Requiring the owners of each project investment request to articulate the business objectives being enabled using a more standard set of metrics defined for each capability
- Allowing the portfolio leaders to make more informed investment decisions for the enterprise, and changing, combining, pausing, or denying project investment requests where applicable

Project Portfolio Management as a Strategy Alignment and Execution Tool

The strategic planning process typically produces a strategic plan. The strategic planning process is meaningless without the successful implementation of the strategic plan. According to J. R. Turner, project management is the "art and science of converting vision into reality."[2] This definition highlights the strength of the relationship between strategy creation, project management, and strategy implementation. The confluence of these disciplines has evolved into the modern science of PPM. The role and purpose of PPM is 1) a tool to implement the organization strategy, 2) a process for the projectification of business strategy, 3) a means to balance overall risk, and 4) a tool for optimizing resource allocation across projects. The portfolio management process is a very important tool for successful enterprise architecture and enterprise alignment.

Although relatively young as a discipline, PPM has greatly matured in the last several years. The number of organizations exploring PPM as a way of adding value to their bottom line continues to grow each year, with projects increasingly viewed as building blocks in the design and execution of strategy.

PPM has been utilized by leading organizations to make their enterprises more competitive and responsive to change. PPM transforms strategy from being reactive to a sense-and-respond operating model. Companies that become industry leaders share a common trait: They understand and exploit their specific source of value to customers. The strategy of these companies emphasizes excellence and prioritizes investments according to one of three value areas: customer intimacy, product leadership, or operational excellence. In an era of information-driven business opportunities and increased demand for business flexibility, alignment with strategy has a new meaning and a new level of importance: the ability to support and at times drive sudden direction changes (and associated changes in strategy) to capitalize on changing market opportunities.

Project Portfolio Governance

The governance body that oversees the portfolio management process develops performance improvement options (for example, shifting resources from one project to another, developing new skills, providing user training). The project portfolio should be continually reviewed with respect to external factors and strategic direction. These factors may require changes in the organization's capabilities that, in turn, require changes in the project portfolio.

This process involves defining and monitoring status metrics to keep projects on track and ensuring the engagement of executives and stakeholders. Making adjustments to the project portfolio as strategic and operational plans change is necessary. As such, continuous monitoring of the project portfolio leads to frequent fine-tuning and occasional major shifts in the portfolio.

Generally, project costs are summarized across multiple investment categories and compared with industry benchmarks to create baselines, set targets, and balance the project portfolio. It's important to capture and summarize project value to evaluate and maximize the value of the entire project portfolio. Thus, conducting an inventory of all projects to properly assess resource demands and ensure that the enterprise has enough resources to make the project portfolio achievable is necessary. Mapping projects to business strategies for a better view of the portfolio's strategic alignment is key. This mapping provides the traceability and line of sight between strategy and projects needed for effective strategy execution. Maximizing value, finding balance, and aligning with corporate strategy while ensuring achievability in the project portfolio is challenging. Focusing on either one of these four goals in the absence of the others leads to very different results. For instance, fully maximizing the value of the project portfolio may lead to a poorly balanced portfolio that is neither aligned nor achievable. Therefore, to reasonably optimize the project portfolio in the face of multiple goals, approach optimization as an interactive review process.

This process begins with a review of the findings uncovered during the portfolio analysis. Strategic alignment issues may have been identified, or overallocated resources may indicate that the project portfolio is not achievable. Before making any changes to the project portfolio, enterprises must define clear objectives that target the desired outcomes. A review of cost and resource impacts will uncover adjustments to make before arriving at an achievable project portfolio. This process continues by reviewing strategic alignment and balance. Through multiple iterations, consider trade-offs and make final adjustments to arrive at the optimal project portfolio.

Assessing Project Portfolio Execution

Enterprises typically use financial models to measure the value of their projects. These models use metrics, such as net present value (NPV) and the internal rate of return (IRR)—which consider the value of money invested over time and the cost of the company's capital—to evaluate the cost of implementing projects along with a stream of future benefits. Depending on the project, the financial benefits may be in the form of expected operating cost reductions, revenue growth, or both. While financial modeling is an important aspect of determining value, it is not the only aspect of value. Non-financial benefits like increased market share, improved customer satisfaction, and reduced defects can be quantified and measured using nonfinancial metrics. Scoring models that use nonfinancial metrics and ratings provide another form of value measurement. As enterprises mature their value measurement, they often employ a mixed model that combines financial metrics with nonfinancial scoring to rank projects.

There are two major challenges in determining project value:

- **Defining a method that allows for the comparison of the value of one project to another:** Most projects have many intangible benefits making it difficult to compare one to another. Also, very large projects often have even larger costs so the net benefit minus costs is important for comparing projects.
- **Compensating for the time value of costs and benefits:** Generally, project costs precede the benefits, and the value of the benefits are greater if received today versus in the future.

Financial models address both these issues by translating costs and benefits into offsetting streams of discounted cash flows (DCFs).

NPV and IRR are the most common models; however, there are several variants with application to capital budgeting decisions in general and to PPM in particular. NPV incorporates the opportunity cost of capital, also called the *discount rate,* into the discounting equation for calculating an absolute economic value. It is widely considered the best absolute measure of value. IRR is a rate or ratio, not an absolute amount. This ratio is useful for comparing dissimilar investments. It is also useful for making comparisons between different periods, for making comparisons between different sized projects, and for making international comparisons.

In most cases, the benefits from each project do not start accumulating until the project has been completed and then the benefits often extend months or maybe years beyond the end of the project. Therefore, to accurately measure a project's ROI, it is important to keep the project in the portfolio well past the completion date. Having captured the actual costs and benefits attributed to each project, some financial models for estimating value (for example, NPV, IRR) can be used to calculate a project's ROI over time. More important, capturing actual costs and benefits at a project level allows for measuring ROI for the entire project portfolio. This provides an objective measure of the value that the project portfolio is delivering and helps executives understand how to balance projects in the portfolio.

Where financial models make use of only a few key criteria, scoring models are free to use many more criteria in assessing a project's value. Scoring models have the added value of using subjective measures but can be more complex to implement since the model relies on decision-makers providing much of the data in the form of ratings assigned through a review process. With scoring models, projects are rated on a number of questions that distinguish superior projects, typically using 0–5 or 1–10 scales. An understanding of how many core business capabilities are positively impacted by each project should be one of the major criteria for superior projects. These ratings are weighted and summed to yield a single score. This score is a proxy for the value of the project to the enterprise and incorporates strategic alignment and balance considerations beyond pure financial measures.

Why Start with Project Portfolio Management?

There are several reasons why you should begin your strategic portfolio management journey by building out a solid PPM ability. PPM provides visibility into projects and constraints. When project portfolio practices are nonexistent or poorly functioning, people will often go around the portfolio process to get work done. In these cases, resources are incorrectly prioritized by stakeholders who have circumnavigated the process. Without the project intake process and project prioritization/reprioritization processes inherent in PPM, the projects they are working on are likely to be the wrong projects that are not aligned with current strategic needs.

An effective way to prioritize is for the PPM function to establish an investment committee to prioritize projects with information on current strategic priorities provided by the strategic business architecture process. The committee should include key cross-functional stakeholders, such as heads of the relevant units such as finance, strategic planning, IT, and operations, to curate the relevant information to support organization investment decisions.

A quantitative decision model removes some of the emotion surrounding decision-making.

The prioritization model should inform initial and ongoing decisions about what projects to advance and how to make trade-offs with resource constraints that are in support of current strategic objectives.

The PPM process maintains visibility through execution and benefits realization. The project portfolio provides comprehensive insights into what is being delivered, priorities, timelines, constraints, interdependencies, and risks to the portfolio. The value realization process will determine whether the expected strategic benefits were delivered. Executives can use this information to inform strategic decision-making and evolve strategy. Projects are the manifestation of the business strategy and the corresponding enhancements needed to capabilities and value streams, and all strategic change happens through projects and the products of those projects. When projects are siloed and not managed as a portfolio, enterprise-wide strategy execution is very likely to fail.

Capability, Process, Value Stream, IT Asset, and Human Capital Portfolios

Strategic portfolio management is more than just PPM. Capabilities, processes, value streams, IT assets and human capital all should be managed as investment portfolios using the same thinking, processes, governance, and discipline applied to PPM. These portfolios are interrelated and dependent on one another. For example, a change in strategy often requires a change in the implementation of core organizational capabilities. In cases of significant transformation, new capabilities may be developed, existing capabilities may need to be modified, or some existing capabilities may need to be decommissioned. These changes in core organizational capabilities will likely require changes in key business processes and may require new or modified hardware and/or software as well as new or modified human resource requirements. All of these changes will likely combine to form needs for a new set of projects required to implement the identified changes to the capability portfolio. All strategic portfolios are modified during this process—changes in one portfolio often result in changes in the other portfolios. Balancing delivery with organizational change management is vital to the success.

Successful portfolio management leads to quicker uptake and an increased appetite for further change that, over time, creates a change-enabled culture. Continuous change is part of the portfolio management process, and effective change management is crucial for success. There are multiple layers of change at the portfolio level where strategic investment decisions are made that affect resources, agendas, and organizational performance. There are additional layers of change for program, product, and project managers accountable for delivering new or enhanced capabilities and ensuring the adoption of the new processes or technologies. When a change in strategy occurs, a rippling effect cascades to portfolio managers and their teams. We will discuss effective change management in more detail in Chapter 8.

Without this level of strategic portfolio management capability, effective strategy execution is difficult to say the least. If an organization can't manage key areas, such as projects and capabilities, as investment portfolios and keep those portfolios aligned with the current needs of business strategy, it is very likely that it will be, at least in part, expending resources on the wrong projects. Achieving this level of strategic portfolio management maturity takes time, resources, discipline, and the right people in the right roles. We will discuss assessing maturity in key organizational areas, as well as organizational structures and roles needed for success, in Chapter 8.

Strategic Portfolio Management and Value Realization

Value management and communication is one of the greatest challenges facing many areas in the organization today—everyone wants to show how what they do adds value to the business strategy, but few understand how to do so or even understand what the strategy is at that point in time. Value measurement and management is often reported as one of the lowest areas of organizational maturity. We will discuss value management, realization, and communication in more detail in Chapter 7.

In the context of portfolio management, you should be able to assess whether value is being delivered by the portfolio. We will discuss a process for accessing value in Chapter 7.

Without this recognition of value, portfolio management may become nonstrategic, irrelevant, and administrative. The main value proposition for strategic portfolio management is the effective execution of strategy—ensuring that investment portfolios are aligned with changes in strategy to ensure that we are investing in the right projects, and related resources, at the right time.

Today's fast-changing environment makes effective portfolio management and measuring results more important than ever. The increasing pace of change means that your organization will expect faster results. These results are organizational benefits delivered as a steady stream, focused on stakeholder expectations. A critical part of effective strategic portfolio management is learning from mistakes and sharing this information to better inform future decisions. By doing this the organization learns to make better assumptions and improve future investment and prioritization decisions.

A value-driven culture is vital for success. However, many organizations don't understand what they should be measuring and what the real sources of value are for the organization. You will find more on this topic in Chapter 7.

Next Steps

Strategic portfolio management is a central component of the overall strategy execution equation. We now need to understand a few other critical factors in building an effective strategy execution function in your organization because it's not enough just to get portfolio management right. It's also important to keep in mind that it takes time, discipline, appropriate resources, and a strategic vision and plan to complete the marathon and cross the finish line with an effective strategy execution function in your organization. These are the topics of coming chapters.

STRATEGY EXECUTION ORGANIZATIONAL ASSESSMENT

Reflect on the following questions to assess how well strategy execution is working in your organization based on the concepts from Chapter 5. Please refer to the scoring guidance provided in Chapter 1.

1. Our organization has an enterprise PPM function, and it is effective.
2. Rate the level of integration between PPM and the strategic planning or related strategy execution function. *(Score 0 if PPM does not report to the strategic planning/strategy execution.)*
3. Rate the organization's maturity with utilizing PPM techniques.
4. Rate the organization's maturity with utilizing portfolio management techniques in other areas (business capabilities, processes, value streams, technology assets, and human capital).
5. Our organization leverages a capability perspective to assess strategic alignment (strategy to project comparison) and project alignment (project-to-project comparison for gaps, overlaps, and so on) within and across portfolios.
6. Our organization is able to align execution-level projects with strategy and ongoing changes in strategy.

Chapter 6

Linking Strategic Business Architecture with Other Architectural Domains and Other Business Functions and Disciplines

Successful strategy execution requires many different business functions and disciplines working together hand in hand to turn strategy into a reality. This includes business functions such as human resources and finance, and strategy execution disciplines such as strategy development, strategic business architecture, experience design, and organizational change management. Effective strategy execution also requires interaction with execution-level disciplines such as program and project management and solution design and delivery. All these teams form a cohesive ecosystem spanning from strategic to tactical and operational—linked together through strategic business architecture. Strategic business architecture is the bridge discipline that creates the enterprise perspectives, understanding, and connections needed for successful strategy development and execution.

In addition, to realize the full benefits of strategic business architecture, it must be embedded into the very fabric of an organization. This includes embedding the mindset and enterprise views of strategic business architecture into processes and practices across an organization, such as strategy formulation, innovation, strategic planning, strategic portfolio management, and project and solution delivery. This also includes incorporating strategic business architecture into the approaches of other teams. In fact, one of the hallmarks of maturity with strategic business architecture is that the discipline is tightly integrated into an organization—to the extent that it becomes expected, and just how people think and work.

This chapter will describe how different functions and disciplines connect and work together to deliver strategy execution from end to end, and how they need to be organized to achieve the most effective results. It will also explore how strategic business architecture interfaces with other parts of an organization to enable effective strategy execution, and how it brings new value to other functions in the process.

Linking Strategic Business Architecture with Other Architectural Domains

We will begin by exploring how strategic business architecture interacts with execution-level business architecture and enterprise and information technology (IT) architecture.

The Continuum of Strategic Business Architecture

As introduced in Chapters 1 and 2 and reflected in Figure 6.1, the contemporary practice of business architecture bridges and plays a role as part of both strategy development and execution, as well as enterprise architecture. Business architecture in the context of

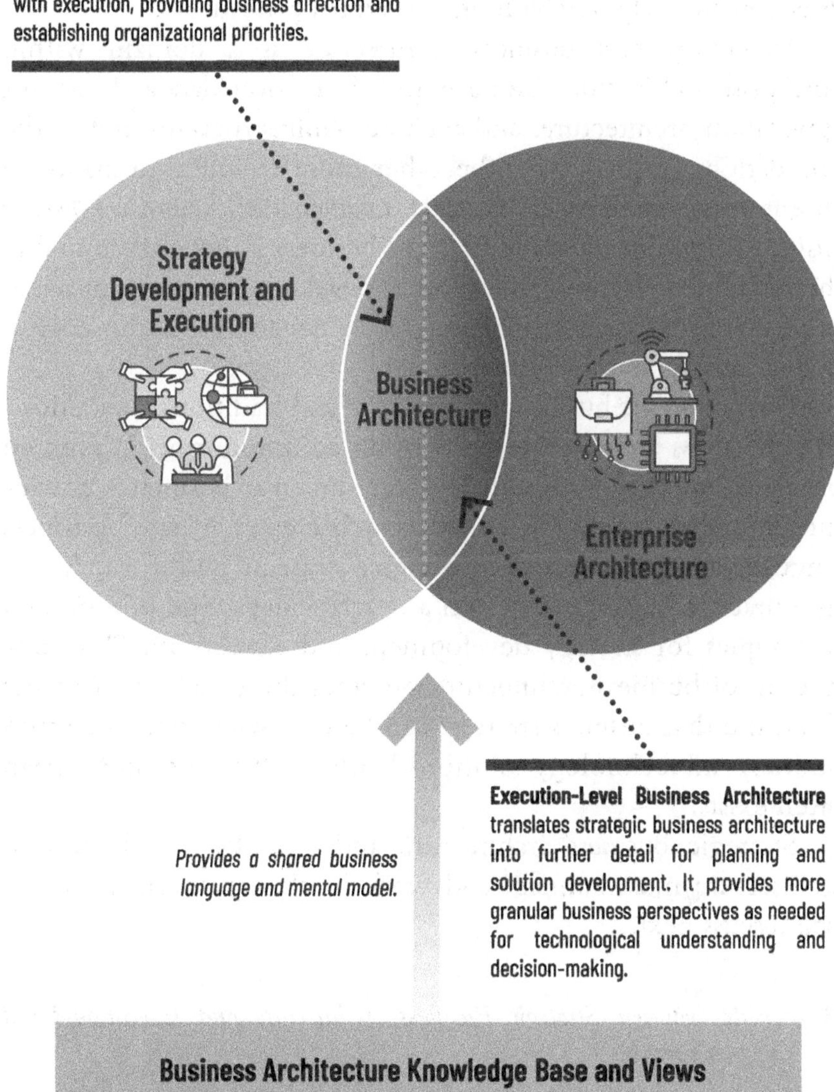
Strategic Business Architecture aligns strategy with execution, providing business direction and establishing organizational priorities.
Strategy Development and Execution
Business Architecture
Enterprise Architecture
Provides a shared business language and mental model.
Execution-Level Business Architecture translates strategic business architecture into further detail for planning and solution development. It provides more granular business perspectives as needed for technological understanding and decision-making.
Business Architecture Knowledge Base and Views

Figure 6.1 The continuum of strategic business architecture.

strategy development and execution, or *strategic business architecture,* has evolved into a vital strategic business discipline that provides a comprehensive approach for effective strategy execution. Strategic business architecture informs and translates strategy and aligns it with execution. Strategic business architecture also provides business direction and helps establish organizational priorities.

Execution-level business architecture is a domain within enterprise architecture (along with information/data architecture, application architecture, and technical/infrastructure) and is the foundation and driver for the other more technical domains. In an enterprise architecture context, *traditional execution-level (legacy) business architecture* translates strategic business architecture into further detail for planning and solution development. It also provides more granular business perspectives as needed for technological understanding and decision-making.

Both strategic business architecture and traditional execution-level business architecture draw upon common roots. Within an organization, they also both leverage the same business architecture knowledge base and views, which creates a shared business language and mental model (though a strategic business architecture practice typically relies on a much wider range of tools and techniques for strategy development and execution). This continuum of business architecture provides the detail and linkages to ensure that business strategy can be cohesively translated into business and technology solutions. Without this continuum, a gap often exists.

Strategic business architecture and execution-level business architecture must connect and work in close partnership, as we will discuss next.

Partnership between Strategic Business Architecture and Execution-Level Business Architecture

While it may seem that strategic business architecture and the other IT architecture disciplines would be enough to bridge the strategy execution gap, in practice, we have found that the execution-level business architecture discipline is also necessary for most organizations. Execution-level business architects play a key role that is not performed by strategic business architects or by enterprise or IT architects to detail the business architecture and connect it to the IT and solution architectures, as required to inform the design of solutions and the technology environment. Execution-level business architects also collaborate with solution architects, program managers, project managers, and other execution roles to enable the delivery of projects and solutions.

Strategic business architecture reports within strategic planning and has an enterprise-wide strategic scope, while traditional execution-level business architecture typically reports within IT, often to an enterprise architecture leader, and often has a narrower, project-level scope. Strategic business architecture represents the full scope of an organization and includes a broader set of tools and views that are used at a strategic level. Execution-level business architecture focuses on what is needed to inform business and technology solutions. This requires detailing the business architecture (for example, decomposing capabilities to lower levels in partnership with strategic business architects) and making connections to (and potentially modeling) adjacent domains such as business processes and system applications. For this reason, the orientation and skills of strategic business architects and execution-level business architects differ, as we will discuss further in Chapters 7 and 8. Together, they help to seamlessly bridge the gap between strategy and planning into execution.

Figure 6.2 summarizes the focus of strategic business architecture versus execution-level business architecture. This phased approach also allows for *just enough* architecture and design to be done in order to inform the next activity, leading to greater agility and speed in the process.

Throughout strategy execution, strategic business architects and execution-level business architects may work together in close partnership to:

- Assess the impact of strategy and inform strategic options.
- Define and translate the strategy into a cohesive set of changes necessary to the organization, ranging from strategic to tactical.

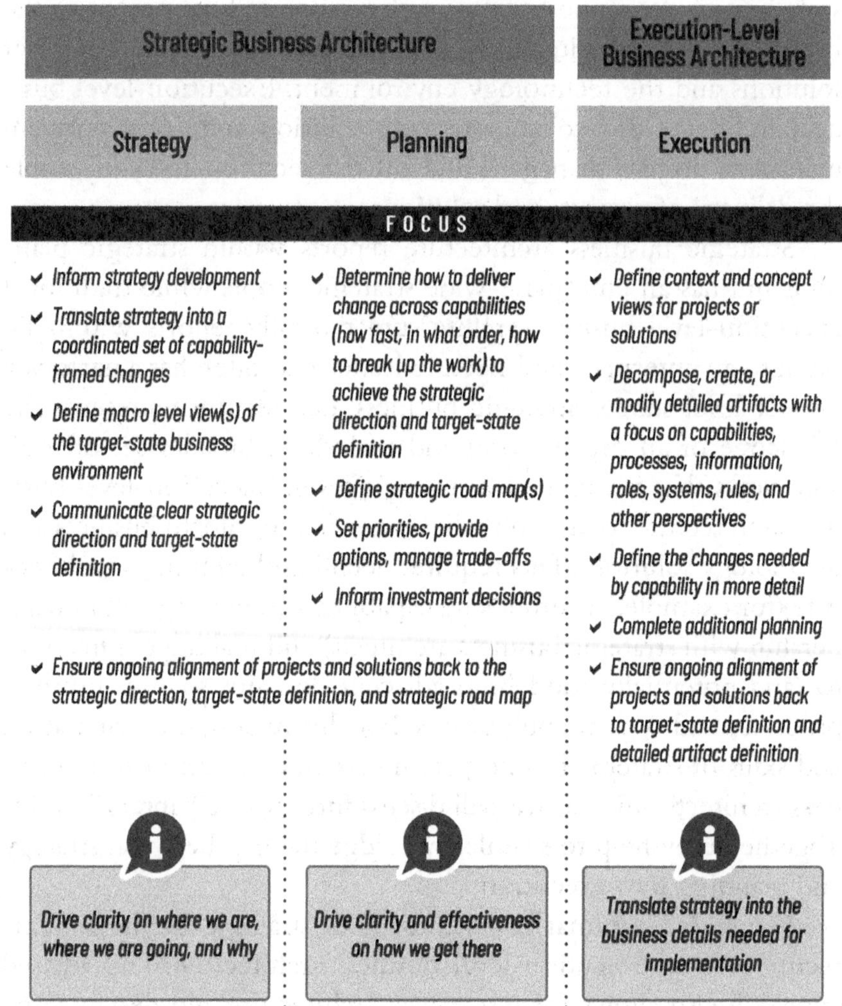

Figure 6.2 A summary of strategic business architecture and execution-level business architecture.

- Assess the ongoing alignment of solutions, projects, portfolios, and initiatives back to the strategic direction, target-state business environment definition (also referred to as a *target-state strategic business architecture*), and the strategic road map.
- Expand and modify the business architecture knowledge base and views as needed.

Table 6.1 The Major Differences between Execution-Level and Strategic Business Architecture

	Scope	**Reporting**	**Primary Orientation**	**Primary Stakeholders**
Execution-level business architecture	Project/program level	IT organization/enterprise architecture	Technical systems	IT organization and IT architects
Strategic business architecture	Enterprise-level strategy execution/enterprise portfolio level	Strategic planning	Strategy execution	Strategic planning, strategy execution stakeholders

Table 6.1 (from Chapter 2) illustrates some of the major differences between an execution-level business architecture practice and a strategic business architecture practice. At a high level, strategic business architecture creates the line of sight between enterprise project portfolios and business strategy and helps to ensure that the organization is doing the "right" projects that are aligned with current business strategy. Traditional execution-level business architecture helps to ensure that projects and initiatives are implemented correctly and achieve their desired objectives.

Partnership between Strategic Business Architecture and Enterprise and IT Architecture

Aligning the Business and IT Architecture Disciplines and Roles

In today's world, nearly every strategy and related execution-level project has a technological component. Technology and business strategy are forever intertwined. Technology not only automates a business, but also now provides an ever-expanding set of opportunities to create strategic advantages. Strategy execution will succeed only if alignment between strategy development and execution and the IT architecture-related disciplines and roles is understood and achieved. Strategic business architecture is the bridge that enables this organizational understanding and alignment. Traditional execution-level business architecture plays an important role to create critical organizational linkages between strategic business architecture and the rest of enterprise and solution architecture. Regardless, though, throughout strategy execution, strategic business architects (together with execution-level business architects) still work in close partnership with enterprise and IT architects to:

- Inform strategy development with an understanding of how technology can be leveraged for strategic advantage.
- Assess the impact of strategy on the technology environment.
- Translate the strategy into a cohesive set of changes needed to applications, software services, data deployments, and infrastructure, framed by capabilities.
- Define macro-level view(s) of the target-state technology environment that corresponds to the target-state business environment view(s).
- Determine how to scope and deliver harmonized business and technology change through programs and projects and, where applicable, develop a strategic road map.
- Assess the ongoing alignment of projects and solutions back to the strategic direction, target-state business and technology environment definitions, and the strategic road map.
- Expand and modify the business architecture knowledge base and views as needed, including the cross-mappings to the IT architecture.

Figure 6.3 shows the approximate timing and levels of involvement for each of the architecture disciplines and roles from strategy to execution. (This does not reflect the high degree of iteration and collaboration that occurs throughout the process.)

As Figure 6.3 shows, **strategic business architecture** is involved most heavily up front in the strategy execution life cycle to inform strategy development and evolution, architect changes, and shape initiatives, programs, projects, and investments at a macro level.

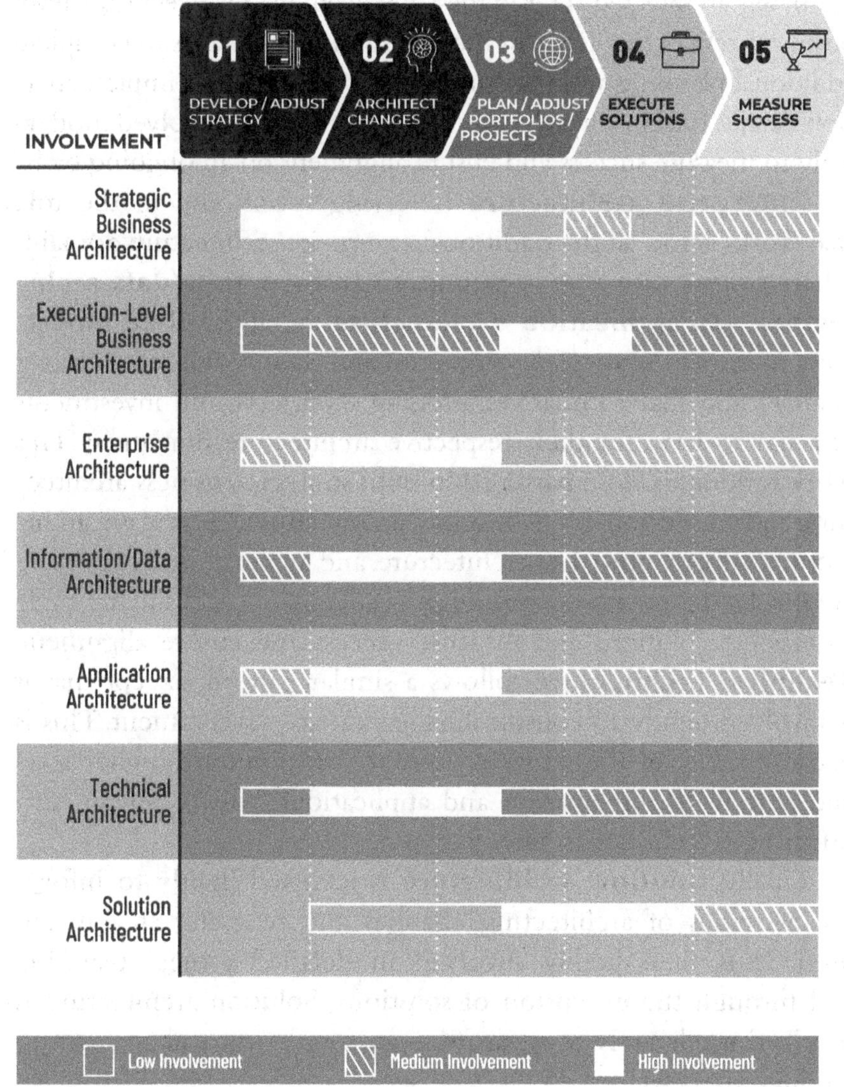

Figure 6.3 Typical architecture involvement from strategy to execution.

There is a moderate level of involvement to consult and guide as solutions are initially being developed and then again to measure success and ensure alignment on an ongoing basis. In contrast, **execution-level business architecture** is involved lightly to consult during strategy development and at an increased level as changes are being architected. The highest involvement for execution-level business architecture is across the third and fourth stages to complete additional planning and translate strategy into business implementation details. Execution-level business architecture is involved moderately to measure success and ensure alignment on an ongoing basis.

Enterprise architecture (referring specifically to the role that works across all the traditional enterprise architecture domains when it exists within an organization), **information/data architecture**, and **application architecture** are all involved moderately to inform strategy development and then heavily to architect changes and shape initiatives, programs, projects, and investments at a macro level for their respective architecture domain(s). This work is done in close partnership with strategic business architecture and execution-level business architecture. Enterprise architecture, information/data architecture, and application architecture are involved moderately throughout the remainder of the life cycle to execute solutions and measure success and ensure alignment. **Technical architecture** follows a similar pattern, except that it is involved lightly to consult during strategy development. This is because many of the conversations at that point are higher level and pertain to information and applications, which will in turn inform the technical architecture.

Finally, **solution architecture** is involved lightly to inform the activities of architecting changes and planning at a macro level. It is then highly involved in detailed project planning and through the execution of solutions. Solution architecture is involved moderately to measure success and ensure alignment on an ongoing basis.

Aligning the Business and IT Architectures

Beyond partnership between the roles and disciplines, the business and IT architectures themselves should also be linked together in the knowledge base. This not only creates a shared business language and mental model, but it is also the mechanism by which the business and IT strategies and the business and IT architectures become aligned and stay aligned.

Figure 6.4 shows a subset of key business and IT architecture domains and how they are related.

Figure 6.4 frames value streams, capabilities, and processes as key focal points, highlighting capability as the central connector. Applications, software services, and data are the domains within the IT architecture that connect to the business architecture. Applications and software services automate capabilities. (Though not shown, business units may use different applications for the same capability.) In addition, the business architecture information map in its entirety informs the data architecture. This includes business information concepts, their relationships, and basic attributes such as types and states.

Figure 6.4 also highlights the formally defined business and IT architecture domains that are described by the reference to *people, process, information, and technology:*

- Changes to *people* are targeted through the business unit and stakeholder domains.
- Changes to *processes* are targeted through the process domain.
- Changes to *information* are targeted through the information domain (specific elements are framed by an information concept such as a customer or product).
- Changes to *technology* are targeted through the application and software service domains.

The linkages from strategic business architecture to the IT architecture are key to enabling strategy execution. Recall from Chapter 4 that strategy (and its decomposition into goals, objectives, metrics, and courses of action) targets capabilities within value stream context. As Figure 6.4 reflects, the impact of changing a capability can be readily assessed by analyzing its related stakeholders, business units, processes, information, applications, and software services (and other business perspectives not shown such

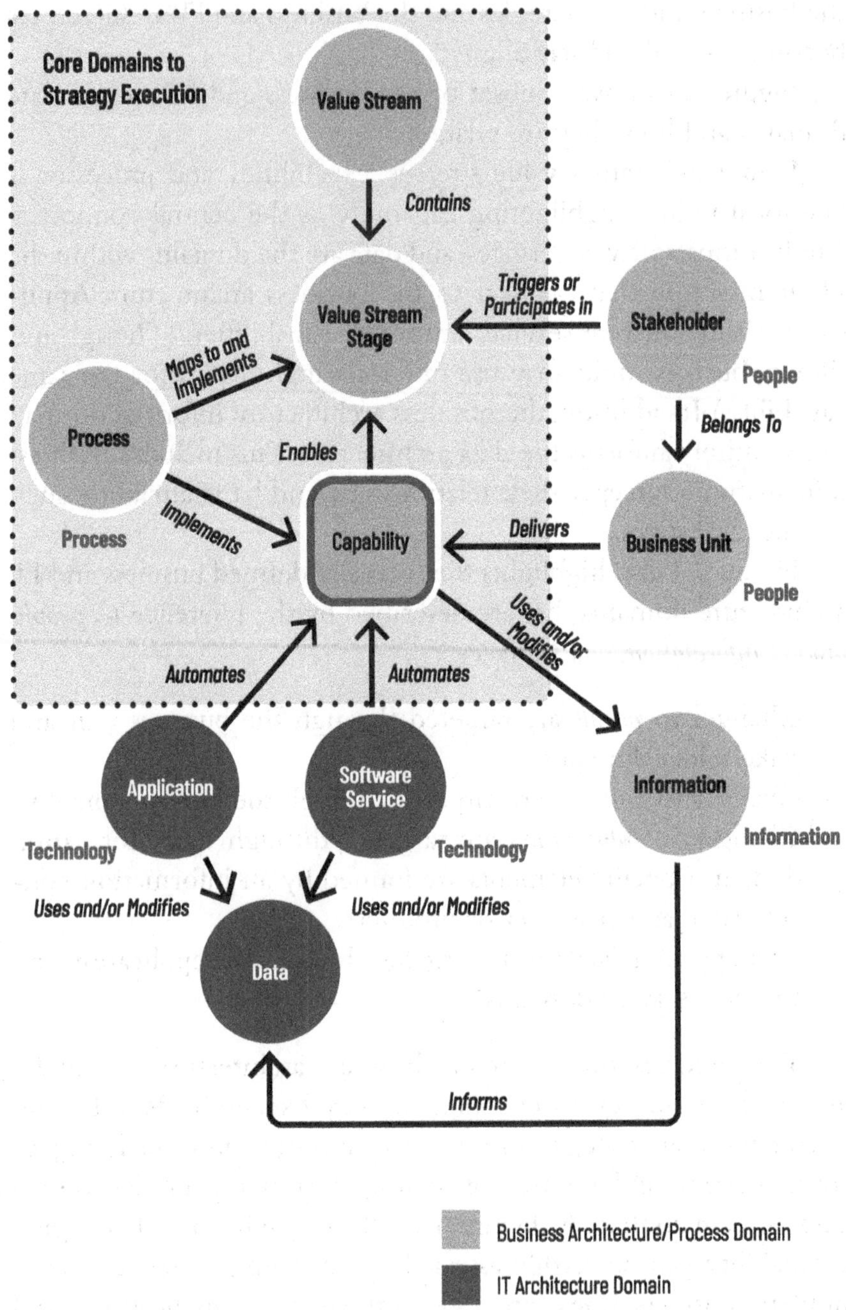

Figure 6.4 Alignment of key business and IT architecture domains.[1]

as products or policies). This impact assessment can be performed any time strategy changes as well to quickly formulate a response.

These linkages also help identify opportunities to create a composable business. Capabilities provide clearly defined, modular business building blocks that illuminate where reusable software services and applications can be created. Since capabilities enable value streams, value streams also play a role in orchestrating the usage of software services and applications.

Aligning the Business and IT Architecture Practices

For strategy execution to work effectively, there must be alignment between strategic business architecture, execution-level business architecture, and the other enterprise architecture functions. This includes aligning the roles and interactions, as well as the domains in the knowledge base, as discussed previously. The third area for alignment is between the practices. This includes intentional coordination on activities such as the following:

- Creating a cohesive understanding and playbook to describe how all architecture disciplines work together to deliver value within strategy execution and other relevant business scenarios
- Defining a shared set of architectural standards and methods (see the next aside, "Creating a Shared Architecture Framework")
- Selecting tool(s) to manage all aspects of the architecture and its linkages
- Developing and aligning road maps to mature and scale the practices over time

While this may sound obvious, a large majority of business and enterprise architecture teams are highly disjointed and do not align across any of the three areas. However, strategic business architecture and its close partnership with execution-level business architecture can be a good starting point to reinvigorate these important linkages and partnerships necessary for effective strategy execution.

Creating a Shared Architecture Framework

Some of the most commonly used industry frameworks include *The Guide to the Business Architecture Body of Knowledge* (known as the *BIZBOK® Guide*) with a focus on business architecture, as well as enterprise architecture frameworks such as the Zachman Framework, The Open Group Architecture Framework (TOGAF®), the Department of Defense Architecture Framework (DoDAF), the Ministry of Defense Architecture Framework (MoDAF), and the Federal Enterprise Architecture Framework (FEAF).

These frameworks are often primarily focused at the execution level and provide a structured approach to developing, managing, and using execution-level business and enterprise architecture to create consistency and leverage industry best practices. The frameworks may include methods, principles, guidelines, standards, notations, *metamodels* (a definition of architecture components and their relationships), reference models, and more.

Most organizations develop a hybrid architecture framework by blending and evolving components from one or more industry business and enterprise architecture frameworks to meet their needs. For example, an organization may leverage the *BIZBOK Guide* as a foundation for its business architecture practice and combine it with an enterprise architecture framework such as TOGAF as the foundation for its IT architecture disciplines.

Linking Strategic Business Architecture across the Business Ecosystem

It takes an entire ecosystem of functions and teams working together across an organization to execute strategy. Considering the vast number of teams and people involved, it underscores why the execution challenges often exist and how critical it is to have a comprehensive approach to strategy execution and the clear foundation that strategic business architecture can provide.

To execute strategy, each of these teams must:

- Understand the strategic and architectural direction.
- Inform on any relevant considerations or implications (for example, Human Resources may inform on workforce considerations or Legal may inform on compliance considerations).
- Plan and carry out the relevant changes for their function or discipline.
- Understand their interactions with related functions and disciplines and create tight linkages between them.

As Figure 6.5 shows, it can be helpful to think about the teams in two different categories, as they have similar patterns of involvement in strategy execution:

- **Business functions:** These teams carry out the major core and supporting activities of an organization. Examples of these teams include research and development (R&D), product development, marketing, sales, customer service, operations, human resources, finance, procurement, legal, risk, sustainability, and IT. Within a strategy execution context, these teams are the ones that are actually making the changes to implement the strategy. In addition, they may be informing and guiding the organization on key considerations related to the change (for example, risk, compliance, workforce, cost, or sustainability implications).
- **Strategy execution disciplines:** These teams report to the strategy execution function. They help design the organization and enable the end-to-end process from formulating ideas to delivering upon them. Examples of these teams include strategy development and evolution, innovation, business relationship management, experience design, organization design, portfolio management, business process management, business analysis,

Strategy Execution Team Involvement

Business Functions
Strategy Execution Disciplines
Business Functions make changes to the core and supporting functions of an organization to implement the strategy. They also inform and guide key considerations (e.g., risk, compliance, workforce, cost, or sustainability implications).
Strategy Execution Disciplines work closely with each other and the business functions to translate business direction into the changes needed to the design of the organization, as well as facilitate the delivery of changes from end to end.
Examples: R&D, Marketing, Sales, Operations, Customer Service, Human Resources, Finance, Risk, Legal, Procurement, Sustainability, IT
Examples: Strategy Development and Evolution, Innovation, Portfolio Management, Organizational Change Management, Experience Design, Organization Design, Business Process Management, Business Analysis

Figure 6.5 Categories of team involvement in strategy execution.

organizational change management, and of course, strategic business architecture. Within a strategy execution context, these teams work closely with each other and the business functions to translate business direction into the changes needed to the design of the organization, as well as facilitate the delivery of changes from end to end.

We will now explore these two categories of teams along with their involvement in strategy execution and their interaction with strategic business architecture.

Interaction with Business Functions

The functional areas of a business are critical for executing strategy, because as mentioned, this is where the real change happens. For context, Figure 6.6 shows a set of business functions that are common to many organizations. However, this is not an industry-specific or fully inclusive list. For example, industry-specific functions, such as manufacturing or claims, are not included. In addition, organizations may have other functions such as public relations or facilities management.

Strategic business architecture could interface with some or all of these teams on an ongoing basis throughout the strategy execution life cycle. This could include activities such as the following:

- Collaborating with Human Resources on the management of the human capital portfolio to ensure the right roles and skills are in place to enable strategy execution
- Collaborating with Corporate Finance on the many financial aspects of strategy execution, including areas such as the management of the asset portfolios of the organization discussed in Chapter 5 (projects, business capabilities, value streams, processes, technology assets, human capital, and other assets)
- Identifying and discussing impacts to the business for the purpose of informing strategic decision-making and defining a coordinated set of changes to implement strategy
- Assessing the various aspects of the business that contribute to capability effectiveness and maturity
- Collaborating on what the target-state business and technology environments should look like
- Collaborating on the scope and sequence of initiatives, portfolios, programs, and projects needed at a macro level
- Aligning on the progress of work to ensure the ongoing alignment of strategy and execution

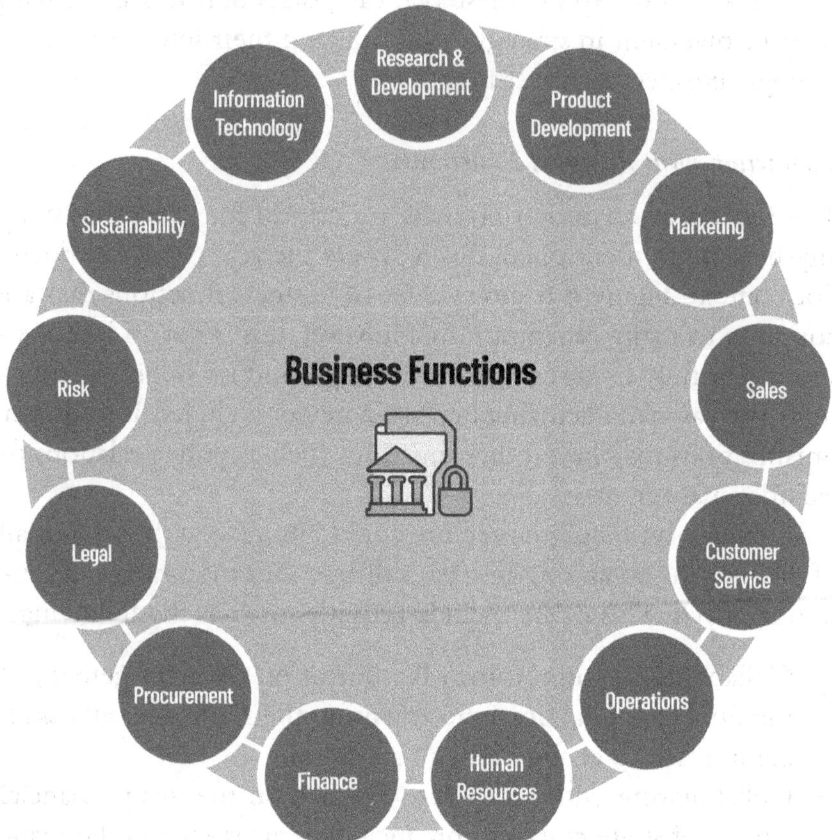

Figure 6.6 Common business functions.

- Updating the business architecture knowledge base and views to reflect updates and new information as needed (for example, adding product or policy information)

A brief description of strategy execution involvement for each of the common business functions follows.

As part of strategy development, **R&D** may be consulted to inform on market, industry, technology, or other trends. R&D identifies any intellectual property, invention, or patent considerations or impacts related to the strategy or its execution. Finally, R&D plans and executes any relevant changes necessary to implement the strategy (for example, adjusting the R&D strategy or enhancing the team's skills and expertise to best support the strategy). Strategic business architecture can facilitate the generation and sharing of innovation ideas, and identify focus areas where innovation is needed, resulting either from business priorities or from known areas of improvement. Strategic business architects also provide the tools to analyze opportunities for value to the organization and potential associated risks. They can assess the viability and impact of innovation ideas on an ongoing basis and provide a perspective on how those ideas fit within the bigger-picture strategy and priorities of the organization.

An organization's **Product Development** function may be engaged heavily during strategy development and execution, especially if the strategy and any planned business model shifts will impact the organization's current set of products and services or require new ones. Product Development also plans and executes any relevant changes necessary to products and services, as well as the capabilities that enable them (in collaboration with other business functions). ***Note:*** To inform holistic decision-making, products can be captured as part of the strategic business architecture along with their enabling capabilities.

As part of strategy development, **Marketing** and **Sales** may be consulted to inform on market segments, target audiences, and key opportunities. They also identify any considerations or impacts of the strategy and its execution, such as those related to the customer experience or salesforce. Finally, Marketing and Sales plan and execute any relevant changes necessary to implement the strategy (for example, branding modifications, promotional activities and campaign development, team training and enablement).

New or changing strategies can have a profound impact on functions such as **Customer Service** and **Operations.** These functions identify any considerations or impacts of the strategy and its execution, such as those related to the customer and omni-channel experience or the customer service and operational teams. They also plan and execute any relevant changes necessary to implement the strategy (for example, modifying processes or enhancing the teams' skills and expertise to best support the strategy).

An organization's **Human Resources** function may be engaged heavily during strategy development and execution to consult on any considerations or impacts related to the organization design, culture, workforce, workplace, compliance, diversity and inclusion, or other factors. Human Resources plays a significant role in ensuring that the right people are in the right roles and are appropriately skilled and staffed in order to effectively implement the strategy. In fact, the Human Capital portfolio focuses on prioritizing and funding these types of investments. (See Chapter 5 on strategic portfolio management for more information.) In addition, Human Resources plans and executes other relevant changes such as modifying organizational structures, reward systems, culture, talent acquisition and retention approaches, and employee experience and engagement approaches. Finally, Human Resources plays a key role in communications and organizational change management throughout strategy execution.

Finance identifies any financial, capital, tax, or compliance considerations or impacts related to the strategy or its execution. Finance also plays a key role throughout strategy execution to manage and oversee the budgets and funding for the required investments and projects. Finally, Finance plans and executes any relevant changes necessary to implement the strategy (for example, adjusting financial reporting or compliance processes).

As part of strategy development, **Procurement** may be consulted to inform on strategic sourcing strategies, supply chain strategies, and other market intelligence. Procurement identifies supply chain, sourcing, supplier, risk, or compliance considerations or impacts related to the strategy or its execution. Procurement also plays a key role throughout strategy execution to manage and oversee the vendor management and procurement processes for the required investments and projects. Finally, Procurement plans and executes any relevant changes necessary to implement the strategy (for example, implementing new sourcing strategies or selecting and managing new suppliers).

Legal identifies any corporate structure, licensing or regulatory approval, government relations, employment law, intellectual property, risk, compliance, or contractual considerations or impacts related to the strategy or its execution. Legal plays a key role throughout strategy execution to provide counsel and to ensure compliance with applicable laws and regulations. Legal also plans and executes any relevant changes necessary to implement the strategy (for example, adjusting the team's composition of skills and expertise). ***Note:*** To inform holistic decision-making, policies and regulations can be captured as part of the strategic business architecture along with the capabilities they guide and the business units that are involved.

Risk provides a comprehensive perspective on the potential strategic, market, financial, operational, supply chain, compliance, or technology risks related to the strategy and its execution. Risk also plays a key role throughout strategy execution to help the organization assess, monitor, mitigate, and respond to risks. ***Note:*** To inform holistic decision-making, risks can be captured as part of the strategic business architecture along with the value streams and capabilities they pertain to and the business units and stakeholders that are involved.

The **Sustainability** function may take different forms within an organization, such as an Environmental, Social, and Governance (ESG) or Corporate Social Responsibility (CSR) department or team. Sustainability identifies environmental or social considerations or impacts related to the strategy or its execution. Sustainability plays a key role throughout strategy execution to provide guidance on designing for sustainability and circularity, adhering to ESG standards, and reporting to and communicating with stakeholders. Finally, Sustainability plans and executes any relevant changes necessary to implement the strategy (for example, adjusting the sustainability strategy or incorporating new sustainability practices into business operations to best support the strategy). ***Note:*** To inform holistic decision-making, sustainability performance can be measured and targeted for improvement within a value streams and capability context. The strategic business architecture views (for example, business model, value network, value chain) also provide a useful canvas for redesigning an organization around sustainability and circularity.

IT identifies any technological and data considerations or impacts related to the strategy or its execution. This includes consulting on how to leverage technology for both strategic and operational advantage. IT also plays a significant role in procuring, designing, developing, delivering, and securing the technology (applications and services, data deployments, infrastructure) needed to effectively implement the strategy. In fact, the Technology Assets portfolio focuses on prioritizing and funding these types of investments. (See Chapter 5 on strategic portfolio management for more information.) IT also plans and executes any relevant changes necessary to implement the strategy (for example, adjusting the IT strategy or enhancing the team's skills and expertise to best support the strategy).

Interaction with Strategy Execution Disciplines

As we have emphasized, strategy execution needs to be approached comprehensively to achieve different and better outcomes. Fragmented organizational structures, functions, processes, and accountabilities are significant contributors to the poor strategy execution results cited earlier. Intentional collaboration among teams is valuable and necessary but has continually proven to be not enough, especially because the teams typically report to different leaders. What works is having all the relevant disciplines report to an enterprise-wide strategy execution function with centralized accountability for strategy execution outcomes.

Figure 6.7 shows a set of the main disciplines that are required to successfully align project/initiative portfolios with strategy and maintain this alignment as strategy evolves. This alignment is the heart of successful strategy execution.

Figure 6.7 does not reflect a fully inclusive list of disciplines, and the presence and naming of each may vary by organization. For example, an organization may not have a business process

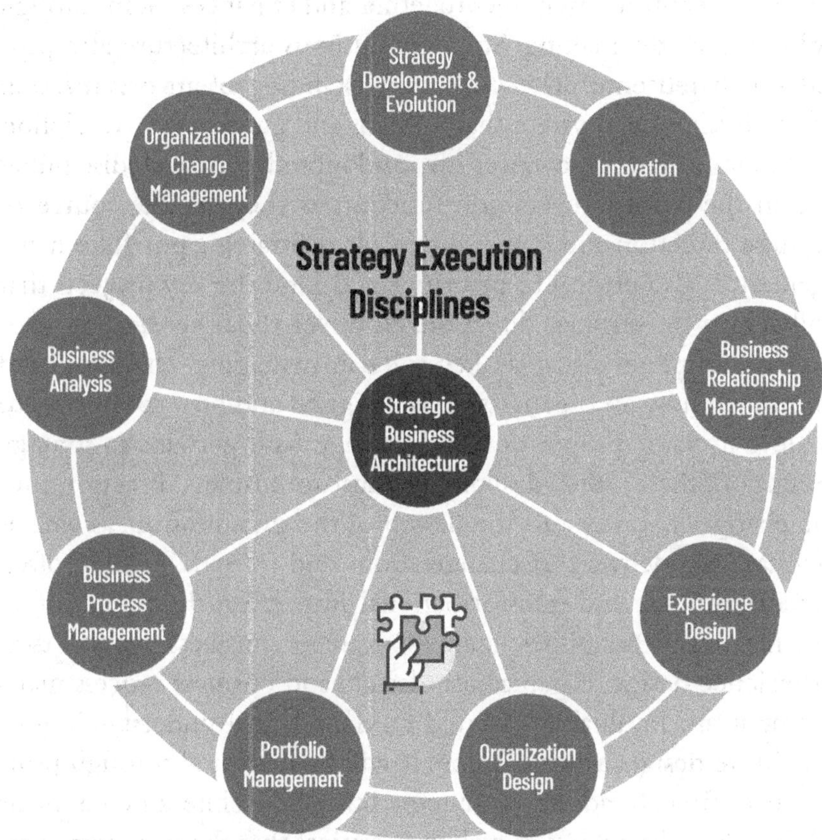

Figure 6.7 Primary strategy execution disciplines.

management discipline (or may not refer to it as such), but instead may have a lean Six Sigma discipline or an operational excellence team.

Strategy execution is truly multidisciplinary, and every team plays a unique and important role. However, Figure 6.7 shows strategic business architecture in the center as an orchestration hub for the other disciplines. This is because strategic business architecture is at the heart and is the integrating bridge discipline that brings everything together in a strategic, methodological manner. Strategic business architecture not only plays a unique orchestration role that informs and translates strategy, but also connects all the strategy execution disciplines together and enhances them through holistic decision-making. Strategic business architecture also provides a shared enterprise-wide understanding of an organization and its business ecosystem that informs and guides every discipline.

Strategy and innovation are undoubtedly critical disciplines within the strategy execution function as they are the source of business direction and new business ideas. Strategic portfolio management is also critical to prioritize and fund the key projects that will deliver the business direction. However, the other strategy execution disciplines also play key roles in managing, changing, and improving how an organization is designed and how it operates to achieve its value proposition and strategy. As it pertains to strategy execution, these other disciplines translate business direction into the changes necessary to the design of the organization, as well as facilitate the delivery of changes from end to end. Strategy often has a significant and transformational impact on the design of an organization. Disciplines such as strategic business architecture, experience design, organization design, and business process management are invaluable to build consensus and understanding of the future design, as well as how it will be delivered through projects over time. In addition, strategic business architecture connects all the other disciplines as well. It is critical that these strategy execution disciplines/functions have a common reporting structure within the strategy execution function to (1) avoid duplication of effort, (2) effectively organize and coordinate resources and efforts, and (3) ensure that all functions are "rowing in the same direction" and effectively executing current business strategy. Without a common reporting structure, the chances of these three outcomes happening consistently is very low; the organizational fragmentation that often results is a leading cause of poor strategy execution.

Figure 6.8 lists each strategy execution discipline along with an indication of high, medium, or low in terms of its level of involvement within each stage of the strategy execution process. Strategic business architecture interfaces with every one of these teams at one point during the strategy execution life cycle and on

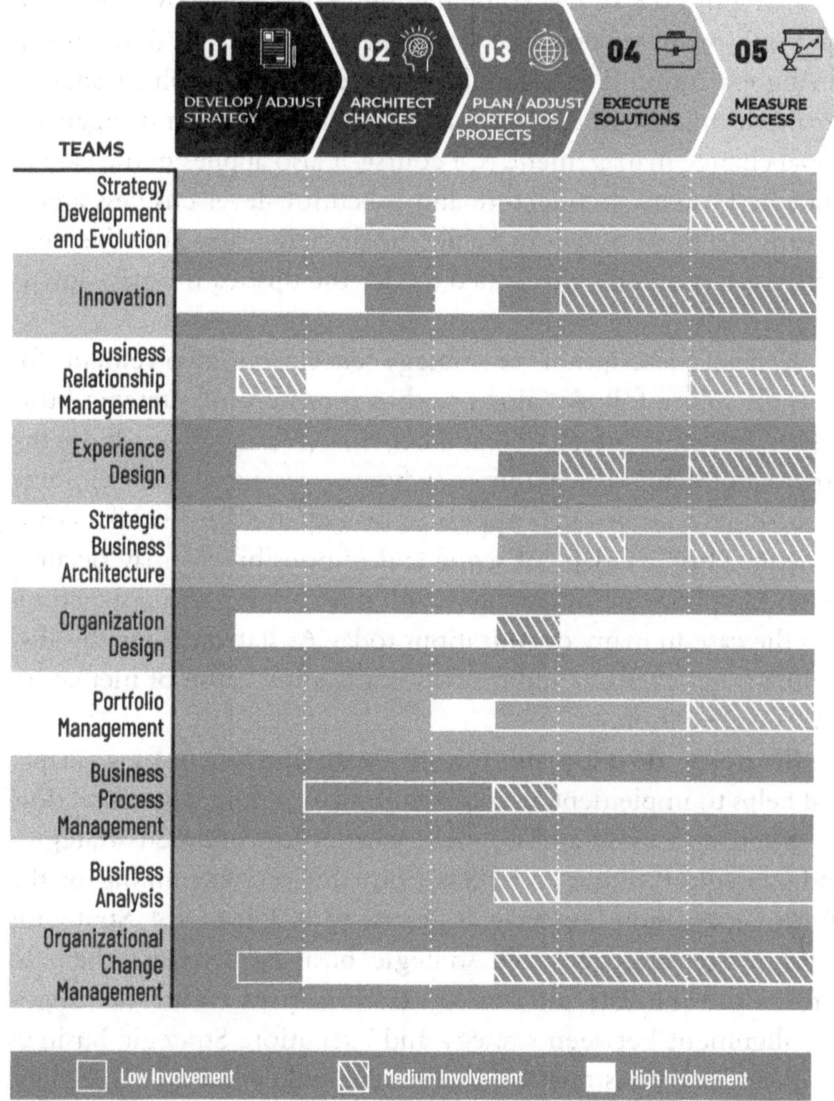

Figure 6.8 Discipline involvement in the strategy execution process.

an ongoing basis as strategy changes and evolves. For this reason, strategic business architects need to be highly fluent in other strategy execution disciplines. Some strategic business architects may even play blended roles across more than one discipline.

As Figure 6.8 shows, some disciplines play an active role both up front prior to portfolio investment, as well as downstream during execution. For example, this applies to disciplines such as organization design, business process management, and organizational change management. (Of course, it also applies in the case of strategic business architecture and execution-level business architecture.) In these situations, while the disciplines are cohesive, very different sets of skills are needed to play the upstream versus downstream roles.

A brief description of strategy execution involvement for each discipline follows, along with a summary of strategic business architecture interaction and benefits. (***Note:*** This excludes the other architecture disciplines as they were discussed earlier.) Some of these descriptions may appear to overlap and have similar components. This "overlap" of scope and responsibilities may occur if these disciplines are fragmented with different reporting structures as is the case in many organizations today. As stated earlier, this discipline fragmentation and overlap is a leading cause of ineffective strategy execution.

Strategy development and evolution formulates, adapts, and helps to implement an organization's overall strategic direction.

There is a close and ongoing partnership between strategists and strategic business architects from the very beginning of the strategy execution life cycle as described in Chapter 4. Strategists develop the strategy while strategic business architects help to inform and translate the strategy. Both help to ensure the ongoing alignment between strategy and execution. Strategic business architecture helps strategy development and evolution succeed by:

- Informing the development of strategy through an understanding of the organization's capabilities and impact analysis for different strategic options
- Consistently deconstructing strategy into its requisite components for clarity and making the information available through a reusable and scalable knowledge base

- Ensuring that the strategy is clearly communicated throughout the entire organization and in an actionable context
- Ensuring that the strategy is realized through a prioritized and rationalized set of projects

The linkages between strategy and strategic business architecture are as defined in the golden thread from Chapter 4. However, the most critical linkage is from business objectives to value streams and capabilities.

Innovation drives and facilitates the ideation, development, and implementation of creative solutions and transformative ideas within an organization. From a strategy execution context, innovation ideas can feed into planning and portfolio management when proven to be viable and relevant. Strategic business architecture should be the nexus for strategy and organizational innovation in an organization.

Innovation team members and strategic business architects can work together across the entire innovation life cycle, even outside the strategy execution life cycle. Strategic business architecture helps innovation succeed by:

- Methodically leveraging the business architecture perspectives to generate new innovation ideas (for product and service innovation, business model innovation, organizational improvement, and so on)
- Cataloging innovation ideas by capabilities to organize them and facilitate sharing
- Assessing the viability and business impact of innovation ideas
- Identifying additional business contexts and scenarios in which existing innovation ideas can be leveraged
- Defining the business priorities, needs, and timing for innovation ideas

By integrating an innovation function within the strategy execution and/or strategic business architecture functions, many organizational synergies may be fostered. Strategic business architects are typically very well connected in the organization and have identified critical subject matter experts and strategic thinkers within the organization. They often are the people who are the "clearinghouse" for ideas and are in a unique position to connect dots for internal innovation opportunities. For example, business architects can help to generate or facilitate sharing of innovation ideas and identify focus areas where innovation is needed, either resulting from business priorities or known areas of improvement. These opportunities can be framed around defined aspects of the strategic business architecture.

Business architects also provide the tools to analyze opportunities for value to the organization and potential associated risks. As mentioned earlier, they can assess the viability and impact of innovation ideas on an ongoing basis and provide a perspective on how those ideas fit within the bigger-picture strategy and priorities of the organization.

Business relationship management provides a strategic interface between a business function and one or more business partners to stimulate, surface, and shape business demand for the function's business assets and capabilities.[2] Business relationship management is included in the strategy execution function because of its key role in defining business needs and taking business direction forward into action.

Business relationship managers partner closely with strategic business architects to translate the strategy and ensure its ongoing alignment with execution. Business relationship managers and strategic business architects share a focus on improving relationships and connectivity across the organization and maximizing business value. Strategic business architecture helps business relationship management succeed by:

- Providing a go-to source of knowledge about any area of the organization, including how it connects to others, can be enhanced for value delivery, and can be optimized and aligned
- Providing a framework for understanding the internal and external relationships of an organization

- Identifying opportunities to optimize the value of strategic investments by means of a resilient, integrated environment

Strategic business architecture provides the multidimensional organizational perspectives that can better inform business relationship management and make this discipline more effective in defining business needs and taking business direction forward into action.

The **customer experience design** discipline designs the experience of a customer across all touchpoints of an organization's brand. It may be considered part of the broader umbrella of *human-centered design,* which encompasses not only experience design but other disciplines and practices such as service design, design thinking, and user experience design. Though the primary emphasis is often on an organization's customers or constituents, experience design can and should be leveraged to design employee and partner experiences as well. Experience designers typically work closely with functions such as Marketing, Customer Service, Human Resources (for employee experience), and others.

Experience design is included in the strategy execution function to bring a human-centered perspective, empathy, and experience focus to the forefront of strategy, design, and investments. It also ensures that experience design is approached holistically for the enterprise.

Strategic business architecture and experience design have a natural affinity. Strategic business architecture already provides an outside-in perspective by positioning around an external view of an organization's business ecosystem, which puts the customer and value delivery at the center. However, experience design takes it further and brings the human perspective and empathy to the forefront to truly facilitate design from the customer perspective. Experience designers and strategic business architects work in concert to translate strategy. In fact, both the strategy and the target-state customer experience design are input to the translation through the business architecture. In addition, these roles work together to assess and optimize customer, partner, and employee experiences on an ongoing basis.

Strategic business architecture helps experience design succeed by:

- Translating experience designs (for example, journeys), needs, and improvements into actionable changes that can be made to the business and technology environments
- Providing an enterprise business perspective on customer experience priorities that are harmonized with other investments, initiatives, and projects within the organization
- Creating reusable business components (capabilities) that are seamlessly orchestrated (through value streams and processes) to deliver consistent and efficient journeys to customers, employees, and partners
- Providing an enterprise-wide framework that supports shared decision-making, investment, and governance around the customer experience (and employee and partner experiences) across business units

The key linkage between experience design and strategic business architecture is from journey stages to value stream stages (which flow through to processes). Typically, multiple value streams enable a journey. (The capabilities that apply to a journey stage are obtained from the corresponding value stream stages.)

The **organization design** discipline is defined as "The deliberate process of configuring structures, processes, reward systems, and people practices and policies to create an effective organization capable of achieving the business strategy. The discipline is strategic, and its focus goes far beyond just defining the organizational structure."[3] Organization designers may be part of an organization's Human Resources department or part of a stand-alone team. If a stand-alone team exists, it typically works closely with Human Resources.

Organization design is included in the strategy execution function to bring the people perspective to the forefront of strategy, design, and investments. For example, it helps to ensure that an organization's structure, processes, and culture can support its strategy. Organization design can also offer considerations for strategic decisions such as global expansion or mergers and acquisitions.

Organization designers and strategic business architects work together at various points across strategy execution. They are both involved early on to inform strategy and then work together to translate strategy. Organization design may play an additional role downstream during execution to facilitate or deliver on the people-related changes necessary to achieve a strategy. In addition, organization designers and strategic business architects work together on an ongoing basis to assess and optimize various aspects of an organization's design as needed.

Strategic business architecture helps organization design succeed by:

- Clarifying the organization's value proposition and business direction, which is the cornerstone of the design process
- Informing organization structure decision-making by providing clarity and transparency about how an organization is structured and identifying opportunities for organizational improvement and redesign at a high level
- Identifying opportunities for lateral mechanisms to bridge silos for information sharing, decision-making, collaboration, and reusable solutions
- Providing traceability from the objectives and metrics of the enterprise, to the objectives and metrics of business units, to those used to measure the performance of individuals

The key linkage between organization design and strategic business architecture is from roles (and potentially competencies) to stakeholders. Business units and capabilities also provide highly relevant business perspectives for organization design.

Strategic portfolio management forges a critical link between the strategic planning process and the project execution process, enabling management to reach consensus on the best use of resources by focusing on the projects that are strategically aligned with the goals of the business. The role of strategic portfolio management and its interaction with strategic business architecture was discussed at length in Chapter 5. This interaction is particularly important to ensure that an organization's investments are appropriately selected, prioritized, and funded to realize the strategy. The linkage also ensures that the enterprise portfolios can be continuously *realigned* as strategy changes so that the projects in execution do not become out of date or misaligned with the organization's direction over time.

Business process management designs, optimizes, continuously monitors, and improves an organization's business processes to enhance efficiency, agility, and overall performance. Strategic business architecture helps an organization to realize its business model, and business processes help an organization to realize its operating model. As a result, these two important disciplines work together to implement change from the high-level perspective to the details.

Business process management is included in the strategy execution function because of the critical role that processes play in the strategic and operational activities that ultimately realize a strategy. It also ensures that business process management is approached holistically for the enterprise.

Strategic business architects and business process managers may collaborate (or, minimally, business process managers may consult) to identify the impacts of strategy and translate it into a set of business changes and projects—which, of course, includes business process as a key aspect. Execution-level business architects are also likely to be involved. Business process managers will play an important role downstream during execution to facilitate or deliver on the process-related changes necessary to achieve a strategy. In addition, business process managers and strategic business architects work together on an ongoing basis to design and optimize business processes and resolve issues as needed.

Strategic business architecture helps business process management succeed by:

- Providing a framework for process governance at an enterprise level (through the shared perspective of value streams)
- Identifying areas for process improvement or collaboration
- Providing an enterprise business perspective on process optimization priorities and ensuring that any improvements do not lead to suboptimization of value streams or journeys

The key linkage between business process management and strategic business architecture is from processes to value streams and from processes to capabilities. Processes map to value streams and implement the capabilities within them.

Note that when business process management is not in place or fully mature within an organization, execution-level business architects may play aspects of this role.

Business analysis analyzes and interprets business needs, facilitating communication between stakeholders, and recommending effective solutions to improve processes, systems, and outcomes within an organization.

Business analysis is included in the strategy execution function because of its key role in translating strategic business architecture into concrete requirements for projects and solutions.

When strategic business architects (and other roles) have translated the strategy into a set of business architecture–framed projects, business analysts consume the changes related to their specific project(s) (with the key inputs being capabilities and their value stream context) and stakeholders. There may be additional inputs from execution-level business architects as well. Business analysts, in collaboration with execution-level business architects and in consultation with strategic business architects, translate the changes into a set of business architecture–framed requirements for their project(s). Business analysts also may link each requirement to the business architecture capabilities and stakeholders they enable for traceability.

Business analysts should be conversant in an organization's strategic business architecture. They play a critical role in bringing its vocabulary and thinking into projects and execution teams. Business analysts can also serve as valuable stewards for the strategic (and execution-level) business architecture. For example, business analysts may uncover gaps that need to be addressed in the business architecture.

Strategic business architecture helps business analysis succeed by:

- Accelerating the definition of requirements and improving their quality and consistency
- Ensuring that requirements align back to strategy through the clear traceability from requirements to capabilities and value streams to business objectives—and that requirements can be realigned if the strategy shifts
- Facilitating the reuse of requirements (when linked to capabilities) and, thus, accelerating future projects

The key linkage between business analysis and strategic business architecture is from requirements to value streams, capabilities, and stakeholders.

Organizational change management helps organizations prepare, equip, and support individuals to successfully adopt change, ensuring a smooth transition and maximizing stakeholder engagement.

Organizational change management is included in the strategy execution function to ensure that it is treated as a strategic discipline, not an afterthought or simply a communication and training effort that occurs at the end of an project. The successful execution of strategy requires understanding, buy-in, and adoption from all stakeholders involved, so the importance of this discipline—and its up-front engagement—cannot be overstated.

The discipline of strategic business architecture is very much about change, and strategic business architects are change agents themselves. Organizational change managers and strategic business architects partner continuously from strategy to execution. Organizational change managers should be engaged early on when business direction is still being shaped so that they can consult on an organization's capacity for change. Organizational change managers and strategic business architects partner closely to assess the potential scope and impacts of change as strategy is being translated.

Strategic business architecture helps organizational change management succeed by:

- Informing the assessment of what will change, for whom, how, and when
- Ensuring that the collective set of changes delivered across projects is consumable by individual stakeholders

Organizational change managers use strategic business architecture to help assess the impacts of change and to inform the change management strategy. For example, value streams and capabilities convey what is being changed and the scope of impact. Other domains (such as products, policies, information, or initiatives) may be used to assess impacts along with corresponding changes to jobs, organizational structure, processes, technology, or even experiences. Business units and stakeholders convey who will be impacted by the changes, both internally and externally.

Figure 6.9 visualizes the key linkages within the business knowledge base described throughout this section between strategic business architecture and other disciplines. These linkages enable the flexible and continual evolution of an organization's strategy and its execution along with it. For example, if strategy changes, the impacted capabilities and value streams can be traced to their related components shown in the figure, such as portfolios/projects and requirements, roles, journeys, processes, and technologies (applications, software services, and data entities).

Strategic and Execution-Level Business Architecture and the Strategy Execution-Level Disciplines

Project portfolio management is one of the main bridges from strategic business architecture to tactical, execution-level projects and execution-level business architecture. There are a few key

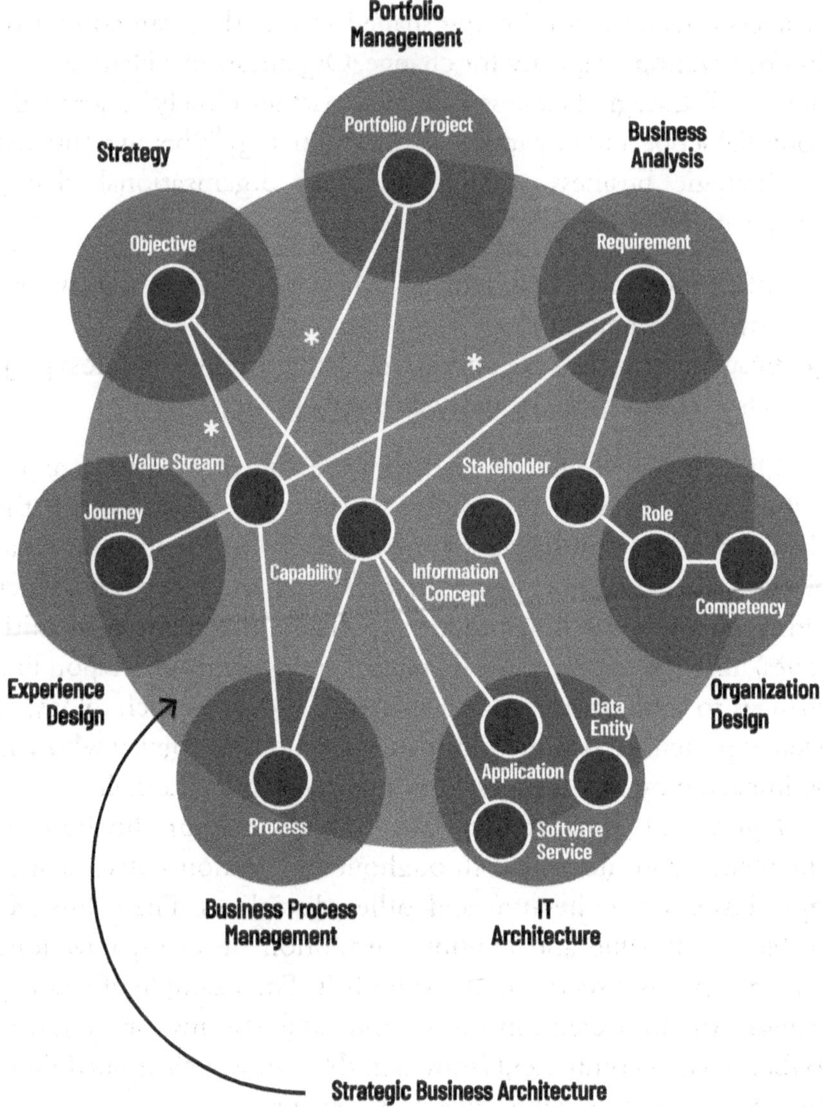

Figure 6.9 Linking strategic business architecture with other strategy execution disciplines.[4]

execution-level disciplines that are critical to further driving the strategic direction and strategic business architecture into execution. These include program and project management, IT architecture (covered earlier), and solution architecture. While these teams may not be the focus of interactions for strategic business architects, they certainly are for execution-level business architects.

Project management plans, organizes, and oversees the successful execution of projects, ensuring that they are completed on time and within budget and that they meet predefined objectives. **Program management** strategically aligns and coordinates a set of related projects to achieve an organization's overarching goals. Strategic business architecture's role in strategically shaping and prioritizing work as part of strategy translation can be invaluable downstream to program and project managers. When a large scope of work is being defined, such as in the case of a strategy or transformation, strategic business architects may work in partnership with enterprise or IT architects and program managers to scope, shape, and estimate programs and projects at a macro level. Execution-level business architects collaborate to help plan projects at a micro level downstream. Program and project managers, strategic business architects, and execution business architects also work together on an ongoing basis to ensure that the projects being executed align back to the strategy—and can be realigned if the strategy shifts.

Strategic and execution-level business architecture helps program and project management succeed by:

- Ensuring that projects are defined with clear, mutually exclusive scopes and are anchored back to the specific business focal points that are changing
- Maximizing resource utilization by scoping and sequencing projects in the most logical way from an enterprise perspective
- Aligning projects to strategy, ensuring that the most important initiatives are prioritized at the right time
- Harmonizing solution reuse and facilitating integration across initiatives, programs, and projects
- Ensuring that the collective changes delivered across programs and projects are consumable by individual stakeholders
- Identifying stakeholders, policies, risks, and any other aspects tied to capabilities up front as projects are defined

- Accelerating the definition of requirements and improving their quality and consistency
- Providing a common business language shared by all roles (business or technology)

The key linkage between program and project management and strategic business architecture is from initiatives to value streams and capabilities (and also back to objectives).

Solution architecture defines solutions within the context of an project, informed by a relevant slice of input across the traditional enterprise architecture perspectives, but informed by the full enterprise view as well for context. Since solution architects are truly working in the execution space, their primary interaction is with execution-level business architects, though strategic business architects may consult on strategic and architectural direction. Together, execution-level business architects and solution architects ensure that business needs are met and that solutions delivered align with the business architecture and business direction.

Strategic and execution-level business architecture helps solution architecture succeed by:

- Defining clear scope and business needs for solutions that directly align with business strategy and priorities
- Providing a comprehensive view of how the organization is structured and what its direction is to enable solution architects to design solutions that consider the broader business context
- Identifying opportunities for reusable solutions

Next Steps

The broad collection of teams and disciplines involved in executing strategy brings a robust and diverse set of abilities and perspectives to the process. Each function and discipline has a unique purpose and approach, and together they can deliver great strategy at scale, especially when they are connected and orchestrated by strategic business architecture.

However, to maximize the value of these teams, they must share a common understanding of the end-to-end strategy execution process and how to work together within it. The "how to work together" requirement is best resolved with a common reporting structure that is designed to minimize duplication of skills and efforts and maximize strategy execution efficiency and effectiveness. As discussed in Chapter 1, the five-stage strategy execution approach can provide a valuable organizing construct to help integrate the teams. For example, organizations have created strategy execution engagement models within the context of this approach and even full playbooks that describe the outcomes, activities, inputs, outputs, roles, and interactions for each stage.

Organizations must see strategy development and refinement to execution as a critical and cohesive process, just as important as any other. In fact, at the end of the day, isn't it the responsibility of everyone in the organization to execute the business strategy? No other goal or objective is more important to the success and viability of the organization, and structuring to effectively execute the business strategy should be the paramount concern of all leaders. This means there must also be transparency and executive ownership and accountability from end to end.

With a solid understanding of the comprehensive approach to strategy execution and how to organize the teams for success, we will now focus on how to build the strategic business architecture function to effectively support the process in Chapters 7 and 8.

STRATEGY EXECUTION ORGANIZATIONAL ASSESSMENT

Reflect on the following questions to assess how well strategy execution is working in your organization based on the concepts from Chapter 6. Please refer to the scoring guidance provided in Chapter 1.

1. All relevant strategy execution–related disciplines (including strategic business architecture) report to an enterprise-wide strategy execution function with centralized accountability for strategy execution outcomes.
2. All relevant strategy execution–related functions and disciplines understand their role and how to interact with other teams within the context of a defined, comprehensive end-to-end approach from strategy development through strategy execution.
3. Our organization has an execution-level business architecture function, it operates effectively, and it works in close partnership with strategic business architecture throughout strategy execution.
4. Our strategic business architecture function works in close partnership with our enterprise and IT architecture function throughout strategy execution.
5. Our strategic business architecture, execution-level business architecture, and enterprise/IT architecture practices share common architecture standards, methods, and frameworks where applicable.
6. Our knowledge base includes linkages from the strategic business architecture domains to the IT architecture domains, and this information is kept current.
7. Our knowledge base includes linkages from the strategic business architecture domains to the domains of other relevant strategy execution disciplines, and this information is kept current.

Chapter 7

Building the Strategic Business Architecture Function and Integration with Strategic Planning

Building a truly strategic business architecture function is a difficult task because there are very few solid exemplars to study. As we've discussed in earlier chapters, a strategic business architecture function that informs enterprise-wide strategy and facilitates the execution of the enterprise strategy must be integrated with strategic planning. This chapter will explore major success factors for strategic business architecture, especially effective value measurement and communication. We will also discuss critical competencies and skills needed for success, as well as the significant potential for innovation facilitation across the organization.

Major Success Factors for Strategic Business Architecture

Several critical factors enable successful strategic business architecture. Strategic business architecture requires the leadership of the strategic planning function to understand the value that such a practice brings to the strategy execution process. As you start out in this journey, it's often not enough for senior leadership to "get it"; you must also be able to demonstrate and communicate the value strategic business architecture brings to the strategy execution process. We will explore this topic in depth later in this chapter. First, let's look at several critical success factors for strategic business architecture.

Integration with Strategic Planning and Structuring the Strategic Business Architecture Practice

For strategic business architecture to inform strategy development and facilitate strategy execution, it must have a strategic position that spans the enterprise. Strategic business architecture provides an enterprise-wide set of information that informs strategy development and execution and must report to the strategy execution function in order to effectively facilitate this critical role. This integration is happening in some organizations today but is in its early stages. One of the first steps in the integration process is the realization by the leaders of the strategic planning function of the many benefits that a strategically oriented business architecture practice brings to the strategy execution challenge. This is one of the main purposes of this book. Next, the strategic business architecture professionals need to demonstrate (and measure) that the business architecture process can produce greatly enhanced effective strategy execution. A process for measuring this value, as well as a process for thinking about how to progress through this process, will be discussed later in this chapter.

In Chapter 6, we discussed many aspects of building a strategic business architecture function. A strategic business architecture practice must be positioned to have the same scope of authority as the strategic planning group in which it is located. For example, in a larger organization, strategic planning might be organized with a corporate strategic planning group that has oversight with divisional strategic planning functions. Strategic business architecture should be organized the same way with a corporate function that has oversight and integration with divisional functions.

Building the Right Competencies, Skills, and Staffing

In addition to the correct positioning in the organization, the right mix of competencies and skills must be built for an effective strategic business architecture practice to flourish. Many legacy execution-level business architecture practices define what they do and how they organize their resources based on a one-size-fits-all model rather than with a view toward strategic stakeholder value. We will discuss the concept of strategic stakeholder value later in this chapter.

The strategic business architecture operating model creates an outside-in operating model that focuses on strategic stakeholders and ensures that your strategic business architecture ecosystem delivers the appropriate value. An effective strategic business architecture ecosystem is essential for resolving possible conflicting objectives and priorities of strategic stakeholders and the effects on possible changes to strategy. Each service provided by the strategic business architecture practice requires a set of capabilities that the strategic business architecture ecosystem must mature for the operating model to become effective. Soft skills are the foundation of an effective strategic business architecture ecosystem. Successful strategic business architecture ecosystems require deep business domain knowledge and analysis skills, as well as the soft skills of facilitation, diplomacy, negotiation, and communication. Having technical skills without these soft skills is a recipe for failure.

The strategic business architecture function should contribute to the development and ongoing evolution of strategy, as well as be the owner of the resulting strategic road maps and strategy execution process. In this context, the strategic business architecture operating model needs to address strategic stakeholder needs, provide accountability, and be the source for different layers of enterprise-wide business knowledge and understanding. Key strategic stakeholders, and their needs, will vary throughout the strategy-to-execution process. The strategic business architecture ecosystem performs various roles and delivers specific value for each activity within this end-to-end process.

Common roles for strategic business architecture in the strategy execution process include strategy informer, strategy influencer, strategy translator, portfolio shaper/executor, and strategy to execution aligner/orchestrator. Each role has a different set of strategic stakeholders, each requiring a different engagement model that includes an understanding of value expected, as well as information needed and produced.

The strategy influencer role assists strategic planning by analyzing internal and external business environment data to help define strategic objectives. As discussed in Chapter 3, business architecture techniques and tools are ideal for providing this contextual data. For example, strategic business architecture will provide the information and enterprise-wide perspectives that highlight the areas, such as business capabilities, that need investment to enable the strategy. In addition, strategic business architecture can uncover new innovations, customer value, and products and services through evolving the business model or reconfiguring existing capabilities and value streams in different ways. The strategy influencer role provides data, insights, and recommendations to strategic planning efforts that help guide strategy and changes to strategy.

The strategy translator role defines the changes to the business environment that are necessary to achieve the strategy, oriented around capabilities. This requires close collaboration with all business functions and strategy execution disciplines discussed in Chapter 6. The strategy translator role then clearly presents the investments required at each stage of the strategy execution process and helps investment boards make better funding decisions that are better aligned with strategic priorities and based on an enterprise perspective. This role also requires a good working relationship with the finance organization and related internal investment/asset management functions that provide information such as the consolidated costs of resources, assets, and processes across the organization.

The portfolio shaper/executor role works with portfolio management functions to inform and guide the strategy execution road map into a set of actionable and executable projects. Portfolio managers are the access points for a holistic view of an organization's capacity to change. The portfolio shaper/executor role requires good relationships with business and information technology (IT) subject matter experts. Line-of-business executives, operations managers, and business process analysts provide information about business and operations, including underlying value streams, workflows, and procedural guidelines needed to develop the enterprise-wide understanding needed for effective strategy execution.

The strategy to execution aligner/orchestrator role works with portfolio managers and strategic planners along with execution-level business architects, enterprise architects, and execution teams to ensure that the projects and solutions being delivered continuously stay aligned to the strategy and ultimately achieve the defined business outcomes.

The strategic business architecture function must not only see the big picture when looking across multiple change initiatives, but also must have a balance of hard and soft skills. Core hard skills are essential for developing and analyzing the architectural artifacts that assist decision-making. Soft skills enable the strategic business architect to collaborate effectively with the various contributors to the strategic business architecture and its evolution.

It is common in many professions for an individual to wear many hats. However, in large organizations, professional responsibilities may disperse across a number of people due to the specialized skills required. The strategic business architect role is one of those professions—it often spreads across a number of business architects and subject matter experts. The set of strategic business architecture role competencies includes the following:

- **Business and organization knowledge:** Strategic business architects must understand the enterprise business model and the organizational structure of the enterprise. They must have a solid understanding of environmental challenges, strategic objectives, and organizational strengths and weaknesses and be able to provide solid data and insights to help guide changes in strategy and provide the organizational understanding needed to effectively execute strategy.
- **Proficiency in strategic business architecture ecosystem components:** To develop the organizational understanding and perspective needed to create and maintain the alignment between the project execution layer and strategy, strategic business architects must be proficient in models and methods that comprise the strategic business architecture ecosystem. An understanding of these components and how they interrelate with each other will enable the multifaceted organizational analysis and understanding needed for effective strategy execution. They must also be able to apply holistic and architectural thinking to organization design and strategy execution.
- **Strategic planning process literacy:** To work effectively with strategic planning, an understanding of the strategic planning process followed in one's organization is needed.

- **Problem-solving techniques:** Strategic business architects often rely on techniques such as strengths, weaknesses, opportunities, and threats (SWOT) analysis, root-cause analysis, and scenarios analysis to understand complex problems and address incomplete and conflicting information, which is common in a business strategy setting.
- **Financial analysis:** Strategic business architects must have financial analysis and reporting skills. Making the right investment decisions is an important part of the overall strategy execution equation.
- **Enterprise technology literacy:** Strategic business architects must communicate and collaborate with technology executives and technical architects to ensure alignment of business and technology strategy, planning, and road maps. They must also have a command of how technology can be leveraged for strategic advantage and operational effectiveness. Almost all initiatives today involve technology, and strategic business architects must have a working knowledge of enterprise-level technologies to maximize effectiveness.

The preceding set of competencies include the core hard skills needed for success as a strategic business architect, but hard skills alone are not enough for success. Effective strategic business architects also must excel at a set of softer skills. Soft skills are often considered people-oriented skills, as well as abstract reasoning skills. These soft skills are not innate and can be learned. They include skills such as the following:

- **Communication skills:** Strategic business architects need to communicate effectively with a wide variety of stakeholders at different levels in the organization. This includes communicating in verbal and written format, with the ability to tell stories and create visualizations that simplify the complex and bring people together. Strategic business architects will need to possess empathy and identify appropriate tools and methods of communication that are appropriate for each stakeholder.

- **Negotiation and influence skills:** Strategic business architects must operate effectively in environments where they meet many stakeholders, each with different goals, agendas, values, and beliefs. They must build a good rapport and level of trust with all stakeholders to ensure that conflicts are resolved in a reasonable and timely manner. The strategic business architect must understand when to compromise and when to be assertive.

  Influencers have a unique skill set, and there is often a positive energy about them. They understand how to generate a buzz about the things they want to change. They have the ability to gain support, inspire others, and create relationships, but more important, they engage peoples' imaginations.
- **Diplomacy skills:** Strategic business architects must have skills to persuade others, particularly skeptics, to build consensus and win allies who can be valuable contributors. Diplomacy skills often go hand in hand with negotiation skills, but they are not the same—someone can be an effective negotiator but a poor diplomat, and vice versa. The combination of these skill sets makes for a very effective strategic business architect.
- **Facilitation skills:** Strategic business architects should have strong skills to facilitate problem solving and collaboration among groups of key internal and external stakeholders.
- **Innovation and creativity:** Strategic business architects are positioned to have unique views into the larger enterprise and to connect dots that others are not in a position to see. These connections can be the source of great internal innovation if identified and connected.
- **Leadership skills:** Effective strategic business architects must inspire confidence and garner respect from a wide variety of stakeholders while knowing that it is not possible to please all the people all the time—those who attempt to please everyone

please no one and are very often ineffective leaders and managers. Strategic business architects are leaders for change.

- **Decision-making skills:** Decision-making can be hard. Decisions have consequences—and decision-makers must be willing to take on that responsibility. Decision-making requires skills such as fact finding, big-picture thinking, creativity, analytical ability, emotional intelligence, and assertiveness. Good decision-making often requires the ability to quickly locate and process information.

While it might not be possible for one person to possess all these critical hard and soft skill sets, it is important that your strategic business architecture team has members with these skill sets and that you have the people with the right skills in the right roles for success.

Value Measurement for Strategic Business Architecture

Another critical success factor for strategic business architecture is the establishment of a strategically oriented value measurement program. A well-developed value measurement program that is aligned with your key stakeholders and core business capabilities keeps your strategic business architecture practice in alignment with the value measures of the key components of your organization. Strategic value measurement is consistently cited as a top area of importance in a wide variety of organizations, but unfortunately, it is also consistently cited as one of the areas of lowest maturity. Developing an effective value measurement and communication strategy for strategic business architecture is the single most important thing that you can do to ensure the strategic success of business architecture in your organization.

This section describes a process for deriving value metrics that align with the strategic value drivers particular to an organization—those important to both the core business capabilities of the organization, as well as its key stakeholders. This process ensures that an organization will select the optimal set of metrics—those that have the greatest likelihood of demonstrating the value that strategic business architecture has produced for the organization. The process also ensures that the metrics selected align with the strategic value measures utilized by the core capabilities of the organization as well as the measures utilized by key stakeholders. Aligning the strategic business architecture value measurement program this way allows you to directly show how strategic business architecture positively impacts measures that matter to the rest of the organization.

According to the maxim often (incorrectly) attributed to Peter Drucker, "What gets measured gets managed." A corollary to this maxim might be, "What gets measured gets executed."

The path that your strategic business architecture practice takes is in large part dependent on what you measure and how effectively you communicate the strategic value of your efforts to those who matter.

Measurement is not a new concept. We deal with measurement in some form or another in our daily lives. Organizations rely on metrics to assess and improve customer satisfaction, time-to-market factors, and other innovative processes for improving their performance. The term *metrics* refers to a series of measurement steps: defining the measure, deciding how the measurement will be carried out (which may involve mathematical calculations), choosing who will be involved in the measuring process, and knowing the source/origin of the data. The key to effective strategy execution is not just data, but also people with the proper skills and perspectives to utilize the data for effective strategy execution.

A Comprehensive Approach to Establishing Strategic Value Measures

Strategic business architecture, as defined and explained throughout this book, requires measures of success that are aligned with the strategic objectives of the organization. Identifying these measures and keeping them aligned with changes in strategic objectives is the challenge. This requires thorough and thoughtful analysis. It also requires a logical and repeatable process that all involved understand. The following strategic value measurement framework provides guidance on where to focus value measurement efforts for maximum strategic impact. The framework consists of the following seven steps:

1. **Key stakeholder analysis/value mapping:** Determines what value measures are the most important and most frequently cited among the organization's key stakeholders. This step answers questions such as:
   - Who are our stakeholders, and which ones are key strategic stakeholders?
   - What do the key stakeholders value?
   - What value measures do we use?
2. **Core business capability analysis/value mapping:** Helps in the understanding, categorizing, and prioritizing of key strategic business capabilities and then determining what value measures are needed for identified high-value business capabilities.
3. **Key stakeholder and core business capability value measures mapping and analysis:** Determines how much of an intersection exists between identified key stakeholder value measures and core business capability value measures.
4. **Metrics selection:** Helps select those metrics that are of importance to key stakeholders and core business capabilities and that strategic business architecture can impact.
5. **Project selection:** Selects which projects will best demonstrate their strategic value to the organization. This step creates a strategic progression of projects designed to progress and expand the demonstration of the strategic value to the organization.
6. **Performance-improvement considerations:** Ensure that the strategic value measurement set continually aligns with

changes in the composition and value sets of the key stakeholders and core business capabilities.

7. **Communications considerations:** Ensure that effective strategic value communications plans are developed for different key stakeholder groups.

These steps are performed on an ongoing basis and are closely interconnected. The results of this process are: (1) a set of metrics that are valued by key strategic parts of the organization that can be positively impacted by strategic business architecture, (2) a strategic progression of projects related to this set of metrics, (3) a communications plan that will ensure that value is properly communicated to the key strategic parts of the organization, and (4) a metrics-governance plan that ensures that the strategic value metrics stay aligned with organizational and strategic changes. There are many dozens of possible metrics for adoption that measure different aspects of the strategy execution process. The organization should adopt no more than 8 to 10 metrics initially.

Process for Determining Strategic Business Value Metrics

Value measurement is consistently cited as a top area of importance for many organizations, but it is also consistently cited as one of the areas of lowest maturity. Robert Kaplan and David Norton state that "strategy is based on a differentiated customer value proposition. Satisfying customers is the source of sustainable value creation." The key to a successful value measurement program is to identify metrics that correlate to business key performance indicators (KPIs). While this makes sense to most people, correctly identifying a reasonable number of high-value metrics that are meaningful to the greatest number of strategic areas of the organization is a very difficult endeavor.

The problem is not a lack of metrics; it is knowing which metrics make sense for your organization and will provide the most strategic "value" for the effort required. According to Michael Porter, there are three components of stakeholder value:[1]

- **Economic value:** The financial impact of the investment. What will be your return on investment (ROI)? What will it do for the company financially?
- **Business value:** The primary consideration to the user of the solution. What can the investment do for the organization and how can it increase productivity, efficiencies, and effectiveness for those who use the solution?
- **Personal value:** More of an intangible value that answers the questions: What will the decision do for me personally? Will I get a promotion, a bonus, or peace of mind, or will I improve my influence with other organizations?

Many metrics measure aspects of economic and business value. Personal value, while an important consideration, is not easily quantifiable.

There are many stakeholders and value propositions to consider, and it is not feasible to align the value measurement program to each and every one. So, how do you select those key stakeholders and value propositions with which to align your efforts? The strategic value measurement framework provides guidance on where to focus value measurement efforts. The next sections explore the seven steps mentioned in the previous section in greater detail.

Stakeholder Analysis/Value Mapping

First, we must define and identify the key strategic stakeholders. A stakeholder is anyone who can affect or is affected by an organization, strategy, or project. Mind mapping is a useful way of visually identifying stakeholders. There are many methods of stakeholder analysis, and any method can be utilized as long as the method analyzes two major characteristics of stakeholders:

- Interest/impact of stakeholders
- Influence/power of stakeholders

Once the stakeholders' interests have been mapped, they can then be prioritized in order of importance. Different methodologies suggest different ways of analyzing stakeholders, some complex and some very simple. A common approach is to map the interest and power or influence of each stakeholder group on a four-quadrant graph, as shown in Figure 7.1.

Key stakeholders are identified as those stakeholders who have high interest/impact in the strategy execution process and who also have high influence/power in the organization. This process identifies which of the many stakeholders in a given organization are key stakeholders. Strategic value measurement efforts should focus on the value measures that are important to the key stakeholders.

The process then analyzes the economic and business values of the identified key stakeholders and determines which of these value measures strategic business architecture can most directly impact. Personal value considerations are typically nonquantifiable but should still be tracked to provide an overall picture of the value considerations for each key stakeholder. Next, list each financial and economic value consideration and how often each occurs between the different key stakeholders. A frequency diagram is produced for the financial and economic value considerations. A frequency diagram could also be produced for the personal value considerations to determine which personal/political value considerations occur most frequently between the different key stakeholders. The frequency is a count of the number of times the consideration is cited in the analysis.

Business Capability Analysis/Value Mapping

Next, identify core strategic business capabilities by conducting a capability mapping exercise to understand, categorize, and prioritize business capabilities. (Refer back to the rating approaches discussed for capability assessments in Chapter 4.) The goal in this step is to identify the economic and business values associated with each high-value capability and identify which of these values strategic business architecture can most directly impact.

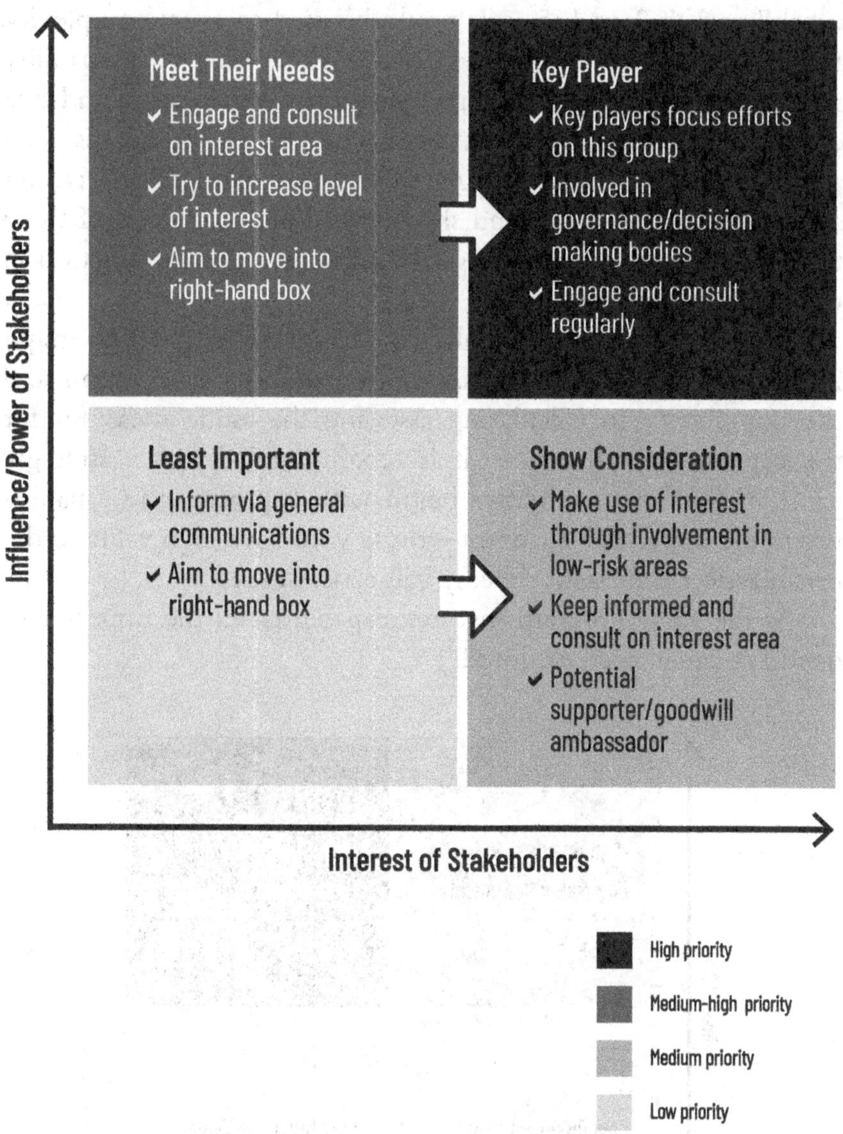

Figure 7.1 Sample stakeholder quadrant graph.

Strategic value to the organization is determined by having the leadership of the organization rank the relative value to the organization of identified capabilities. The complexity of assessing the value of the capability is determined by accessing the amount, type, and location of data needed to assess the value of a given capability. A 1–3 or 1–5 scale could be used to assess complexity. For example, if the data needed to assess the value of a capability resides in three different departments of the organization and two of these departments are difficult to access on a regular basis, then this capability would rate a higher complexity rating. These ratings are somewhat subjective and should be done by a team of three to five people from the strategic business architecture function in order to achieve consensus.

Figure 7.2 shows a sample four-quadrant graph. The graph illustrates the value of the capabilities to the organization and the complexity in calculating/assessing the value measures for the capability. In this case, it is recommended that a strategic value measurement initiative begin with exploring the capabilities in the upper-left quadrant—those who have high value to the organization and relatively easy value assessments.

As the value program matures, capabilities in the upper-right quadrant can also be explored.

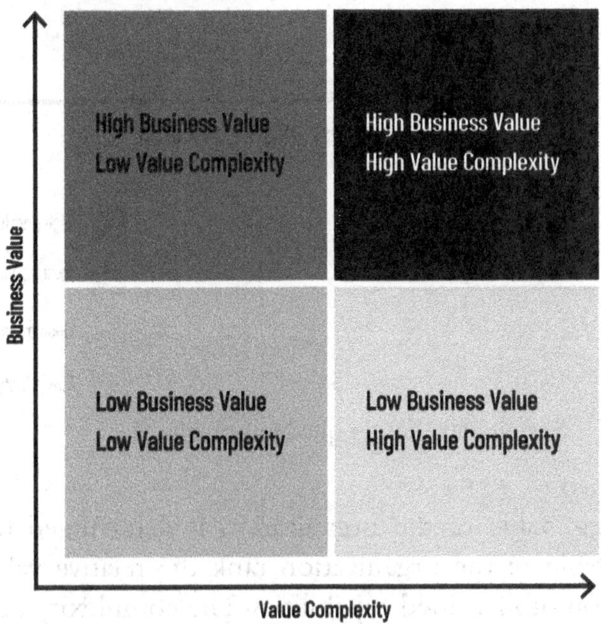

Figure 7.2 Sample capability quadrant graph.

Next, key capabilities with high business value and reasonable value complexity should be assessed for their financial, economic, and personal value considerations. As with key stakeholder value analysis, key business capability value analysis includes metrics, such as ROI, for financial and economic value considerations. Personal value considerations are typically nonquantifiable but should still be tracked to provide an overall picture of the value considerations for each key capability.

Next, just like the key stakeholder value analysis, list each financial and economic value consideration and how often each occurs between the different core capabilities. A frequency diagram should be produced for the financial and economic value considerations. A frequency diagram could also be produced for the personal value considerations to determine which personal/political value considerations occur most frequently between the different key capabilities.

> Note that in some organizations, capabilities may not be well understood and/or have associated value metrics. This should be viewed as an opportunity rather than a setback. This is an opportunity to assist the organization in better understanding strategic capabilities and helping the owners of these capabilities to better demonstrate their value to the organization by establishing value metrics for the capabilities (and value metrics that strategic business architecture can positively impact).

Stakeholder and Business Capability Value Measures Mapping and Analysis

Next, the identified key stakeholder value metrics are compared with the identified key business capability value metrics. Those metrics that appear in both areas are the business value metrics that have the greatest potential for impact on the largest portion of the organization. In most organizations, there will be considerable overlap between the value measures of the key stakeholders and the value measures of the core capabilities, as shown in Figure 7.3.

Metrics Selection

If more than 10 metrics fall into the area of high-impact metrics, then a discussion on which 10 metrics can be most positively impacted by strategic business architecture is needed in order to determine which 10 metrics to include in the initial strategic value measurement program. Those metrics that occur more frequently have greater potential to impact the organization.

If the strategic business architecture practice can demonstrate an ability to positively impact these metrics, value demonstration to the organization will be apparent.

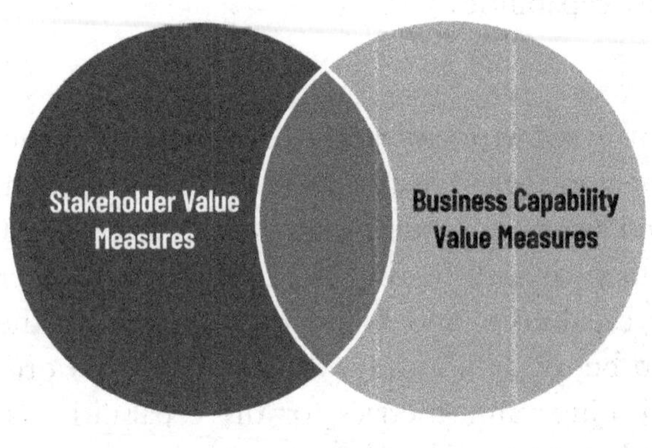

Figure 7.3 Overlap area between key stakeholder and core capability value measures.

Metrics Aggregation

Aggregation of different in-kind metrics is a common value measurement challenge. The most common aggregation problem is the use of nonquantitative (or qualitative) metrics. Quantitative metrics are the numbers that are readily measured and are often financial in nature. Quantitative metrics help crunch the numbers and determine ROI. While quantitative metrics focus on the hard numbers, qualitative metrics are based on the quality of responses derived from documents, interviews, and surveys. Qualitative metrics are often "fuzzier" and hard to quantify and, as a result, are often not used in value measurement. However, some of the biggest impacts made from strategic business architecture initiatives are in qualitative areas.

There are many methods for deriving quantitative measures and results from qualitative data. We will not go into that detail here but will simply emphasize that qualitative data should not be ignored simply because there are no associated hard measures. Qualitative research is important because it generates data that can provide in-depth insight into a question or topic, and techniques exist to quantify the data obtained from qualitative research. Qualitative data is often very insightful and important for true value measurement.

Metrics Governance

A periodic review of the selected metrics should include representatives from key strategic stakeholder groups, as well as representatives from the core strategic business capabilities. These groups are included to ensure that the set of selected metrics is in alignment with any changes in the values of the key stakeholders and key business capabilities. It is important to annually review metrics for their continued relevance. These annual meetings should be conducted strategically and serve multiple purposes. These meetings are a chance for the strategic business architecture practice to demonstrate how much it has learned about these key areas of the organization and how much their efforts have positively impacted these areas over the last year, as well as to discuss plans for further positive impact over the next year.

Another purpose of these meetings is to demonstrate that the strategic business architecture team plans to keep its value measure program (and knowledge of the organization) continually aligned with these key areas of the organization and intends to focus on helping these areas improve the metrics that they are measured on as business priorities and strategies change over time. Once the strategic business architecture practice achieves these goals through a strategically developed value measure program and process, the role of an indispensable strategic advisor and partner is assured.

Project Selection

Once the initial strategic value metrics set is selected, a liaison from the strategic business architecture practice will need to approach the owners of the selected value metrics and express the desire (and ability) to work with them to positively influence the metrics. The liaison must demonstrate a solid understanding of the value metric owner's area of the organization and current issues; without this understanding, gaining the initial trust and willingness to work with strategic business architecture practice will be difficult. Most areas of the organization will give anyone a chance who claims that "I can help positively impact metrics that you're measured against." However, you will get only one chance to demonstrate that you can make a positive impact, so strategically selecting the initial projects and subsequent projects is key to long-term success. The goal is to have great initial success and build upon that success with other successes to eventually become viewed as an indispensable strategic resource. This journey typically takes two to four years, depending on the organization and people involved, and will be successful only with a strategic approach to selecting projects that build the reputation of the ability of the strategic architecture practice to execute and impact the greatest number of selected value metrics possible.

It is also important to select projects of moderate complexity at first. If a project is deemed too simple, critics may claim that anyone could have generated success, and if a project is too complex, the risk of failure is greater. It is also important to work with "friendly" areas of the organization at first, if possible. When you are just starting out on this journey, you will make mistakes and encounter issues as your skills and business knowledge mature. Working with friendly parts of the organization initially helps when unexpected issues arise as the strategic business architecture practice matures. Save the complex projects in less friendly parts of the organization for later in the journey, after the practice has built its reputation and matured its skills and understanding of the organization.

Performance Improvement Considerations

The metrics identification process should be performed annually to examine any changes in the key stakeholders or core business capabilities of the organization, and the metrics selected for strategic value measurement should be updated accordingly. This process ensures that time is not wasted in calculating and tracking metrics no longer valued by the organization and that the value metrics set reflects changes in the composition and value sets of the key stakeholders and core business capabilities.

Communications Considerations

Do not confuse deliverables with value. Successful strategic business architects focus on the value received and communicate in terms of value to the stakeholder. The recommended process includes the development of a communications strategy/plan for each of the key stakeholders and owners of core business capabilities—one size does not fit all. This communications plan should be updated annually to reflect any changes to the target audiences. It is important to present information in the manner most appropriate to the data represented and in the presentation format the audience is used to. It is also important to adjust reporting frequency, presentation format, and level of detail to the needs of different stakeholder groups. The underlying data should remain consistent, but the presentation format doesn't have to be the same. Effective communication of strategic value is a critical (and often overlooked) component of an effective value measurement program. In most organizations, perception is reality, and without effective communications, incorrect perceptions are often formed.

There is no such thing as too much communication, only too little communication. The perception that is created with the communications plan becomes reality in most people's minds. Successful development and execution of an effective strategic communications plan cannot be left to chance; the strategic business architecture practice must have people with communications expertise (or be able to leverage such people in the organization). Ideally, the practice would have this critical function developed internally rather than rely on external people with limited understanding of strategic business architecture.

Strategic Value Measurement and Strategy Execution

The framework outlined in this section emphasizes that the design, development, and execution of an effective strategic value measurement is the single most important factor to long-term strategic business architecture success in any organization. Strategic value measurement cannot be an afterthought or a minor task assigned to someone under the banner of "other duties as assigned." If done correctly, strategic value measurement is a significant job that requires a significant set of skills.

The process ensures that an organization will select the optimal set of metrics, those with the greatest likelihood of demonstrating the value that strategic business architecture has produced for the organization. This process also helps select metrics that align with the value measures utilized by the core capabilities of the organization, as well as those measures utilized by key stakeholders. Aligning the strategic value measurement program with these measures allows the strategic business architecture practice to directly show how it positively impacts measures that matter to those parts of the organization that directly impact the organization's ability to execute strategy.

A strategic value measure program demonstrates that the strategic business architecture group understands how key parts of the organization function and understands how these areas are evaluated. Through an ongoing value measurement process, solid connections and relationships are built as key parts of the strategy execution process are aligned at the performance management level.

Other Strategic Business Architecture Success Factors

In addition to the skills and roles mentioned so far in this chapter, several other factors contribute to strategic business architecture success.

Agreement on Strategic Business Architecture's Definition and Scope

Because of the influence of legacy business architecture in some organizations, there may be different ideas and definitions of what business architecture is and its potential scope and value. A critical best practice is to reach an agreement on what strategic business architecture means and its scope and value. The key point is to ensure that there is a well-defined and well-understood definition of strategic business architecture that is understood by all key stakeholders. This definition should include an enterprise-wide scope for informing strategy and for facilitating strategy execution.

Strategic business architecture is very rarely involved in the day-to-day operations of the organization. The practice focuses mainly on informing strategy development and evolution, as well as translating strategy into actionable and executable portfolios of projects. These activities form the value stream discussed throughout this book, often referred to as *strategy-to-execution,* in which strategic business architecture works in close partnership with many other business functions and strategy execution disciplines.

Define and Socialize a Common Organizational Understanding

A common understanding of the organization and a related common vocabulary is needed between key stakeholders in terms of the strategic business architecture process, scope, information needed and produced, and requirements for defining the strategic business architecture. Agreement on common terms and language is important to ensure that different parts of the enterprise use the same terms to mean the same things.

Understanding Key Stakeholders and Maintaining Buy-In

The value measurement process outlined earlier in this chapter is a key part of understanding your key stakeholders. Understanding how people derive value from their association with your efforts can be very revealing and helps develop a deep understanding of motivations, politics, and spheres of influence. Understand who your key stakeholders really are and what they value.

This understanding and alignment at the value measurement level helps to maintain the buy-in and support of key stakeholders. Many organizations report the need for a two-part approach to gaining stakeholder support during the early years of supporting strategic business architecture. The first part of the approach is to garner high-level buy-in of the overall goals, objectives, and potential business value of strategic business architecture and to ensure that there is alignment on the goals, objectives, and potential business value of business architecture efforts. This buy-in is primarily focused on very specific benefits that are based on shorter-term (one-year) business goals and objectives; it is demonstrated with specific metrics and examples.

While focusing on producing short-term benefits to quickly demonstrate value, a focus on the second part of the approach must occur in parallel. This part focuses on the longer-term strategic goals for strategic business architecture that may take multiple years to achieve. These are the goals that often produce the largest value to the organization but take longer to produce. The balancing act is to produce high-value shorter-term benefits while laying the strategic foundation for longer-term value.

Trust with key stakeholders is built over time as you build your track record of delivering value. As discussed in the value measurement section of this chapter, build trust by initially selecting projects that:

- Have the potential to positively impact multiple key stakeholders.
- Have a high probability of success and are of moderate complexity. If the project is too easily done, it will be discounted by critics, and if it is too hard to accomplish, the risk of failure (and reputation damage) increases.
- Have data for the value measures that matter to the key stakeholders from before the project was initiated. Project benefits can't be measured without baseline data.

A well-developed strategy for gaining trust by demonstrating value and success in a systematic and thoughtful manner will cause the strategic business architecture practice to be viewed as a valuable, strategic resource over time by multiple key stakeholders.

Business Architecture Leadership Is Key

Ideally, the person chosen to lead strategic business architecture efforts within the strategy execution function should have a solid understanding of the organization and be focused full-time on establishing and leading the strategic business architecture function. There is a big difference between an effective manager and an effective leader. Management is more about controlling, organizing, staffing, reducing risk, and coping with complexity to accomplish a specific goal. Leadership is more about influencing, setting a vision and strategy, aligning, motivating, inspiring, and coaching to enable other employees to make contributions that make the organization more successful. A good manager does not necessarily make a good leader. We will discuss effective leadership in Chapter 8.

Focus on Higher-Level Core Business Capabilities

Strategic business architecture practices often start by focusing on higher-level core business capabilities. These higher-level capabilities support the enterprise business context, and this provides the foundation for the analysis that takes place in strategic business architecture. Core capabilities are often thought of as the cornerstone of a strategic business architecture.

Starting with this higher-level view provides a layer of abstraction from the specific details of the organization (people, processes, organizational structure, and so on) and allows strategic business architecture efforts to focus on understanding the organization and evolving toward a desired future state without getting bogged down in the potential political and detailed issues. Once this analysis is completed, further analysis may be done to produce a gap analysis and a migration road map.

Become the Unifying Bridge between Strategy Execution Disciplines

As discussed in Chapter 6, there are many functions/disciplines that need to work together to achieve effective strategy execution. As also discussed in Chapter 6, consolidation of these fragmented (and sometimes overlapping) functions/disciplines under the strategy execution function is needed to achieve efficient and effective strategy execution. From this perspective, strategy execution is the umbrella discipline under which all the other "subdisciplines" needed for effective strategy execution reside. As discussed throughout this book, strategic business architecture is the "bridge" discipline/subdiscipline that facilitates the orchestration and collaboration of the strategy execution subdisciplines. Without this bridge discipline, and the organizational understanding and insights that it provides, other disciplines needed for effective strategy execution will likely remain fragmented and partially effective at best. As a result, building close relationships with these other functions/disciplines and defining clear interactions with each is a critical success factor for strategic business architecture.

A Summary of Strategic Business Architecture Success Factors

Strategic business architecture practices mature over time, and their effectiveness improves as they build relationships with key stakeholders and subject matter experts across the organization. When developing the operating model for the strategic business architecture practice, consider the following:

- **Focus on delivering value to a subset of key stakeholders.** The practice will succeed only if it delivers value. We have outlined a process for identifying key stakeholders and accessing what they value in this chapter.
- **Develop a collaborative culture.** A collaborative culture is based on transparency and trust. Build an informal environment that focuses its energy on informing changes to strategy, facilitating strategy execution, and facilitating internal innovation.
- **Build team accountability.** High-performance strategic business architecture occurs when peers in the strategic business architecture ecosystem immediately and respectfully communicate with one another when problems arise. This culture drives greater innovation, trust, and productivity.

Strategic Business Architecture as a Facilitator of Innovation

Strategic business architecture (if properly staffed and properly positioned in the organization) could (and should) be a "hub" for innovation within the organization. Innovation is driven by different thinking and can accelerate organizational performance. Often, we think of organizational improvements in terms of effectiveness (producing the desired results), efficiency (decreasing waste), or improving (making things better). While these are desirable outcomes, they are not the organizational improvements that will propel your organization to great heights. When we can do things or produce things that are very different from our competitors and do or produce things that were once considered impossible, we add the most value to our organization.

Strategic business architecture should be the nexus for strategy *and* organizational innovation in the enterprise. Organizational innovation often refers to improving the way the organization is structured and the way it works. While this is typically where strategic business architecture contributes the most value, it is also possible that strategic business architecture could add value and insights into new or existing product or service innovations.

Strategic business architects are typically very well connected in the organization and know the strategic thinkers and critical subject matter experts in the organization. As a result, they can quickly bring together the right people to explore a possible area of innovation. Strategic business architects also have the skills and perspectives needed to conduct an opportunity analysis of the possible area of innovation, as well as a comprehensive risk analysis. Strategic business architecture can help weave innovations into the fabric of the organization and identify potential problem areas.

As with any idea or defined business direction, strategic business architecture also plays an important role in assessing the viability and impact of innovation ideas, and then making them real by translating them into a coordinated, actionable set of projects across the organization.

Strategic business architecture helps the organization understand how any potential innovations fit with the bigger-picture strategy and helps to ensure that pursuing the potential innovation makes sense for the strategic priorities of the organization.

In summary, strategic business architecture can play a valuable role throughout each of the typical stages of the innovation process:

- **Stage 1: Idea generation and mobilization.** As mentioned earlier, strategic business architects are well positioned to *generate* *new innovation ideas.* In addition, the business architecture framework (especially value streams and/or capabilities) can be leveraged to *facilitate the sharing of innovation ideas across the enterprise.* Think about all the great ideas that are generated through innovation challenges and efforts. If they are tied to the reusable business architecture, they can easily be found and used. Business architecture can also help to *identify focus areas where innovation is needed,* either resulting from business priorities or known areas of improvement. It can even help to provide specificity and clarity on the problem to be solved or an opportunity to be pursued.

- **Stage 2: Advocacy and screening.** Business architecture can be used to *assess initial viability and impact of innovation ideas,* narrowing the focus on only those that are worthy of your precious resources and mindshare. It can also be used to *identify additional applications for innovation ideas.* For example, using the business architecture, a business architect can readily identify other business units, products, and/or scenarios that might have use for the same innovation idea in other contexts. This could even help to increase the support and funding for an innovation idea.
- **Stage 3: Experimentation.** Based on an understanding of overall business priorities, as well as applicable scenarios (as mentioned in the previous item), business architecture can *inform priorities, timing, and scenarios for innovation idea experimentation.*
- **Stage 4: Commercialization.** Once an innovation idea is ready for commercialization, it hits the sweet spot of how business architecture translates ideas into concrete enterprise actions to make them real. Business architecture can be used to *assess the final impacts on the organizational operating environment.* In addition, it can *provide a structure for and inform the cost-benefit analysis.*
- **Stage 5: Diffusion and implementation.** Strategic business architects, IT architects, and other team members from other strategy execution disciplines will architect the organizational changes needed to create and maintain the innovation idea. From there, they will define and scope projects required to implement the idea and ensure that the implementation of the innovation idea achieves the defined business objectives.

Strategic Business Architecture, Design Thinking, and Agile Enterprise Transformation

In addition to considering the possible innovation role for the strategic business architecture function, you should also consider the role strategic business architecture could play in fostering design thinking in the organization. As discussed in Chapter 2, design thinking is a mindset and approach that can be applied at various points across the strategy execution process.

Strategic business architecture facilitates the four general types of design:

- **Business design** creates a model of the mechanism for value creation. Strategic business architecture provides the modeling approaches for effective business design, such as the value proposition canvas and business model canvas.
- **Enterprise design** elaborates the architecture and elements needed for value creation across the enterprise. Strategic business architecture provides the enterprise-wide modeling and understanding needed to identify new opportunities for value creation or uncover areas for improvement to reduce friction or fragmentation in value creation. For example, strategic business architecture can provide new perspectives on organizational and business ecosystem design, or value delivery through value streams and processes.
- **Product design** articulates a deliverable, marketable tool that serves a purpose for particular stakeholders. Strategic business architecture provides the ecosystem-level understanding of market trends and stakeholder needs and value. It also ensures that the appropriate capabilities are in place to effectively deliver the goods and services that an organization offers in the market.
- **Execution design** refers to the flow of activities, ideas, and engagements necessary for the production of a product or service. Strategic business architecture informs the definition and priority of projects and creates the line of sight to ensure that an organization is doing the right projects that support the current business strategy.

As discussed in Chapter 2, design thinking enables agile enterprise transformation through the creation of *composable business*—the creation of an organization from interchangeable "building blocks." Composable business enables the organization to maximize the design and delivery of the resilience and agility needed to rapidly respond to market opportunities and challenges.

Strategic business architecture enables the four basic principles of composable business:

- More speed through discovery
- Greater agility through modularity
- Better leadership through orchestration
- Resilience through autonomy

Enabling innovation, design thinking, and agile enterprise transformation through strategic business architecture is not easy and will likely require some reorganization as innovation and design groups may have sprung up in various parts of the organization. As we saw with portfolio management, integration of key related disciplines, such as innovation and design thinking, with strategic business architecture is key to effective, enterprise-wide success in these areas. If strategic business architecture is an enterprise-wide strategic function under strategic planning, it makes sense to have related key areas, such as innovation and design thinking, be integrated into the strategic business architecture function.

Beyond Strategy Execution: Business Architecture Should Inform Strategy Development

The strategic business architecture function should be structured so that it can be leveraged to shape and evolve corporate strategy. Figure 7.4 presents an integrated model of strategic business architecture and strategic planning.

As Figure 7.5 suggests, if the strategic business architecture practice is positioned correctly in the organization and staffed appropriately, it becomes a critical input into the formulation of an effective corporate strategy that is actionable and executable.

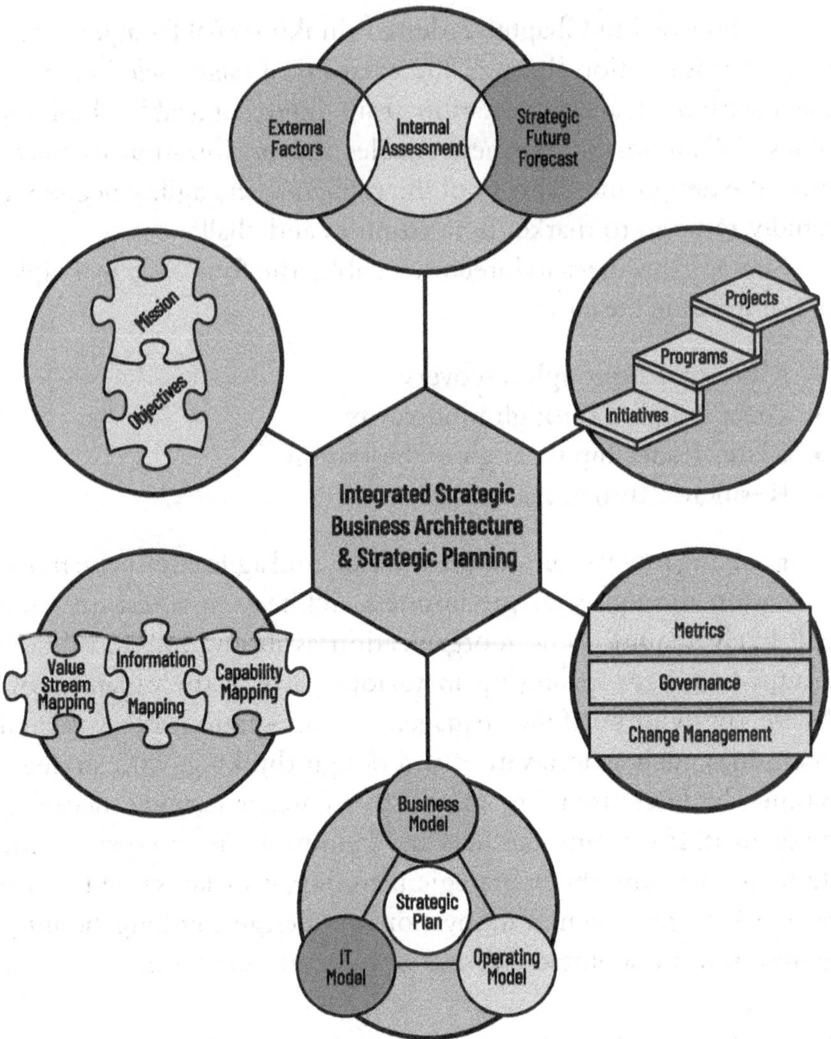

Figure 7.4 Strategic business architecture informs strategic planning.

Next Steps

This chapter outlined critical considerations as you determine the scope, roles, and structure of your strategic business architecture practice. Your practice will likely start with a subset of these possible roles and grow over time. However, you should have an

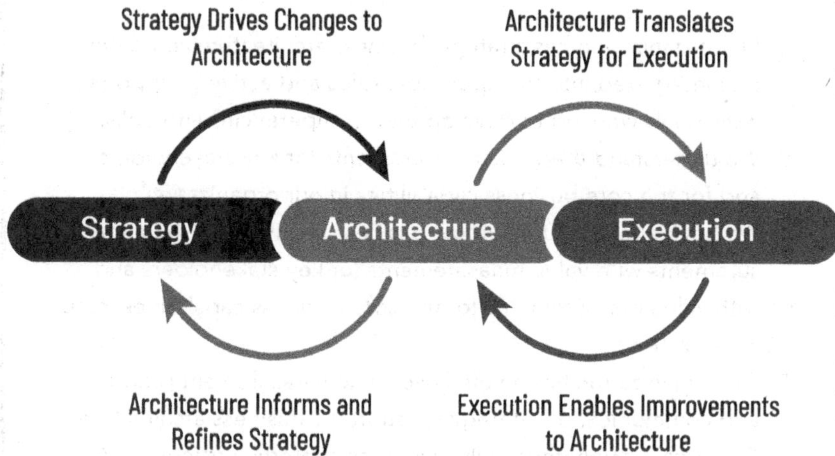

Figure 7.5 The positioning of strategic business architecture.

agreed-upon vision and strategy for the long-term scope, roles, and structure for strategic business architecture in your organization and a plan and timeline for achieving these objectives. The development of this plan is the focus of Chapter 8.

STRATEGY EXECUTION ORGANIZATIONAL ASSESSMENT

Reflect on the following questions to assess how well strategy execution is working in your organization based on the concepts from Chapter 7. Please refer to the scoring guidance provided in Chapter 1.

1. Our strategic business architecture function is formalized, reports to an enterprise-wide strategy execution function, and has the appropriate positioning and scope of authority.

(continued)

2. Our organization has strategic business architecture competencies integrated into the applicable roles and actively supports individuals working to develop their competencies and skills.
3. We understand the value measurements for key stakeholders and for the core business capabilities in our organization.
4. We have aligned our strategic business architecture value measurements with value measurements for key stakeholders and with value measurements for the core business capabilities in our organization.
5. Our organization has an effective value measurement program and communication strategy for strategic business architecture.
6. Our organization effectively leverages strategic business architecture to foster innovation and enable the innovation life cycle.
7. Our organization effectively leverages strategic business architecture for all types of design—business, enterprise, product, and execution.

Please also refer to the Strategic Business Architecture Maturity Model in Chapter 8 *for additional assessment questions pertaining to the strategic business architecture function.*

Chapter 8

Scaling and Maturing the Strategic Business Architecture Function

In this chapter, we will bring the key concepts and components together into a cohesive plan for scaling and maturing a strategic business architecture function that can successfully support strategy execution across an organization. This is a journey, and one that needs to be pursued with intent, vision, leadership, empathy, and persistence. Introducing a comprehensive approach to strategy execution enabled by strategic business architecture is a human journey more than an architecture journey. It's about changing the ways of thinking and working within an organization, and that takes time, demonstration of value, and careful management of change.

We will also explore how to build a career path for strategic business architecture and how to govern the architecture to support business decision-making and change. Finally, we will discuss the important role of leadership in creating a strategic business architecture function that is truly visionary and transformative.

Components of a Strategic Business Architecture Function

The most critical component of a strategic business architecture function is, of course, **value realization.** The entire reason for investing in the creation of a strategic business architecture knowledge base and function is for the unique value and insights that it brings to strategy execution. As Chapter 7 highlighted, value measurement is key to ensure that the strategic business architecture function is contributing tangible results that are aligned with the organization's direction and stakeholder needs. Demonstration of value is even more important to create understanding and buy-in considering the relative newness of the strategic business architecture discipline, comparatively speaking.

However, in order to deliver this value, there are two key enabling components for strategic business architecture: the **strategic architecture** itself (the business knowledge base) and the **people and organization** that comprise the function. With value realization as the guiding light and focus, the architecture and the supporting aspects of the function are built out *just enough, just in time,* in direct support of the intended business outcomes. Strategic business architecture presents a unique challenge: Unlike the buildings in which we live or work that were a blueprint before they were built, organizations rarely have a cohesive, documented business architecture. This means we must create one before we can start using it. The practical *just enough, just in time* approach allows for a robust architecture and function to be built over time while simultaneously delivering business results and exploring how the discipline can be leveraged most effectively within an organization.

Two additional components amplify all the others. **Governance** manages the creation and evolution of strategic business architecture to align with business direction, usage, and stakeholder needs. Finally, **commitment** is the essential component that ensures the understanding and adoption of strategic business architecture across an organization.

Figure 8.1 shows these five key components of a strategic business architecture function and how they relate to each other.

Getting Started: A Practical Approach That Works

How do you get started on this journey? There is a practical approach to introducing and scaling strategic business architecture

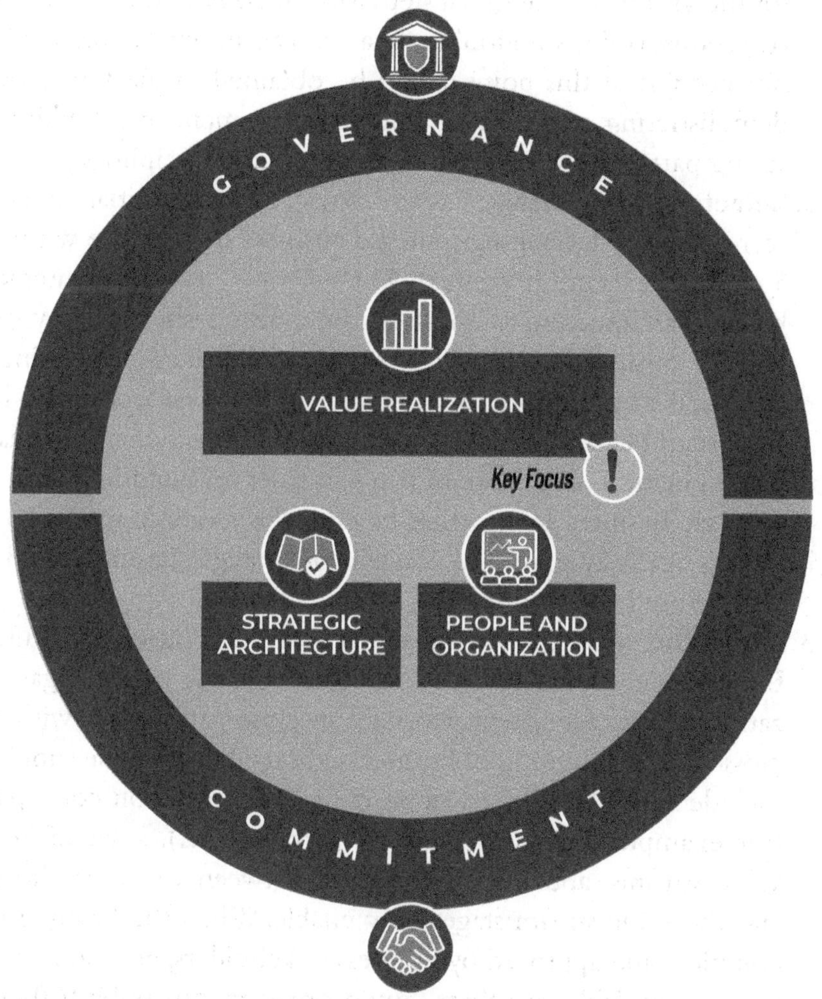

Figure 8.1 Key components of a strategic business architecture function.

that has continued to prove successful for organizations, led by the principle of being value-driven.

The approach can be summarized in five steps:

1. **Build the business case.** Build a case for a comprehensive approach to strategy execution and strategic business architecture as a key enabling and connecting discipline. Build understanding, buy-in, advocacy, and executive business sponsorship for the vision and the initial steps forward. (***Note:*** While executive sponsorship is undoubtedly a critical success factor, if it is not possible at this point, it can be obtained in the future by demonstrating results with value measurement and building strong partnerships with other functions and disciplines.)
2. **Select initial usage scenario(s).** Select initial usage scenario(s) for leveraging strategic business architecture within a strategy execution context. For example, leverage strategic business architecture to translate a new or refreshed strategy, or apply a capability lens to strategic portfolio decision-making, as described in Chapter 5. Selecting initial usage scenario(s) is important because it helps to provide context in conversations, guide practical usage, and inform priorities for building out the strategic business architecture baseline. In addition, most people do not fully grasp the concept of strategic business architecture until they can see it.
3. **Build the strategic business architecture baseline.** Build the business architecture baseline for the scope of the organization and its ecosystem, working in close partnership with a cross-functional group of business experts. The baseline should include capabilities based upon defined information concepts (for example, customer, product, partner, asset), a set of key value streams, and a cross-mapping between the capabilities and the value stream stages they enable. When the baseline is complete and approved by business stakeholders, publish it and make it available to others. Some organizations publish their

initial baseline widely, while other organizations share it among a smaller group of people until strategic business architecture gains traction. Introduce a light process to manage changes to the baseline on an ongoing basis.

4. **Leverage strategic business architecture.** With clear direction, commitment, and a baseline in place, leverage the strategic business architecture on the first usage scenario defined in Step 2. Deliver the intended business outcomes, and measure and communicate the value and learning to others. Continue leveraging strategic business architecture for expanded usage scenarios, and repeat the cycle of delivering business outcomes, measuring value, and telling the story and building advocates as you go.
5. **Create a strategic plan for strategic business architecture.** As momentum increases, build out the strategic plan for your strategic business architecture function. Start by performing an initial maturity assessment and creating a road map for establishing and maturing the strategic business architecture function within the organization over the next 6 to 12 months (discussed in the next sections). The key is to be intentional and invest for long-term success by building a robust discipline that can scale to support strategy execution for the organization.

Assessing Strategic Business Architecture Maturity

An organization's level of maturity in the strategic business architecture discipline can be assessed across each of the key components. As with most maturity models, an organization does not need to strive for the top level of maturity (level 5) in each category, but higher maturity leads to greater embeddedness, transformation, and value to strategy execution. The model also helps to convey a vision of what a fully integrated and effective strategic business architecture function looks like.

The Strategic Business Architecture Maturity Model

The Strategic Business Architecture Maturity Model has five categories (the components introduced earlier) and five levels of maturity. The categories are described in Table 8.1.

The strategic business architecture maturity levels are described in Table 8.2. They adhere to common delineations within maturity models and are also reflective of the stages that organizations typically go through on their strategic business architecture journeys.

A visual representation of the Strategic Business Architecture Maturity Model is shown in Figure 8.2.

The full Strategic Business Architecture Maturity Model is shown in Table 8.3, with the key characteristics of each category described by level.

As the maturity model reflects, the hallmark of a fully mature strategic business architecture function is that the discipline is fully embedded into the fabric of an organization, where it becomes just how the organization works—no longer a separate concept requiring special attention. As part of this process, strategic business

Table 8.1 Strategic Business Architecture Maturity Model Categories

Maturity Category	Description
Value realization	The delivery and measurement of business value using strategic business architecture
Strategic architecture	The creation, management, and automation of the strategic business architecture knowledge base and views used in support of business decision-making
People and organization	The formalization of the strategic business architecture function and role and its integration with other functions and strategy execution disciplines
Governance	The decision-making and oversight of strategic business architecture to ensure alignment with business direction, usage, and stakeholder needs
Commitment	The sponsorship, support, adoption, and use of strategic business architecture by people at all levels of the organization

Table 8.2 Strategic Business Architecture Maturity Model Levels

Maturity Level	Key Characteristics
Initiation	**Unaware:** Limited awareness and recognition of strategic business architecture within the organization
Exploration	**Informed:** Basic understanding of strategic business architecture and its potential benefits **Experimental:** Systematic exploration of strategic business architecture value through intentional usage scenarios **Ad hoc:** Informal and inconsistent strategic business architecture practices
Adoption	**Standardized:** Adoption of strategic business architecture as a formal discipline with active management and enforcement of consistent practices **Integrated:** Seamless integration into strategy development and execution processes and structures
Optimization	**Optimized:** Continuous improvement and optimization of strategic business architecture practices **Innovative:** Pioneering new and advanced uses of strategic business architecture
Transformation	**Transformative:** Radical transformation of strategy development, strategy execution, and business design **Visionary:** Continuous and proactive vision, innovation, and leadership as it pertains to strategy development, strategy execution, and business design trends and directions

architecture becomes fully integrated into a cohesive approach from strategy to execution along with other business functions and strategy execution disciplines. Strategic business architects become highly skilled strategic resources. Leveraging strategic business architecture for decision-making becomes part of everyone's role. Strategic business architecture is seen as a core capability of the organization and as a source of competitive advantage. Finally, strategic business architecture takes on a leadership role to drive continuous innovation and transformation.

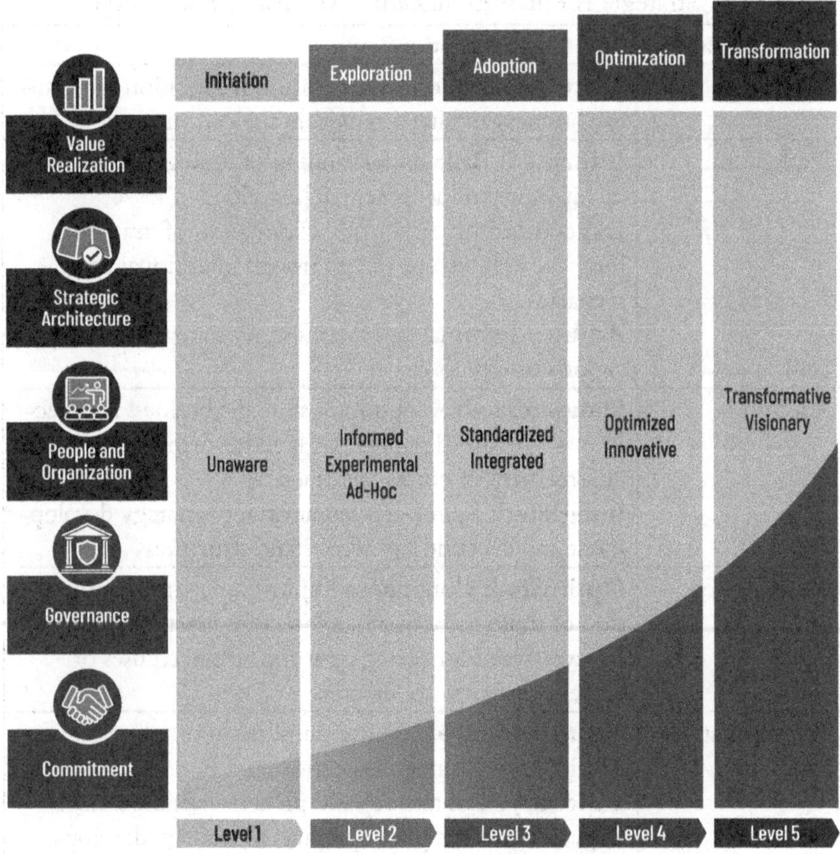

Figure 8.2 Strategic Business Architecture Maturity Model.

The Strategic Business Architecture Maturity Assessment Process

Strategic business architecture maturity is typically assessed annually, and the results are used to communicate progress to stakeholders, as well as inform the road map to mature the practice over the next horizon. Even if you're just getting started, it can be useful to perform an initial maturity assessment. This helps you to become familiar with the concepts, as well as understand any underpinnings for the discipline that may already exist within the organization (for example, working models or views, people playing the role, and so on).

Table 8.3 Strategic Business Architecture Maturity Model

Maturity Level	Key Characteristics by Category
Initiation	Value realization: • Limited understanding of how strategic business architecture contributes to strategy development, strategy execution, and business value delivery • Initial identification of potential usage and value areas of strategic business architecture without a formalized approach Strategic architecture: • Initial documentation of high-level strategic business architecture concepts without a structured approach • No formalized strategic business architecture framework or methodology People and organization: • Limited competencies related to strategic business architecture • Limited organizational structure to support strategic business architecture Governance: • Initial discussions on the need for strategic business architecture governance without established processes • Limited accountability for strategic business architecture outcomes Commitment: • Leadership awareness of strategic business architecture but limited commitment • Strategic business architecture is not yet seen as a key enabler for strategy execution • Limited allocation of resources and sponsorship for strategic business architecture exploration and investment

(Continued)

Table 8.3 (Continued)

Maturity Level	Key Characteristics by Category
Exploration	Value realization: • Basic understanding of how strategic business architecture contributes to strategy development, strategy execution, and business value • Initial exploration of specific usage and value areas for strategic business architecture and their potential benefits • Initial efforts to measure and communicate value of strategic business architecture Strategic architecture: • Documentation of key strategic business architecture content and views • Adoption of a basic strategic business architecture framework and standard practices People and organization: • Increased awareness and initial competency development programs for strategic business architecture • Formation of the core or foundational organizational structures to support strategic business architecture • Initial efforts to integrate strategic business architecture into job roles and responsibilities Governance: • Early establishment of a governance structure for strategic business architecture • Initial definition of processes and responsibilities within the governance framework • Limited measurement and reporting on business architecture governance effectiveness Commitment: • Growing leadership commitment and recognition of the strategic importance of strategic business architecture and its role in strategy development, strategy execution, and business value • Increased resource allocation and sponsorship for exploring strategic business architecture usage and value areas • Formal communication of the benefits and value of strategic business architecture

Maturity Level	Key Characteristics by Category
Adoption	Value realization: • Strategic business architecture leveraged to inform and translate strategy, shape projects and enterprise portfolios, and facilitate holistic and ongoing alignment of strategy and project-level execution • Understanding and adoption of value measurement metrics that are aligned with key parts of the enterprise and the establishment of a communications strategy for strategic business architecture targeting these key parts of the organization (described in Chapter 7) • Recognition of strategic business architecture as a key driver of value across strategy development and execution Strategic architecture: • Strategic business architecture baseline (capabilities, information concepts, and value streams) defined for the enterprise and captured within a shared, automated business knowledge base • Adoption of a comprehensive business architecture framework and standardized processes, methods, and practices • Active integration of strategic business architecture content with content from other enterprise architecture domains and strategy execution disciplines • Strategic business architecture becoming a valuable enterprise asset with the knowledge base and views being used by different roles throughout strategy development and execution People and organization: • Establishment of formal strategic business architecture function with clearly articulated goals and the appropriate executive leadership and sponsorship

(Continued)

Table 8.3 (Continued)

Maturity Level	Key Characteristics by Category
	• Establishment of formal strategic business architect role(s) and integration of strategic business architecture competency into other organizational roles • Dedicated strategic business architecture team staffed appropriately based on business needs • Formal competency model defined (described in Chapter 7) and comprehensive competency development program for strategic business architecture in place • Strategic business architecture actively integrating into strategy development process, strategy to execution process, and with related business functions, strategy execution disciplines, enterprise architecture, and execution-level disciplines Governance: • Well-defined governance structures and processes for strategic business architecture with regular reviews • Integration of strategic business architecture governance with other enterprise governance processes Commitment: • Strategic business architecture seen as an enabler of strategy execution • Strategic business architecture seen as a contributor to strategy development • Strong leadership commitment to leveraging strategic business architecture for strategy execution and strategic advantage • Dedicated resources and ongoing sponsorship for strategic business architecture usage and value areas • Active management of change and organization-wide awareness and understanding of strategic business architecture and its role in strategy execution

Maturity Level	Key Characteristics by Category
Optimization	Value realization: • Strategic business architecture seen as a valued discipline to inform and influence strategy development • Strategic business architecture seen as a facilitator of innovation, business transformation, business performance improvement, strategic initiatives, and enterprise portfolio opportunities • Proactive identification and pursuit of new and advanced usage and value areas for strategic business architecture • Integration of value measurement and realization with key stakeholders and core business capabilities Strategic architecture: • Strategic business architecture leveraged to create a composable business and inform design at all levels (business, enterprise, product, and execution) • Continuous improvement of the business architecture framework and processes, methods, and practices People and organization: • Strategic business architecture career path created and supported by defined learning paths and curriculum • Strategic business architect knowledge excellent with solid competency demonstrated by a majority of team members • Integration of strategic business architecture principles and architectural thinking into the organizational culture

(Continued)

Table 8.3 (Continued)

Maturity Level	Key Characteristics by Category
	• Strategic business architecture function fully operationalized and operating effectively • Strategic business architecture fully integrated into the strategy to execution process and strategic planning and decision-making, as well as integrated with related business functions and disciplines • Strategic business architects recognized as valued, strategic partners, and formal processes in place for engaging them across strategy execution and business decision-making Governance: • Strategic business architecture governance structure and processes well managed and metrics-driven with real-time feedback loops • Enterprise-level governance managing the current- and target-state strategic business architecture and the investments to it • Active business ownership and stakeholder participation in the strategic business architecture governance process Commitment: • Strategic business architecture seen as a critical enabler of strategy development and execution • Continuous reinforcement of leadership commitment to strategic business architecture that is strong, consistent, and adequate across the organization • Optimization of resource allocation based on demonstrated value

Maturity Level	Key Characteristics by Category
Transformation	Value realization: • Strategic business architecture driving radical transformation of strategy development, strategy execution, and business design with significant impact on business outcomes • Strategic business architecture driving proactive and continuous innovation, leadership, and vision as it pertains to strategy development, strategy execution, and business design trends and directions • Full integration of value measurement/realization with key stakeholders and core business capabilities • Value measurement and delivery deeply embedded in the organizational DNA Strategic architecture: • Innovative strategic business architecture approach that anticipates future needs for business strategy and resilience • Proactive identification and pursuit of architectural innovations People and organization: • Visionary skill development program for strategic business architecture professionals • Integration of strategic business architecture and architectural thinking principles into talent management • A culture of continuous learning, innovation, and adaptability across the organization Governance: • Adaptive strategic business architecture governance responding to rapid changes in the business environment • Stakeholder-driven governance ensuring alignment with evolving strategies and strategic priorities

(Continued)

Table 8.3 (Continued)

Maturity Level	Key Characteristics by Category
	Commitment: • Strategic business architecture seen as a core capability of the organization and as a source of competitive advantage • Strategic business architecture fully embedded as part of the fabric of the organization and how it develops and executes strategy • Fully engaged and ubiquitous leadership support and commitment to continuous innovation and transformation

Maturity is typically assessed by the strategic business architecture team, though an external expert may perform the assessment to provide an objective perspective and additional recommendations. Strategic business architecture stakeholders may be consulted for input or even included through a survey component in more mature practices.

Consider three ratings for each category of the maturity model:

- The current level of maturity for the category
- The long-term target-level maturity for the category
- The next horizon target level for the category

The difference between the current level and next horizon target level ratings within each category drives the activities included in the road map for maturing the strategic business architecture function over the next 12 months. For example, if an organization currently has a maturity level 2 for the strategic architecture category but would like to achieve a level 3 during the next horizon, then the road map may include activities focused on building out the strategic business architecture knowledge base and capturing it in an automated tool.

Remember that establishing and maturing a strategic business architecture function within an organization is a journey that takes time. This is especially true for large organizations where reaching a maturity level of 4 or 5 can take years, but each step brings new value and experience to build upon.

Developing the Business Architecture Strategic Plan

A strategic business architecture charter is a highly useful collaboration and communication tool when establishing the function. It defines the intent of strategic business architecture for the organization along with key aspects of the function. The process of creating a charter can be a valuable way for a team to fully think through and come to consensus on the value they deliver to the organization and how they do it. The charter also creates consistency in how team members communicate with others about strategic business architecture and is invaluable for onboarding new team members. (***Note:*** This is an internal document for the function. The next section addresses socialization with others.) The charter may include information such as the definition of strategic business architecture, its value and role in strategy execution, measures of success (see Chapter 7 on value measurement), the services offered by the team, principles, the engagement model, and more.

Like other functions, strategic business architecture should also have a purpose and direction definition. For example, this may include a vision, mission, and/or purpose statement to define the overall aspirations of the function. In addition, this should include goals and objectives that are set and measured regularly to assess the advancement progress of the function (for example, team expansion and development goals) along with value delivery as defined in Chapter 7. The direction for the function should, of course, be aligned with the direction of the strategy execution function and the organization overall.

Finally, a road map provides the action plan to implement both the current set of goals and objectives, as well as the targeted advancements for the next horizon within the Strategic Business Architecture Maturity Model. The road map is typically refreshed annually to correspond with the timing of the maturity assessment and an organization's planning rhythm. The strategic business architecture road map should include activities for each of the key components described earlier. Value realization activities (for example, engagements or services being provided within a strategy execution context) are the focal point of the road map. Activities related to the other components (strategic business architecture development, people and organization, governance, and socialization and change management for commitment) should be defined to achieve *just enough, just in time* to support the value being delivered by the function.

Change Management for Strategic Business Architecture

Strategic business architecture changes the way that the people within an organization work and think. As is often said, organizations don't change, people do. This means that the activities related to socialization, relationship building, and organizational change management are essential to the success of a strategic business architecture function. They ensure that the discipline is fully understood, adopted, and resourced across the organization.

Building Buy-In for Strategic Business Architecture

The leader of the strategic business architecture function plays a key role in socializing the discipline and its value. In addition, the entire team helps to socialize with the people they interact with on a daily basis. Teams typically create engaging assets to help visualize and tell their story in a consistent way, such as with presentation decks, infographics, animations, or videos. Executives within the strategy execution function also play a critical role to actively and visibly support and advocate for strategic business architecture and its usage.

The decision of when to socialize strategic business architecture and with whom depends on an organization's specific situation and dynamics. Some strategic business architecture teams build buy-in quickly and share with executives at the C-level and wider audiences throughout the organization relatively early in their journey. However, most teams socialize within a smaller sphere of the organization initially and then socialize more widely once they have proven successes to share and the ability to scale.

The most effective way to socialize strategic business architecture is to simply demonstrate and effectively communicate the results. Showing an example of how the views and insights contributed measurable value within a strategy execution context conveys more about the role and potential of discipline than words ever could. These examples can be summarized and shared as success stories, and even presented together with the stakeholders involved.

Additionally, there is always a need for informational communications around the "what" and "why" of strategic business architecture to a variety of audiences. This includes executives, the board, stakeholders, and consumers involved throughout strategy execution, as well as all the functions and disciplines that strategic business architecture partners with. Communications should be tailored to each audience, both in format and relevant takeaways. They can be delivered through engaging methods ranging from presentations during team meetings to focused sessions during offsite events or training sessions.

Managing Change

Strategic business architecture introduces organizational change from two perspectives. The first is through the introduction of a new function. The level of change here is magnified by the fact that the discipline is often unfamiliar to many people at this stage of its evolution. The second source of change is more significant and is attributed to how strategic business architecture challenges behavior and norms. It enables a new and comprehensive approach to strategy execution, and it introduces a holistic enterprise mindset that can challenge the structures and culture around ownership, decision-making, funding, and motivation.

For these reasons, it is imperative that intentional change management is performed as soon as an organization decides to establish a strategic business architecture function. An experienced change manager from within the organization (or externally) can be engaged as an objective expert to perform the key activities for the strategic business architecture team. Alternatively, the change management activities can be performed by member(s) of the team who have the appropriate knowledge and training.

Organizational change management should define a compelling case for change and then focus on building relationships with key stakeholders and partnering with them throughout the change over time. This includes the activities of identifying, assessing, and managing stakeholders, as well as creating and executing communication and change management plans.

Building the Strategic Business Architecture Career Path

The strategic business architecture knowledge base and views can and should be used by anyone in an organization for strategy execution and business decision-making. In fact, widespread usage unlocks the value of strategic business architecture and is a key indicator of maturity. In addition, the architectural thinking mindset and strategic business architecture competencies may be embodied in many different roles from executives to strategic planners and other roles involved throughout strategy execution.

However, just as there has been a gap between strategy and execution, there has been a gap in a role to help translate and align strategy and execution. A new role and career path have emerged for the strategic business architect. Strategic business architects play a critical and unique role in helping not just to build and steward an organization's business architecture, but more important, to translate strategies into actionable projects, ensure end-to-end strategic alignment, facilitate effective organizational design, and support business decision-making.

Moving into the Strategic Business Architect Role

Strategic business architects can come from a wide variety of roles and diverse backgrounds. There is no single career path for the strategic business architecture professional today. The same can be said for strategic planning professionals. A team with diverse backgrounds typically creates many synergies and strengths. Considering the key competencies discussed in Chapter 7, those in business strategy, planning, and leadership roles are particularly well suited for the role, but strategic business architects can truly come from anywhere. Depending on an individual's background and experiences, they will approach the role differently. For example, a business leader or strategic planner who moves into the role will be a natural at communicating with business stakeholders, will have solid strategic planning process and financial literacy, and will intuitively know how to use strategic business architecture in practical ways throughout strategy execution. They can learn the strategic business architecture mindset and methods. On the other hand, the architectural thinking and methods will come easily to an individual who has worked in an analyst or technology role, but they may need to develop the business acumen, empathy, and communication skills to effectively connect with business stakeholders.

Potential or aspiring strategic business architects can often be identified by a set of recognizable traits and thought patterns. They tend to be structured thinkers with the ability to abstract and synthesize information, recognize patterns, embrace ambiguity, and connect dots that others do not see (or connect them in ways that others do not see). They ask *why,* they bring people together, and they see the big picture and take ownership of it.

Creating the Pathway for Strategic Business Architects

To attract a broad pool of talent and build a strong team, define a clear career path for strategic business architecture that is easy to transition into and out of. Additionally, support that career path with a robust development program.

Strategic Business Architect Role Definition

As the strategic business architecture function becomes formalized, the strategic business architect role definition should also be formalized through human resources. This not only supports hiring, compensation, and performance management, but also brings credence to the discipline. While an organization may just formalize one role to start, as the function grows, ultimately this will expand to include a progression of roles. Chapter 7 describes the common skill sets needed for strategic business architecture roles. Common roles include strategic business architect, senior strategic business architect, lead strategic business architect, and principal strategic business architect. The roles tend to vary by the scope of responsibility, level of strategic involvement and advisory, and mentoring or management responsibility.

When defining the strategic business architect roles, consider the appropriate positioning and organizational context. For example, the role should be positioned at a level high enough for the individuals to be respected and included in strategic activities. In addition, consider parity with other roles such as business leadership, strategic planning, and senior information technology (IT) architecture roles. For example, a top IT architect role should not be defined higher than a top strategic business architect role.

Strategic Business Architect Development

In addition, there are four key aspects of developing strategic business architects: education, experience, mentoring and apprenticeship, and performance management. A robust educational curriculum should be defined that helps individuals to develop the competencies described in Chapter 7. A wide range of educational options may be incorporated into the curriculum, including higher education and formal and informal training sourced from within or outside of the organization. It may include certification as well. Curating these educational options into a cohesive learning path targeted for competency development and practical application is the key. In addition, consider creating specific learning paths that curate education for other roles, such as executives or those within the strategy execution function.

Another key aspect of developing strategic business architects is through experience. Be intentional about cultivating opportunities for strategic business architects to apply the discipline in practice.

This includes building different aspects of the strategic business architecture knowledge base and views, and gaining experience across all aspects of strategy execution. This is also closely related to mentoring and apprenticeship. Because strategic business architecture is a comparatively new discipline, utilize an apprenticeship model and consider establishing a formal mentoring program. The progression of strategic business architect roles described earlier creates a natural mentoring structure for newer team members to apprentice with and be mentored by more experienced ones. This approach not only develops competency but also creates consistency in how strategic business architects within an organization deliver value.

Finally, performance management allows strategic business architects to drive their own growth and advancement with intent. The strategic business architecture competencies from Chapter 7 can be organized into a formal assessment and incorporated as part of an organization's mentoring and performance management processes.

Strategic Business Architecture as a Destination or as a Step to Greater Leadership Roles

A career as a strategic business architect is one of the most unique, exciting, and rewarding roles. Strategic business architects help shape the future and are at the heart of business strategy, transformation, and change. While strategic business architecture is a career destination in itself, the role also makes an excellent stepping stone for other senior leadership–related career aspirations. Regardless, strategic business architecture provides an opportunity to develop strategic and structured thinking skills, gain exposure to a wide variety of business functions and processes, and contribute to transformational initiatives. Very few roles provide the depth and breadth of organizational understanding and enterprise perspective that can be gained through strategic business architecture. This unique experience makes anyone more valuable in their future roles and arguably should be required for all emerging leaders.

The experience and mindset acquired through the strategic business architect role provides a foundation for countless other senior leadership–related roles. This could include roles such as chief executive officers and other C-level executives, vice presidents and other types of business leaders, technology leaders, innovation and organizational design leaders, strategy developers and planners, and many more.

As Figure 8.3 reflects, strategic business architects may take various twists and turns in their careers, often winding up in different and even unexpected positions later in their careers. Career growth also comes not just from moving up, but from moving into lateral positions that can provide the opportunity for developing new skills and perspectives.

Figure 8.3 shows common possible starting points and career path options for strategic business architects. For example, some career paths that could lead into a strategic business architect role include business leadership, strategy development, strategic planning, innovation, portfolio/project management, other design disciplines (for example, business process design, organization design, human-centered design, and others), enterprise architecture (including from an execution-level business architect role), business analysis, and many other possible career paths.

A person can pursue strategic business architecture throughout their entire career with great fulfillment and impact, progressing through increasingly senior roles like the four examples shown in Figure 8.3. Alternatively, they can also diverge from the role at various points in the progression to pursue another career path, with some leading to a top executive position within an organization.

Please note that the options shown in Figure 8.3 are provided to illustrate the dynamic nature of transitioning into and out of the strategic business architect role and should in no way be considered a full representation of the possibilities.

The key for organizations is to be intentional about sourcing and developing strategic business architects—and support them when they move into a new role where they will inevitably continue contributing their unique talents and perspectives. The key

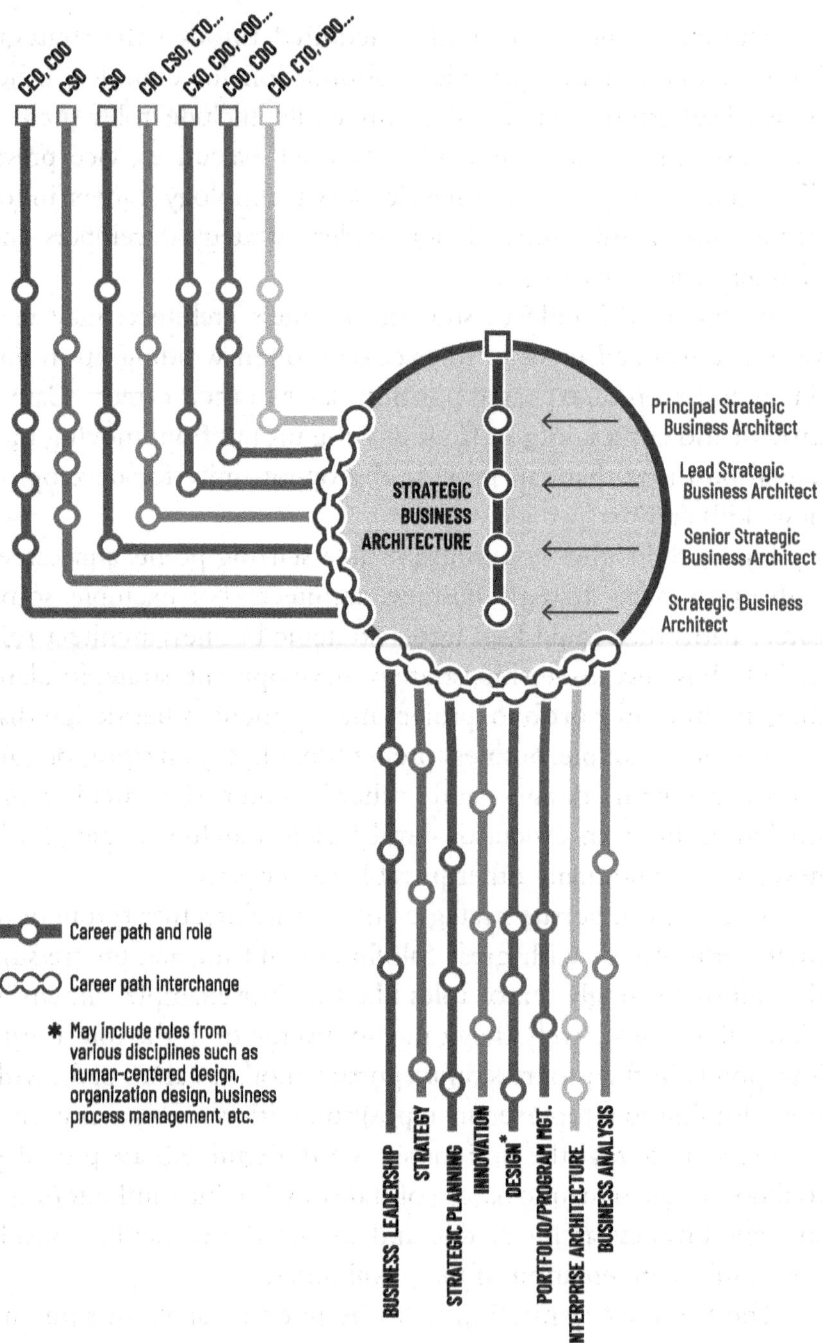

Figure 8.3 A sample of strategic business architecture career path options.

for individuals is to take control of their careers and either continue advancing in the strategic business architect role or leverage it as a unique and valuable step toward another senior-level role or career path in the future.

Strategic Business Architecture Governance

Strategic business architecture governance defines the decision-making structures and processes that ensure an organization is designed to meet the needs of the business today and in the future. An organization's strategic business architecture represents the current structure of the business, but this will be continually reshaped as a result of strategy and other business changes. Strategic business architecture governance provides a methodical way to represent, analyze, build agreement for, and communicate changes across an organization. It allows executives to lead not only by setting strategic direction, but also by guiding the strategic business architecture blueprints and strategic road maps that translate that direction into business solutions and projects.

As the breadth and complexity of strategic business architecture usage expands within an organization, so does the need for governance. However, the establishment of governance should be approached practically and focus on the activities that provide business value and ensure outcomes—not create unnecessary bureaucracy.

Types of Strategic Business Architecture Governance

There are two main focuses of strategic business architecture governance: knowledge base governance and future-state governance. Both focus on the strategic business architecture content itself, but from two different perspectives.

Figure 8.4 summarizes the two key types of strategic business architecture governance.

Knowledge base governance manages changes to the *representation and description* of an organization's strategic business architecture. These changes are more superficial and are focused on how

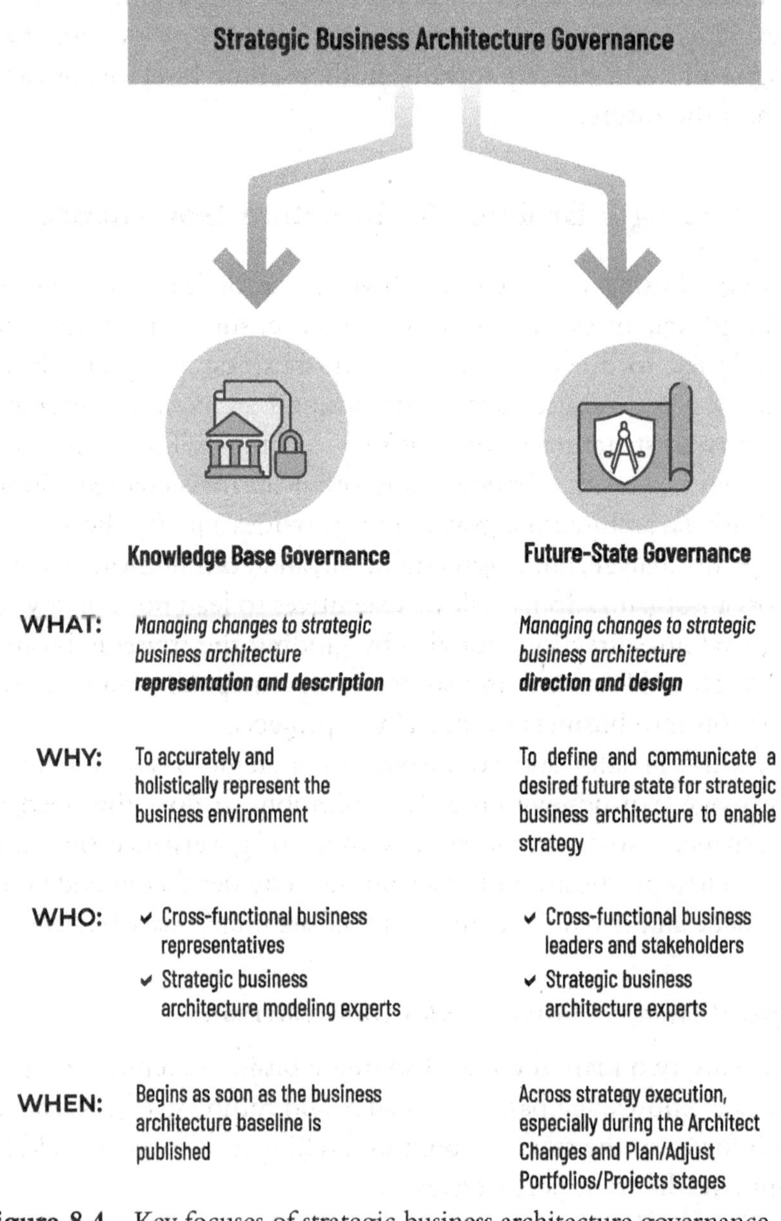

Strategic Business Architecture Governance
Knowledge Base Governance
Future-State Governance
WHAT:
Managing changes to strategic business architecture representation and description
Managing changes to strategic business architecture direction and design
WHY:
To accurately and holistically represent the business environment
To define and communicate a desired future state for strategic business architecture to enable strategy
WHO:
Cross-functional business representatives
Strategic business architecture modeling experts
Cross-functional business leaders and stakeholders
Strategic business architecture experts
WHEN:
Begins as soon as the business architecture baseline is published
Across strategy execution, especially during the Architect Changes and Plan/Adjust Portfolios/Projects stages

Figure 8.4 Key focuses of strategic business architecture governance.

the strategic business architecture is named, defined, and modeled in the knowledge base. For example, this type of governance would decide whether a level 1 capability should be called client management or customer management.

There are two perspectives for review and oversight related to knowledge base governance:

- **Business perspective:** A designated group of cross-functional business stakeholders reviews proposed additions or changes to ensure that they are correct and complete from a business subject matter expertise perspective. This ensures that the strategic business architecture content accurately represents the organization.
- **Architecture perspective:** Designated strategic business architecture modeling experts review proposed additions or changes to ensure that they adhere to strategic business architecture principles and guidelines for modeling. This ensures that the strategic business architecture content remains consistent and high quality and adheres to best practices.

Knowledge base governance is relevant to all organizations. It becomes essential just as soon as the first version of the full or partial business architecture baseline (capabilities, information concepts, value streams) is published. Knowledge base governance manages how proposed changes to the strategic business architecture naming, definition, and modeling will be tracked, reviewed, approved, implemented, published, and communicated to all stakeholders. Knowledge base governance is typically managed through regular releases that occur not more frequently than quarterly. Updated content may be published within the tool that automates the strategic business architecture knowledge base (if available). In addition, refreshed views of the capability map, value streams, and other key components may be published on intranet sites or other shared locations.

Future-state governance focuses on the definition of a desired future state for the strategic business architecture to enable strategy. This type of governance manages changes to the *direction and design* of an organization's strategic business architecture. From a strategy execution perspective, this is a critical point of alignment to build a common understanding and agreement around what the future-state business environment will need to look like. This alignment is key to heading off the downstream execution challenges that can occur. The outcomes of this process have significant bearing on the design of an organization's strategic business architecture and operating model, as well as any corresponding investments.

Since capabilities and value streams frame change, but the actual changes are typically made through aspects of the operating model (people, process, information, technology), *both* strategic business architecture and operating model views are leveraged to communicate the future state. For example, consider an organization that has redundant implementation of its customer information management capability across product areas (that is, multiple people, processes, data, and system applications are doing the same work duplicated across each product area). The capability of customer information management would remain the same in the organization's target-state strategic business architecture, but the *implementation* of that capability would be streamlined into one or fewer instances. This underscores the importance of close partnership between strategic business architecture and other strategy execution disciplines such as organization design, business process management, and IT architecture, as discussed in Chapter 6.

Future-state governance is a more advanced concept that is typically introduced once an organization matures in its use of strategic business architecture to translate strategies and other large-scale changes such as business transformations. The need for a common understanding of the future-state business environment applies across strategy execution, but it is particularly relevant during the Architect Changes stage and the Plan/Adjust Portfolios/ Projects stage.

Future-state governance again has two perspectives for review and oversight:

- **Business perspective:** A designated group of cross-functional business leaders and stakeholders review the future-state strategic business architecture views (sometimes referred to as a *target-state strategic business architecture,* as described in Chapter 4) and other design documents as applicable. They also review the strategic road map(s) that will transform the business environment from the current state to the future state to enable strategy. This ensures that all key decision-makers are aligned to a common vision of the future state prior to funding and implementation. A business executive (or set of executives, such as a cross-functional business steering committee) is ultimately accountable for the direction and approval. Figure 4.20 from Chapter 4 reflected an enterprise-level ownership structure that was oriented around value streams and capabilities (the cube). This ownership structure is particularly useful for future-state governance, which is typically framed around value streams and capabilities at the highest level.

- **Architecture perspective:** A designated group of strategic business architecture experts review the target-state strategic business architectures, design documents as applicable, and design strategic road maps. These experts are typically at the highest level of strategic business architecture experience and authority. This review ensures that the architecture and designs are aligned with architectural guidance and direction for purposes of design integrity. It also ensures that any defined future states are aligned across initiatives, programs, and portfolios where applicable.

These two types of governance interrelate in some scenarios. For example, if an organization's strategy requires an entirely new capability to be performed by the organization, this would certainly fall within the direction provided through future-state governance. In addition, a change would also be required through knowledge base governance to name and define the new capability and add it to the appropriate place within the enterprise capability map.

In addition to strategic business architecture governance, enterprise portfolio governance reflects the changes needed to the enterprise portfolios discussed in Chapter 5 to keep them current with changes in strategic direction. In fact, the defined future state of the strategic business architecture reflecting changes to strategy is an input to enterprise portfolio governance. The decisions made regarding these technology asset, human capital asset, value stream, process, capability asset, and project investment asset portfolios have a direct impact on strategy execution effectiveness. Governance of these portfolios is discussed in detail in Chapter 5.

Leveraging Strategic Business Architecture within Other Governance Processes

Strategic business architecture is valuable far beyond just architecture-specific governance. It can be integrated into other governance processes anywhere across strategy execution to bring new insights and accountability.

For example, submitted investment requests may require an assessment of the capabilities being enhanced so that prioritization and investment decisions can include an aggregated perspective across the organization, as shown in Figure 5.3 in Chapter 5. Innovation ideas that reach a certain point of maturity may require a strategic business architecture impact assessment to determine viability and alignment before moving forward. In addition, strategic business architecture can be leveraged to provide a wide range of holistic, data-based checks on proposed initiatives and projects, from customer experience impact to sustainability impact to technical debt impact.

Integration with Enterprise Architecture Governance

If an enterprise architecture practice already exists within an organization, it is likely that some execution-level governance mechanisms are already in place, such as an architecture review board. Enterprise architecture governance often focuses on projects and solutions, especially from a technology perspective. Execution-level business architecture may be incorporated as an additional layer within these structures and processes. For example, an assessment of the alignment of solutions to execution-level business direction and strategic business architecture direction may be incorporated within the process. Typically, execution-level business architects would perform these governance activities and coordinate with strategic business architects as appropriate.

In contrast, strategic business architecture governance is primarily focused on the effective execution of strategy, is driven within strategic planning, and occurs much further upstream as strategies are being developed and translated, before projects are defined. Enterprise architects and senior IT architects may also be involved upstream, for example, to define the corresponding target-state IT architectures to enable the target-state strategic business architectures.

Leadership: The Essential Element of Successful Strategic Business Architecture

Effective leadership is critical for long-term success in strategic business architecture. It is not only necessary for strategic business architecture to bring the greatest value as a discipline, but also to help lead an organization to new levels of vision, innovation, and transformation.

First, what is leadership? Leadership and management are often delineated as distinct yet interrelated aspects of organizational governance that help to guide people toward common goals. However, *leadership* tends to focus on inspiring, motivating, and mobilizing individuals to achieve their best potential; creating the vision and fostering a sense of purpose; encouraging innovation; and building the culture and teams. On the other hand, *management* is often associated with planning, budgeting, organizing, and controlling resources to ensure efficiency and productivity. A good manager does not necessarily make a good leader, and a good leader does not necessarily make a good manager. Most research has concluded that leadership is more about who one is and management is more about one's position in the organization. While leaders prioritize long-term vision and change, managers are more concerned with day-to-day operations and effectiveness. Both are important for sustained success within an organization, but we will focus on the key role of leadership for strategic business architecture.

Strategic Business Architecture Leadership for the Success of the Function

Strategic business architecture plays the role of a service provider and internal consultancy within the strategy execution function and the organization. The leadership capabilities needed to effectively be the *bridge* between strategy and execution are many and diverse. For example, strategic business architecture needs to:

- Provide leadership, support decision-making, serve as a change leader, and help communicate throughout the entire life cycle of strategy and transformation, especially early in the process as ideas are being formed.
- Set and lead the vision for the desired future state for the strategic business architecture to achieve strategy and influence people to adopt it.
- Inspire, motivate, and mobilize people toward a vision of cohesive, end-to-end strategy execution enabled by strategic business architecture.
- Inspire and influence people to think differently about intentional, composable design for the enterprise and instill a sense of responsibility for business outcomes and the value delivered to customers/constituents across the entire organization, infused into the culture.
- Facilitate innovation and design for the business, enterprise, product, and execution.
- Build the team and culture for the strategic business architecture function, which includes developing, motivating, and mobilizing individuals to deliver value for the organization and succeed in the role.

The strategic business architecture function must have effective leaders to be successful. The models of strategic business architecture are only a means to an end to achieve outcomes for strategy execution and provide new business insights. Key organizational stakeholders need to see strategic business architects as leaders who can help them to address the organization's challenges and opportunities in a fresh, holistic, and effective way. Introducing new ways of doing things that are innovative and different from the status quo builds new trust and confidence in strategic business architecture leadership.

This requires moving into a leadership mindset, having a command of the strategic business architecture competencies defined earlier, and being comfortable in a position of influence. Influence is a key lever through which change is made, especially in strategic business architecture–related roles. As Figure 8.5 shows, many people assume that power comes from position or politics, but the greatest power—and that which is hardest to lose—comes from how one is perceived by others and one's ability to influence.

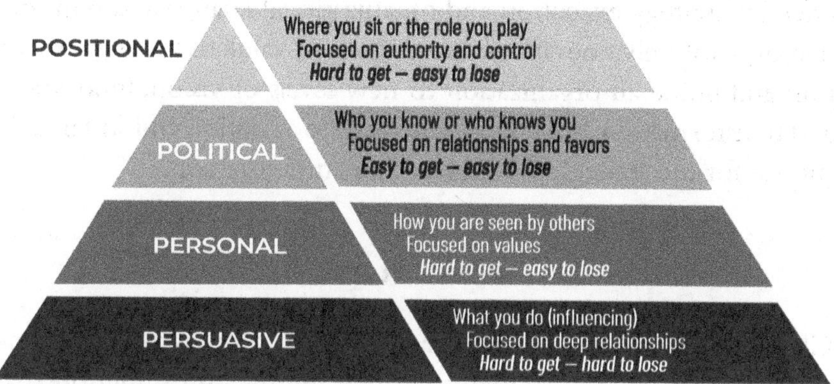

Figure 8.5 Influence is multifaceted.

Source: Jeff Scott, Business Innovation Partners

Strategic Business Architecture Leadership for the Success of the Organization

In addition to facilitating the leadership of strategy development and execution, strategic business architecture can also be a powerful mechanism for transformation and change *across the entire organization*. Strategic business architecture attracts some of the best and brightest people who often see a bigger picture and connections that others do not—and they take responsibility for doing what is best for the enterprise and its stakeholders. As a strategic and emerging function, strategic business architecture often has more latitude than others to take a leading role to introduce change and new ways of thinking and working.

As the Strategic Business Architecture Maturity Model described, the most mature and impactful strategic business architecture functions are those that are transformative and visionary. Organizational change is hard, but that is part of being a transformative leader. Organizations are in desperate need of a holistic approach to enterprise design, strategy execution, and transformation, so think big, step into the role, and lead. The future success of your organization depends on it.

Impactful strategic business architecture leadership is essential for effective strategy execution and organizational change and transformation. Not only does it deliver the greatest value to strategy execution and guide an organization to new levels of vision, innovation, and transformation, but it is also the path to adoption and sustainable success for the strategic business architecture function.

Next Steps

Chapters 7 and 8 described the necessary components and considerations to build a strategic business architecture function that scales, succeeds, and continually delivers value.

To get started, follow the practical approach provided:

1. Build the business case for a comprehensive approach to strategy execution and strategic business architecture. Build understanding, buy-in, advocacy, and executive business sponsorship for the vision and the initial steps forward.
2. Select initial usage scenario(s) for leveraging strategic business architecture within a strategy execution context.
3. Build your strategic business architecture baseline in close partnership with a cross-functional group of business stakeholders.
4. Leverage the strategic business architecture baseline for your first usage scenario. Deliver the intended business outcomes, and measure and communicate the value and learning to others. Continue leveraging strategic business architecture for expanded usage scenarios, and repeat the cycle of delivering business outcomes, measuring value, and telling the story and building advocates as you go.
5. As momentum increases, start formalizing your strategic business architecture function. Perform an initial maturity assessment, create your strategic plan, and develop a road map to establish and mature the strategic business architecture function over the next 6 to 12 months that includes the five key components discussed in this chapter. Leverage value measurement and the Strategic Business Architecture Maturity Model to continue guiding your way forward.

With a solid understanding of a comprehensive vision for strategy execution and strategic business architecture, we will now look toward the future and explore some key trends and closing considerations in our final chapter.

STRATEGY EXECUTION ORGANIZATIONAL ASSESSMENT

Reflect on the following questions to assess how well strategy execution is working in your organization based on the concepts from Chapter 8. Please refer to the scoring guidance provided in Chapter 1.

1. Our organization regularly assesses the maturity of our strategic business architecture function and actively works toward maturing and scaling it with intentional plans.
2. Our organization ensures that strategic business architecture is fully understood and adopted throughout the organization with intentional socialization, relationship building, and organizational change management.
3. The strategic business architecture function is resourced appropriately to meet the business needs across strategy execution.
4. Our organization has a defined career path for strategic business architecture that is easy to transition in and out of, supported by a robust development program.
5. Strategic business architecture principles and architectural thinking are embedded into our organizational culture and talent management.
6. Our organization has defined the relevant governance structures and processes for strategic business architecture, and they are working effectively to achieve our desired business outcomes.
7. Our organization has an enterprise-level executive business ownership and accountability structure (for example, one business leader or a committee of business leaders) to set direction and guide investments oriented around the delivery and enhancement of value streams and capabilities.
8. The leadership of our strategy execution function is effective.

9. Our strategic business architecture function is recognized for its leadership and seen as a powerful mechanism for transformation and change for the organization.

Please also refer to the Strategic Business Architecture Maturity Model presented earlier in this chapter for additional assessment questions pertaining to the strategic business architecture function.

Chapter 9

Strategy Execution Trends and the Application of Strategic Business Architecture

The futures of strategic business architecture and strategy execution are intertwined. In most organizations, most of the focus for strategic planning groups has been on strategy formulation. Only recently has there been more of a shift to strategy execution. Google Trends reports a steady growth of worldwide use of the search term "strategy execution" over the past 10 years.This suggests an increased attention to strategy execution across the globe. Since 2019, research and advisory company Gartner has increasingly covered strategy execution as a key area of increasing global importance. Strategy execution is not a new topic—it has been around for decades and is widely recognized as one of the most challenging aspects of strategy. So, why is there more emphasis on strategy execution today than in the past?

There are many reasons why the importance of strategy execution is growing. Today, strategy cycles have become shorter, and there is more change and uncertainty in most environments. This has required organizations to become more agile and increase attention on effective strategy execution. Also, strategy execution has become more difficult due to the more complex operating environment faced by most organizations today, which often includes fierce competition, greater rate of change, increasing customer and employee demands, working in interconnected business ecosystems, and more organizational complexity and decision points. This increasingly complex business environment increases the stakes of strategy execution as the results of poor strategy execution are more impactful and harder to recover from than in the past.

As we saw in Chapter 1, strategy execution entails much more than just the last minor step of strategy. Organizations are waking up to this fact, and strategy execution is now much more substantive than a vague paragraph or two in the strategic plan. This chapter will explore the major strategy execution trends and how strategic business architecture facilitates these trends.

> *"Most leaders would agree that they'd be better off having an average strategy with superb execution than a superb strategy with poor execution. Those who execute always have the upper hand."*
>
> —*Stephen R. Covey*

More Focus on Developing Executable Strategy

The first trend is that organizations will put more focus on developing strategy that is executable. As we've discussed in prior chapters, strategy execution is notoriously difficult and known for its high failure rates. One contributor to the strategy execution problem that has only recently been recognized is that many strategies aren't very executable in the first place. Unfortunately, the strategy development process can create strategies that are hard, or even impossible, to execute. For a strategy to be executable, it should be understandable, developed in a manner that people want to execute it and make it work, and the strategy should match the reality of the organization and its people. Let's examine each of these three qualities of an executable strategy and how strategic business architecture helps make each quality a reality.

An understandable strategy is not vague, abstract, complex, or otherwise incomprehensible for people to understand. Often people read a strategy but can't relate it to what they do and what it means for them. People at all levels in the organization need to be able to translate the strategy into tactics that they understand and relate to their role in the organization. A strategy is developed to direct a group of people to a shared goal, but if the strategy and goal are not well understood, effective execution will remain elusive. Strategic business architecture provides the organizational views, perspectives, and information needed to create the common understanding and vocabulary of the organization needed to (a) inform strategy development in a manner that the organization understands, and (b) facilitate the development and maintenance of the understandable linkages between strategy and tactical project-level execution.

Often, strategy is developed within smaller groups of senior-level executives and is not understood or embraced across a large parts of the organization. Without broader commitment, buy-in, and comprehension from different levels of the organization, effective strategy execution is very difficult. This is often interpreted as resistance and seen as a change management problem that often results in a variety of persuasive, and perhaps forceful, attempts to get the organization to execute strategy. However, the root cause of the strategy execution problem is not a change management issue, but rather a strategy development issue. Strategic business architecture brings the organizational understanding needed to identify which parts of the organization are central to the strategy execution process so that they can be included in the strategy development process. This early inclusion in the process creates the buy-in needed for effective strategy execution.

Strategy can be difficult to execute when the strategy doesn't really match the reality and values of the organization and its people. This lack of common purpose often results in failed strategy execution. A well-communicated and understood shared strategic purpose, beyond profitability, will create an environment where stakeholders derive meaning from the strategy and understand how they are benefiting others by successfully executing the strategy.

Many strategy development processes begin with an outside-in approach, often starting with a competitor analysis and analysis of external trends. This process often leads to ambitious and perhaps not-so-realistic objectives. These types of external analyses have their place, but when overemphasized, they may lead to the formulation of strategy that is too far off from what the organization and its people can pragmatically achieve. Strategic business architecture provides the organizational understanding needed to produce a strategy that is more closely aligned with the organization's assets, capabilities, and stakeholders and has a much higher likelihood of successful execution. While strategic business architecture does not alleviate all implementation problems, it will help to produce a well-formulated strategy that is executable and will greatly improve the chances of successful strategy execution.

Alignment of Projects with Strategy

Ensuring that project portfolios are aligned with current strategy, and the ongoing prioritization of the projects in the portfolios, will be a major factor in the need to increase performance and effectively execute strategy. With the constant pace of change, strategy development and strategy execution will need to be inextricably linked. Throughout this book, we've discussed how strategic business architecture creates (and maintains) the alignment between strategy and project-level execution.

Continuous Monitoring and Adaptation

In a rapidly changing business environment, the ability to monitor and adapt strategy implementation in real time is crucial. This continuous monitoring involves the use of feedback loops and key performance indicators (KPIs) to ensure that the organization remains on track and can swiftly adjust course when needed. Greater uncertainty means a need for greater flexibility in the execution of strategy and that strategies are now less long term in nature than in the past. Strategy has become a hypothesis to be tested, not a plan carved in stone.

Continuous monitoring and adaptation requires greater degrees of collaboration at all levels of the organization. This enhanced collaboration requires a greater need for a more collaborative working environment, with clear, open communication and access to shared information. It also requires greater degrees of transparency to provide increased clarity on the organization's goals and direction. Transparency not only enables collaboration and communication, but it also enables the organization to be adaptive. Clear direction and focus are critical for effective strategy execution. Strategic business architecture provides the organization understanding needed to assess where feedback loops are needed and what KPIs are needed and where they are most useful in the strategy execution process. Strategic business architecture also helps to foster greater organizational transparency and ensure that a change in direction is quickly understood by all levels of the strategy execution process and that appropriate changes are made to support the change in direction.

Agile Strategy Execution

The discipline of strategy development is undergoing fundamental transformation. Uncertain environments create a need for agility and result in shorter strategy cycles. Scenario planning is more important than ever. Speed and agility are key for survival in fast-paced, ever-changing markets. As a result, there has been an increasing movement toward agile methodologies for strategy execution. Agile methodologies, originally developed in the software development realm, are gaining traction in strategic management. These methodologies emphasize rapid prototyping and iteration, as well as constant communication and collaboration among team members. The iterative nature of agile allows organizations to respond swiftly to changes in the business environment. Agile strategy execution requires an agile organization whose components are well understood and able to be rapidly changed and deployed.

As discussed in earlier chapters, *composable business* is the design of an organization with interchangeable building blocks, which enables it to maximize the design and delivery of the resilience and agility needed to rapidly respond to market opportunities and challenges. Agile methodologies can be leveraged to effectively implement the concepts of a composable business. The foundation for a composable business is the strategic business architecture, with capabilities at the center. Strategic business architecture provides the modular business building blocks with which an organization can be designed. A composable strategic business architecture enables an enterprise to react faster to large-scale organizational transformations. Strategic business architecture enables the business design to be analyzed to see if value creation and the associated strategic business architecture components, such as value streams and capabilities, are modularly designed.

Data-Driven Strategy Execution

In the era of big data, organizations have unprecedented access to information. Leveraging data analytics for strategy execution is increasingly important to provide insights into market trends, customer behavior, and internal operations. This data can help inform decisions on everything from resource allocation and product development to big capital investments. Data analytics is increasingly becoming a cornerstone of effective strategy implementation. Organizations can harness the power of data to monitor progress, identify bottlenecks, and make informed decisions. Strategic business architecture provides the organizational understanding needed to determine what data is needed for effective strategy execution and to understand where gaps in data might exist. The organizational data and analytics produced by the strategic business architecture practice make the strategy formulation and strategy execution process more efficient and effective.

Technology Integration and Transformation

Advanced technologies such as artificial intelligence (AI), machine learning, and blockchain are reshaping the way organizations execute their strategies. From predictive analytics for forecasting to blockchain for supply chain transparency, technology is becoming an integral part of strategy development and its enablement. AI can scan very large datasets, analyze market information, and offer insights that not only aid in the initial development of strategy but also enable organizations to make real-time changes in strategy. In addition, AI is also then able to quickly identify which business capabilities in an organization should be modified or added to reflect the changes in strategy, allowing the organization to react faster and better ensure effective strategy execution. The potential for composable business, as first discussed in Chapter 2, and for overall business agility is immense.

AI is rapidly converging with other technologies, such as machine learning, blockchain, and the Internet of Things (IoT), to enable transformative changes in organizations across all industries. Today's digital enterprises require shorter strategy life cycles in the fast-changing competitive environments enabled by these revolutionary technologies. Strategic business architecture has its roots in enterprise technology strategy and integration. Strategic business architecture provides the framework, tools, and organizational understanding and perspectives needed to effectively integrate advanced technologies into any complex process. Strategic business architecture provides the insights needed to understand where advanced technologies can (and should) be utilized to enhance complex processes such as strategy execution—and how technologies can be leveraged for strategic advantage. Strategic business architecture can also help determine whether a particular technology is appropriate for the needs of an organization. Additionally, strategic business architecture provides traceability and transparency to support stakeholder management and governance for emerging technologies such as AI.

Collaborative and Inclusive Leadership in a Digital World

The future of strategy execution demands a shift in leadership styles toward collaboration and inclusivity. Leaders must engage with diverse stakeholders, both internal and external, to ensure alignment and commitment to the strategic vision. In addition, the rate of transformation (digital and otherwise) has increased exponentially for most organizations and has forced many organizations to rethink their business and operating business models to compete in a digital world. This restructuring of the business and the way it executes strategy has resulted in fundamental shifts in the way leaders operate.

Middle managers are becoming more involved in and accountable for strategy execution and are playing greater roles in the strategy development process. Research has shown that the changemakers in most organizations are in the mid-levels—those who are connected to senior-level leadership but are also connected to the lower, more tactical levels of the organization. These mid-level leaders are often the people who connect the dots and drive innovation in the organization. They are also often the people who inspire and lead the people at the tactical execution layer of the organization. Increased involvement of middle managers will strengthen the strategy development and execution processes, as well as increase understanding, buy-in, and support for strategic directions. Today, leaders need to understand what is happening in the organization at many levels, and strategic business architecture provides the views and perspectives into the organization that produce the comprehensive understanding of the organization that is required to lead in the digital age.

Dynamic Organizational Structures

The hierarchical structures of the past are giving way to more dynamic and flexible organizational models that include networked organizations, cross-functional teams, and decentralized decision-making structures. These organizational models enable organizations to respond swiftly to market shifts and customer demands. These dynamic structures also make understanding the current state of the organization much more challenging than in the past. Organizational structures have shifted to accommodate a workforce that is increasingly made up of knowledge workers who are organized into real and virtual teams. Strategy will be increasingly executed via networks of collaborators who may be largely self-managed.

Increased globalization will make the execution of strategy more complex because it allows organizations many more choices about how and where to execute strategies. This increased complexity coupled with shorter strategy life cycles requires a highly flexible organizational culture. Organizations are also shifting to work in partnership with other organizations in business ecosystems where they can deliver greater value together. Complex organizations build global supply chains and strategic alliances and need to understand the implications of changes in strategy on these complex structures. Strategic business architecture is crucial for developing and maintaining these dynamic organizational structures and ensuring that a current and accurate understanding of the organization is utilized for strategy development and execution.

Culture of Continual Innovation

Leading organizations seek ways to foster a culture of innovation to drive growth and enhance competitiveness. Organizations that foster a culture of innovation experience improved financial performance compared to those that do not prioritize innovation as part of their strategic goals. As discussed in earlier chapters, strategic business architecture can be leveraged throughout the entire innovation life cycle and makes innovation more impactful, effective, and embedded into all aspects of an organization. In fact, strategic business architecture practices are often a hub for internal innovation because of the unique, enterprise-wide understanding and perspective that a well-functioning strategic business architecture practice possesses. Strategic business architects are typically very well connected in the organization and have identified critical subject matter experts and strategic thinkers within the organization. They are often the people who are the "clearinghouse" for ideas and are in a unique position to connect dots for internal innovation opportunities. For example, strategic business architects can help to generate or facilitate sharing of innovation ideas and identify focus areas where innovation is needed, resulting either from business priorities or from known areas of improvement. These opportunities can be framed around defined aspects of the strategic business architecture.

Strategic business architects also provide the tools to analyze opportunities for value to the organization and potential associated risks. They can assess the viability and impact of innovation ideas on an ongoing basis and provide a perspective on how those ideas fit within the bigger-picture strategy and priorities of the organization.

Stakeholder Understanding and Management

Research shows that organizations that effectively manage the needs and expectations of their stakeholders are more likely to achieve their strategic goals. Furthermore, there is also an increasing shift toward stakeholder capitalism, which emphasizes the responsibility of businesses to consider the interests of all stakeholders, including employees, customers, suppliers, communities, and the environment, alongside generating profits for shareholders. This increase is marked by a growing recognition among businesses that long-term success is intertwined with the well-being of diverse stakeholders. This means that there are many stakeholders to consider, including customers, employees, investors, regulators, and others, and not all stakeholders are of equal importance in the strategy execution process. As you saw in earlier chapters, strategic business architecture helps you to understand which stakeholders are key to your success and helps you to understand what they value. Strategic business architecture also helps with the assessment of change impact on different stakeholder groups and ensures their voice and needs have been appropriately considered in strategies and solutions.

Enhanced Strategic Risk Management

Strategic risk management is a critical aspect of enterprise risk management that is often overlooked. *Strategic risk management* is the process of identifying, quantifying, and mitigating risks related to an organization's strategy, strategic objectives, and strategy execution. Dynamic business environments coupled with the increased use of agile practices in strategy execution amplify the requirement for timely identification and mitigation of risks in the strategy development and execution processes. Strategic risks are those risks that could potentially result in a major loss for the organization. The organization needs to be able to determine which strategic risks could have the most impact. There are two major types of risks to consider in the strategy development and execution processes. First are the risks associated with possible strategic choices and directions, and second are organizational risks that might inhibit the successful execution of strategy. Both sets of risks are crucial to understand and evaluate. As mentioned in Chapter 2, strategic business architecture provides the tools and environmental and organizational perspectives needed to analyze potential strategy development– and execution-related risks and develop and implement contingency plans.

Increased Focus on Sustainability

Many organizations are increasing their focus on sustainability in the strategy execution process as they recognize the importance of long-term environmental, social, and economic aspects of strategy. This increased focus may involve adopting sustainable business practices, such as reducing waste and greenhouse gas emissions, and incorporating sustainability considerations into strategy formulation.

As the Ellen MacArthur Foundation states, "Design is a force for change." The problem—and the solution—starts with design. Strategic business architecture provides a holistic and value-oriented framework to design and redesign an entire organization and its products and services around sustainability and circularity. In addition, capabilities (along with their value stream context) provide a focal point for measuring sustainability performance. This means that they can be leveraged to inform strategy development on potential sustainability and stakeholder impacts and considerations. Capabilities can also help to identify targeted sustainability improvements that will have the greatest impact on strategy and are actionable and harmonized across the organization. Strategic business architecture can also help to embed sustainable and circular thinking throughout an organization.

Increased Workforce Diversity and Complexity

As we've discussed throughout this book, effective strategy execution requires people with the right skills, the right understanding of the organization, the right understanding of strategic goals, and the motivation to help the organization attain these goals. Workforces around the globe are becoming more diverse not only in terms of ethnicity, age, gender, and nationality but also in terms of employer relationships—many organizations utilize more free agents, contractors, vendors, part-timers, and working retirees than they did in the past. This increased workforce complexity necessitates the degree of organizational understanding provided by strategic business architecture to better ensure that the components of this complex workforce "row the boat in the same direction." Strategic business architecture can also help to ensure that the needs and perspectives of all stakeholders are considered to ensure that products, solutions, and interactions are aligned and also free from bias.

The Evolution of Strategic Business Architecture as a Separate and Distinct Discipline

As discussed in Chapter 1, it is important to understand the significant differences between traditional execution-level business architecture and strategic business architecture. The discipline of business architecture "grew up" as part of an information technology (IT) strategic planning discipline known as enterprise architecture. Traditional legacy business architecture practices that reside as part of a larger enterprise architecture practice are typically technically oriented and often focus on process and/or capability modeling for the IT organization for the purpose of understanding a part of the organization in order to implement or change an IT system, project, or initiative. These practices are not enterprise-wide in their scope (reporting to the IT organization) and are not closely affiliated with strategic planning or enterprise strategy execution.

In contrast, strategic business architecture practices have an organization-wide perspective, are business oriented, and are typically part of the strategy execution function. For many organizations, these strategically oriented practices represent the critical component needed for effective strategy execution and a component that is missing in many organizations today. Strategic business architecture creates the line of sight between enterprise project portfolios and business strategy and helps to ensure that the organization is doing the "right" projects that are aligned with current business strategy. Traditional execution-level business architecture helps to ensure that projects and initiatives are implemented correctly and achieve their desired objectives.

It is possible (and likely) that an organization may have both an execution-level business architecture practice within the IT organization and a strategic business architecture practice within the strategic planning organization. The execution-level business architecture practice will likely utilize a narrow range of business architecture tools and techniques, while the strategic business architecture practice will likely rely on a much wider range of tools and techniques to inform strategy development and facilitate strategy execution.

As we have emphasized, the backgrounds, skills, and perspectives needed to be successful with strategic business architecture are very different from those needed to be successful with traditional, more IT systems–centric, execution-level business architecture. Both disciplines have value in the organization, but if someone is successful in execution-level business architecture, it does not necessarily mean they will successfully transition to strategic business architecture. In fact, often this transition is not pragmatic due to the vast differences in the two disciplines and the types of people each requires for success. Perhaps a future rebranding of each discipline will occur as they continue to evolve in different directions.

Strategy Execution Evolves into a Distinct Discipline

As we discussed in Chapter 1, most strategic planning approaches do not provide much detail on the *how* of strategy execution. Setting strategy is the easier part—execution is difficult. As discussed in Chapter 6, many functions and disciplines need to work together for strategy execution to succeed from end to end. As also discussed in Chapter 6, consolidation of these fragmented (and sometimes overlapping) functions and disciplines under one strategy execution function is needed to achieve efficient and effective strategy execution. From this perspective, strategy execution is the umbrella discipline under which all the other "subdisciplines" needed for effective strategy execution reside. As discussed throughout this book, strategic business architecture is the "bridge" discipline/subdiscipline that facilitates the orchestration, collaboration, and connection of the strategy execution subdisciplines.

As effective strategy execution continues to advance as an organizational priority and our understanding of what it takes to effectively execute strategy continues to advance, it is natural to expect that strategy execution will evolve into a distinct discipline that is closely aligned with strategic planning yet with its own separate and distinct roles, skill sets, competencies, knowledge bases, education, certifications, professional associations, and other features and requirements of a formalized discipline.

Summary

The landscape of business strategy execution is evolving rapidly, driven by technological advancements, global interconnectedness, and a growing need for adaptability in the face of unprecedented challenges. Effective strategy implementation is paramount for organizations to translate their strategic vision into tangible results and confront an unpredictable future. By embracing agile methodologies, leveraging data, integrating technology for strategic and operational advantage, fostering collaborative leadership, and establishing dynamic organizational structures, businesses can position themselves for success in the fast-changing, ever-evolving, landscape that lies ahead. By fostering innovation and adaptability, organizations can not only execute their strategies more effectively but also build resilience to face the uncertainties that lie ahead.

The future of strategy execution demands a holistic and adaptive approach. As we've emphasized throughout this book, strategic business architecture is central to the creation and implementation of this approach. Without the deep organizational understanding and concrete ability to translate strategy into organized effort that strategic business architecture provides, the holistic and adaptive approach needed for successful strategy execution will remain elusive in many organizations.

Endnotes

Chapter 1: Strategy Development, Alignment, and Execution

1. Robert S. Kaplan and David P. Norton, *The Balanced Scorecard: Translating Strategy into Action* (Boston, MA: Harvard Business School Press, 1996).
2. Robert S. Kaplan and D. P. Norton, *The Strategy-Focused Organization: How Balanced Scorecard Companies Thrive in the New Business Environment* (Boston, MA: Harvard Business School Press, 2000).
3. Robert S. Kaplan and David P. Norton, "The Office of Strategy Management," *Harvard Business Review* (2005). https://hbr.org/2005/10/the-office-of-strategy-management.
4. https://balancedscorecard.org/bsc-basics-overview/.
5. J. Trevor and B. Varcoe, "A Simple Way to Test Your Company's Alignment," *Harvard Business Review* (2016). https://hbr.org/2016/05/a-simple-way-to-test-your-companys-strategic-alignment.

6. J. C. Henderson and N.Venkatraman, "Strategic Alignment: Leveraging Information Technology for Transforming Organizations," *IBM Systems Journal* 38, no. 2.3 (1999): 472–484, https://doi.org/10.1147/SJ.1999.5387096.
7. MBA Roundtable/Business Architecture Guild®, "Strategy Execution Education in Graduate Management Education," (2021). StrategyExecutionEducationinGraduateManagementEducation_Report(1).pdf (gbcroundtable.org).

Chapter 2: The Role of Strategic Business Architecture in Strategy Development and Execution

1. Adapted from the original definition of business architecture in the *BIZBOK® Guide* by the Business Architecture Guild®, which was "A blueprint of the enterprise that provides a common understanding of the organization and is used to align strategic objectives and tactical demands."
2. Michael E. Porter, *The Five Competitive Forces That Shape Strategy*. (Boston, MA: Harvard Business School Press, 2008).
3. Gartner, "4 Steps to Bridge the Strategy-Execution Gap with Adaptive Capabilities," (2021). https://www.gartner.com/en/documents/4009100.
4. IDEO Design Thinking. "Design Thinking Defined." https://designthinking.ideo.com.

Chapter 3: The Strategic Business Architecture Toolkit

1. This set of domains is the perspective of the Business Architecture Guild® and are defined per the *BIZBOK® Guide*.
2. Ibid.
3. The formal OMG standard (the Business Architecture Core Metamodel) is available at: https://www.omg.org/spec/BACM/1.0/Beta1/PDF. Please also see the business architecture metamodel in the *BIZBOK® Guide*.

4. Alexander Osterwalder et al., *Value Proposition Design* (Hoboken, NJ: John Wiley & Sons, Inc., 2010).
5. Alexander Osterwalder and Yves Pigneur, *Business Model Generation* (Hoboken, NJ: John Wiley & Sons, Inc., 2014), 14.
6. Alexander Osterwalder and Yves Pigneur, *Business Model Generation* (Hoboken, NJ: John Wiley & Sons, Inc., 2014).
7. Andrew Campbell, Mikel Gutierrez, and Mark Lancelott, *Operating Model Canvas* (Van Haren Publishing, 2017), 3.
8. Andrew Campbell, Mikel Gutierrez, and Mark Lancelott, *Operating Model Canvas* (Van Haren Publishing, 2017) 19.
9. This is the perspective that is defined in the *BIZBOK® Guide*.
10. Value stream based on the *BIZBOK® Guide* Manufacturing Reference Model with minor adaptations. The *BIZBOK® Guide* reference models are available at https://www.businessarchitectureguild.org/page/INDREF.
11. Capability map is a hybrid, with a combined information concept and functional orientation. This is partially aligned with the *BIZBOK® Guide* Manufacturing Reference Model.
12. Based on the definition referenced in the *BIZBOK® Guide*.
13. Value stream and capabilities are based on the *BIZBOK® Guide* Manufacturing Reference Model with minor adaptations. Processes are based on the APQC Consumer Products Process Classification Framework.

Chapter 4: Leveraging a Capability Perspective for Strategy Translation and Alignment

1. Richard Rumelt, *Good Strategy Bad Strategy* (Crown Business, 2017), 66.
2. Most value stream names are based on the *BIZBOK® Guide* Manufacturing Reference Model. The *BIZBOK® Guide* reference models are available at https://www.businessarchitectureguild.org/page/INDREF.

3. Most capability names are based on the *BIZBOK® Guide* Manufacturing Reference Model. Most processes are from APQC Consumer Products Process Classification Framework. This diagram represents a subset of the applicable capabilities and processes for the value stream.
4. Most capability names are based on the *BIZBOK® Guide* Manufacturing Reference Model.

Chapter 5: Strategic Portfolio Management and Effective Strategy Execution

1. David Stang, "Strategic Portfolio Management Primer for 2023," Gartner Research (February 2, 2023). https://www.gartner.com/en/documents/4022938.
2. J. R. Turner, "Editorial: International Project Management Association Global Qualification, Certification, and Accreditation," *International Journal of Project Management* 14, no. 1 (February 1996): 1–6. https://doi.org/10.1016/0263-7863(96)88794-1.

Chapter 6: Linking Strategic Business Architecture with Other Architectural Domains and Other Business Functions and Disciplines

1. Diagram is not from the *BIZBOK® Guide,* but it is primarily based upon its content that defines domains and relationships, with some modifications.
2. Defined by the BRM Institute at https://brm.institute/about-business-relationship-management.
3. Jay Galbraith, Diane Downey, and Amy Kates, *Designing Dynamic Organizations: A Hands-on Guide for Leaders at All Levels* (New York, NY: AMACOM, 2002).

4. Diagram is not from the *BIZBOK® Guide,* but it is primarily based upon its content that defines domains and relationships. This does not include organization design, as it is not currently defined in the *BIZBOK® Guide.*

Chapter 7: Building the Strategic Business Architecture Function and Integration with Strategic Planning

1. Michael E. Porter, "The Five Competitive Forces That Shape Strategy," *Harvard Business Review* (January 2008), 79–93.

Acknowledgments

We express our deepest gratitude to all the people who made this book possible. Our sincere appreciation goes out to the esteemed team at John Wiley & Sons for helping us to create a world-class book and bring it to a global audience. We see this as just the beginning of a special partnership around the research, writing, and practical application of *The Execution Challenge*.

A special thanks to Bill Falloon, who immediately understood our approach to strategy execution and the power that it brings to organizations of all types and sizes. We are profoundly grateful for his insightful guidance and support throughout this journey.

Thank you to Tom Dinse, our incredible development editor, whose guidance and expertise was invaluable to help us create clarity and achieve our desired outcomes. Thank you also to our copy editor, Elizabeth Kuball, whose meticulous attention to detail and dedication to quality led to the final and polished version of this book that you hold in your hands now.

We also want to thank Richard Samson and Purvi Patel for their continual support and invaluable guidance throughout the entire process.

We extend our sincere gratitude to Christopher Wray of Communique Marketing Solutions, who brought this book to life with an extensive portfolio of graphics. His level of creative and design expertise is unparalleled, as is his commitment to excellence. We deeply valued his partnership and contributions throughout this journey.

We also want to express our profound gratitude to our spouses Denise (Brian) and Asbjørn (Whynde) for their unwavering love, encouragement, sacrifices, and support. They have been our champions, cheerleaders, and partners throughout this journey, and we simply could not have done it without them.

Lastly, we extend our greatest thanks to you, our readers. Thank you for your openness and curiosity to engage with us and explore strategy execution from a fresh, holistic perspective. We applaud your courageous leadership in translating these ideas into practical action for your organization, and we look forward to collaborating with you to shape the future of business together!

Brian H. Cameron
Whynde Kuehn
February 2024

About the Authors

Brian H. Cameron, Ph.D., is the Associate Dean for Professional Graduate Programs and Executive Education in the Smeal College of Business at the Pennsylvania State University. In his current role, Brian led the rapid growth of the Smeal professional graduate portfolio from the four master's programs and one online graduate certificate, representing approximately 300 students, in 2015 to an integrated portfolio of 16 master's programs, an Executive Doctor of Business Administration degree, and 16 online graduate certificates representing more than 2,300 students.

His work has been the topic of several articles in *BizEd,* the publication of AACSB, the international business school accreditation body. He is very active in the professional graduate education community, is a founding member of the Consortium for Online Graduate Business Education, and serves on boards for the

Graduate Business Curriculum Roundtable, the Executive MBA Council, and the Business Architecture Guild®. Brian is the recipient of the 2022 Penn State Commission for Adult Learners' Shirley Hendrick Award for his contributions to significantly foster and increase Penn State's efforts to serve the adult learner. He was also the recipient of the 2023 Graduate Business Curriculum Roundtable Innovator Award for his work at Penn State.

Brian is also a Senior Consultant with Cutter Consortium's Business & Enterprise Architecture practice and is the Founding Director of the Center for Enterprise Architecture in the College of Information Sciences and Technology at Penn State and Founding President of the Federation of Enterprise Architecture Professional Organizations (FEAPO). He designed and implemented the first online Enterprise Architecture master's program in the world. Brian was awarded the NPA Career Achievement Award in 2011 for efforts related to founding FEAPO, building the Center for Enterprise Architecture, and associated service to the enterprise architecture profession.

He has worked with a wide portfolio of companies on a variety of consulting engagements, ranging from systems integration strategy to strategic enterprise and business architecture planning and design. Brian has consulted with Accenture, AT&T Wireless, Avaya, Boeing, EMC Corp, Lockheed Martin, NSA, Oracle, Raytheon, the U.S. Marine Corps, Saudi Telecommunications Corp (STC), and many others. He has served as an expert witness for major U.S. law firms. Brian has taught executive education sessions to audiences around the globe in areas related to enterprise architecture, business architecture, and strategy execution and has published many related professional articles. Brian's current research focus is effective value measurement for strategic business architecture. Brian is currently working on the development of a new strategy execution executive education series.

Brian can be found at:

- **LinkedIn:** https://www.linkedin.com/in/brian-cameron-051814
- **Website:** www.theexecutionchallenge.com

Whynde Kuehn is recognized globally as a highly sought-after pioneer and thought leader in strategy execution, transformation, and strategic business architecture. She has worked with an extensive array of organizations to build their capacity for end-to-end strategy execution, including Fortune 500 and global enterprises, governmental and nonprofit organizations, social enterprises, start-ups, and cross-sector initiatives. With vast experience in enterprise transformation and strategic planning, including leading large-scale transformations and teams, she has a distinguished track record of creating strategic business architecture practices worldwide.

As a long-time educator and community builder, Whynde has also helped countless individuals develop their careers. She has taught executive-level audiences from around the world and is currently working with Penn State Executive Programs on the development of a new strategy execution series. She is also the founder of Biz Arch Mastery, a dedicated online platform that helps professionals master the art and science of business architecture. Whynde is the Managing Director of S2E Transformation and a Senior Consultant with Cutter Consortium's Business and Enterprise Architecture practice. She is a Fellow with the Institute for Digital Transformation and a member of the Fast Company Executive Board. She is cofounder, vice president, and academic chair of the Business Architecture Guild, a not-for-profit professional association that has helped formalize the business architecture discipline. Whynde is cofounder and chair of the Women In Architecture (WIA) global initiative. She is also author of the book *Strategy to Reality*.

Whynde is exceptionally passionate about assisting mission-driven organizations in succeeding and scaling through the application of solid business approaches. Likewise, she routinely inspires corporate entities to use business as a force for good. With a focus on Africa and emerging nations, Whynde has spent years assisting public and private partners in hands-on efforts to drive dreams into action through effective and sustainable design and creating systemic change. Whynde lives with her husband in Norway, where she proudly brings her bold New York spirit, Wisconsin heart, and global ambition for adventure and possibility.

Whynde can be found at:

- **LinkedIn:** https://www.linkedin.com/in/whynde-kuehn
- **Website:** www.theexecutionchallenge.com

Index

C

D